PRAISE FOR *THE ART OF R PROGRAMMING*

"If a person really wants to be able to speak the R language and become a competent R programmer then . . . one can find no better guide than Norman Matloff's *The Art of R Programming*."
—JOSEPH RICKERT, REVOLUTION ANALYTICS

"The book I'd recommend for someone wanting to learn R, especially for someone with more experience in programming than statistics."
—JOHN D. COOK, THE ENDEAVOR

"Good from cover to cover. Enough depth that the experienced R user will find useful things in the later chapters."
—JOHN GRAHAM-CUMMING

"If you are serious about learning R . . . *The Art of R Programming* will be beneficial to you."
—PAOLO SONEGO, ONE R TIP A DAY

"Makes it look easy for those scientists who need to make numerical models based on statistical analysis. Serious stuff for people who are already R programmers, but it has a lot of value for entry level folks too."
—HANK CAMPBELL, SCIENCE 2.0

"If you need to do statistical work as a programmer, I highly recommend buying it."
—BRYAN BELL, MATH AND MORE

"An R programming book that starts from the beginning. If you have at least a vague idea of what programming is, you should find *The Art of R Programming* useful. I'm keeping this one."
—NATHAN YAU, FLOWINGDATA.COM, AUTHOR OF *VISUALIZE THIS*

THE ART OF R PROGRAMMING

PROGRAMMING

A Tour of Statistical Software Design

by Norman Matloff

no starch press

San Francisco

ISBN-10: 1-59327-384-3
ISBN-13: 978-1-59327-384-2

Publisher: William Pollock
Production Editor: Alison Law
Cover and Interior Design: Octopod Studios
Developmental Editor: Keith Fancher
Technical Reviewer: Hadley Wickham
Copyeditor: Marilyn Smith
Compositors: Alison Law and Serena Yang
Proofreader: Paula L. Fleming
Indexer: BIM Indexing & Proofreading Services

For information on distribution, translations, or bulk sales, please contact No Starch Press, Inc. directly:

No Starch Press, Inc.
245 8th Street, San Francisco, CA 94103
phone: 415.863.9900; info@nostarch.com; www.nostarch.com

Library of Congress Cataloging-in-Publication Data
Matloff, Norman S.
 The art of R programming : tour of statistical software design / by Norman Matloff.
      p. cm.
 ISBN-13: 978-1-59327-384-2
 ISBN-10: 1-59327-384-3
 1. Statistics-Data processing. 2. R (Computer program language) I. Title.
 QA276.4.M2925 2011
 519.50285'5133-dc23
                                  2011025598

BRIEF CONTENTS

CONTENTS IN DETAIL

2
VECTORS

3
MATRICES AND ARRAYS

6
FACTORS AND TABLES
121

7
R PROGRAMMING STRUCTURES
139

10
INPUT/OUTPUT   231

11
STRING MANIPULATION   251

12
GRAPHICS 261

13
DEBUGGING 285

14
PERFORMANCE ENHANCEMENT: SPEED AND MEMORY   305

15
INTERFACING R TO OTHER LANGUAGES   323

16
PARALLEL R   333

ACKNOWLEDGMENTS

This book has benefited greatly from the input received from many sources.

First and foremost, I must thank the technical reviewer, Hadley Wickham, of `ggplot2` and `plyr` fame. I suggested Hadley to No Starch Press because of his experience developing these and other highly popular R packages in CRAN, the R user-contributed code repository. As expected, a number of Hadley's comments resulted in improvements to the text, especially his comments about particular coding examples, which often began "I wonder what would happen if you wrote it this way. . . ." In some cases, these comments led to changing an example with one or two versions of code to an example showing two, three, or sometimes even four different ways to accomplish a given coding goal. This allowed for comparisons of the advantages and disadvantages of various approaches, which I believe the reader will find instructive.

I am very grateful to Jim Porzak, cofounder of the Bay Area useR Group (BARUG, *http://www.bay-r.org/*), for his frequent encouragement as I was writing this book. And while on the subject of BARUG, I must thank Jim and the other cofounder, Mike Driscoll, for establishing that lively and stimulating forum. At BARUG, the speakers on wonderful applications of R have always left me feeling that writing this book was a very worthy project.

BARUG has also benefited from the financial support of Revolution Analytics and countless hours, energy, and ideas from David Smith and Joe Rickert of that firm.

Jay Emerson and Mike Kane, authors of the award-winning `bigmemory` package in CRAN, read through an early draft of Chapter 16 on parallel R programming and made valuable comments.

John Chambers (founder of S, the "ancestor" of R) and Martin Morgan provided advice concerning R internals, which was very helpful to me for the discussion of R's performance issues in Chapter 14.

Section 7.8.4 covers a controversial topic in programming communities—the use of global variables. In order to be able to get a wide range of perspectives, I bounced my ideas off several people, notably R core group member Thomas Lumley and my UC Davis computer science colleague, Sean Davis. Needless to say, there is no implication that they endorse my views in that section of the book, but their comments were quite helpful.

Early in the project, I made a very rough (and very partial) draft of the book available for public comment and received helpful feedback from Ramon Diaz-Uriarte, Barbara F. La Scala, Jason Liao, and my old friend Mike Hannon. My daughter Laura, an engineering student, read parts of the early chapters and made some good suggestions that improved the book.

My own CRAN projects and other R-related research (parts of which serve as examples in the book) have benefited from the advice, feedback, and/or encouragement of many people, especially Mark Bravington, Stephen Eglen, Dirk Eddelbuett, Jay Emerson, Mike Kane, Gary King, Duncan Murdoch, and Joe Rickert.

R core group member Duncan Temple Lang is at my institution, the University of California, Davis. Though we are in different departments and thus haven't interacted much, this book owes something to his presence on campus. He has helped to create a very R-aware culture at UCD, which has made it easy for me to justify to my department the large amount of time I've spent writing this book.

This is my second project with No Starch Press. As soon as I decided to write this book, I naturally turned to No Starch Press because I like the informal style, high usability, and affordability of their products. Thanks go to Bill Pollock for approving the project, to editorial staff Keith Fancher and Alison Law, and to the freelance copyeditor Marilyn Smith.

Last but definitely not least, I thank two beautiful, brilliant, and funny women—my wife Gamis and the aforementioned Laura, both of whom cheerfully accepted my statement "I'm working on the R book," whenever they asked why I was so buried in work.

INTRODUCTION

 R is a scripting language for statistical data manipulation and analysis. It was inspired by, and is mostly compatible with, the statistical language S developed by AT&T. The name S, for *statistics*, was an allusion to another programming language with a one-letter name developed at AT&T—the famous C language. S later was sold to a small firm, which added a graphical user interface (GUI) and named the result S-Plus.

R has become more popular than S or S-Plus, both because it's free and because more people are contributing to it. R is sometimes called GNU S, to reflect its open source nature. (The GNU Project is a major collection of open source software.)

Why Use R for Your Statistical Work?

As the Cantonese say, *yauh peng, yauh leng*, which means "both inexpensive and beautiful." Why use anything else?

R has a number of virtues:

- It is a public-domain implementation of the widely regarded S statistical language, and the R/S platform is a de facto standard among professional statisticians.

- It is comparable, and often superior, in power to commercial products in most of the significant senses—variety of operations available, programmability, graphics, and so on.

- It is available for the Windows, Mac, and Linux operating systems.

- In addition to providing statistical operations, R is a general-purpose programming language, so you can use it to automate analyses and create new functions that extend the existing language features.

- It incorporates features found in object-oriented and functional programming languages.

- The system saves data sets between sessions, so you don't need to reload them each time. It saves your command history too.

- Because R is open source software, it's easy to get help from the user community. Also, a lot of new functions are contributed by users, many of whom are prominent statisticians.

I should warn you at the outset that you typically submit commands to R by typing in a terminal window, rather than clicking a mouse in a GUI, and most R users do not use a GUI. This doesn't mean that R doesn't do graphics. On the contrary, it includes tools for producing graphics of great utility and beauty, but they are used for system output, such as plots, not for user input.

If you can't live without a GUI, you can use one of the free GUIs that have been developed for R, such as the following open source or free tools:

- RStudio, *http://www.rstudio.org/*

- StatET, *http://www.walware.de/goto/statet/*

- ESS (Emacs Speaks Statistics), *http://ess.r-project.org/*

- R Commander: John Fox, "The R Commander: A Basic-Statistics Graphical Interface to R," *Journal of Statistical Software* 14, no. 9 (2005):1–42.

- JGR (Java GUI for R), *http://cran.r-project.org/web/packages/JGR/index.html*

The first three, RStudio, StatET and ESS, should be considered *integrated development environments (IDEs)*, aimed more toward programming. StatET and ESS provide the R programmer with an IDE in the famous Eclipse and Emacs settings, respectively.

On the commercial side, another IDE is available from Revolution Analytics, an R service company (*http://www.revolutionanalytics.com/*).

Because R is a programming language rather than a collection of discrete commands, you can combine several commands, each using the output of the previous one. (Linux users will recognize the similarity to chaining shell commands using pipes.) The ability to combine R functions gives tremendous flexibility and, if used properly, is quite powerful. As a simple example, consider this (compound) command:

```
nrow(subset(x03,z == 1))
```

First, the subset() function takes the data frame x03 and extracts all records for which the variable z has the value 1. This results in a new frame, which is then fed to the nrow() function. This function counts the number of rows in a frame. The net effect is to report a count of z = 1 in the original frame.

The terms *object-oriented programming* and *functional programming* were mentioned earlier. These topics pique the interest of computer scientists, and though they may be somewhat foreign to most other readers, they are relevant to anyone who uses R for statistical programming. The following sections provide an overview of both topics.

Object-Oriented Programming

The advantages of object orientation can be explained by example. Consider statistical regression. When you perform a regression analysis with other statistical packages, such as SAS or SPSS, you get a mountain of output on the screen. By contrast, if you call the lm() regression function in R, the function returns an *object* containing all the results—the estimated coefficients, their standard errors, residuals, and so on. You then pick and choose, programmatically, which parts of that object to extract.

You will see that R's approach makes programming much easier, partly because it offers a certain uniformity of access to data. This uniformity stems from the fact that R is *polymorphic*, which means that a single function can be applied to different types of inputs, which the function processes in the appropriate way. Such a function is called a *generic function*. (If you are a C++ programmer, you have seen a similar concept in *virtual functions*.)

For instance, consider the plot() function. If you apply it to a list of numbers, you get a simple plot. But if you apply it to the output of a regression analysis, you get a set of plots representing various aspects of the analysis. Indeed, you can use the plot() function on just about any object produced by R. This is nice, since it means that you, as a user, have fewer commands to remember!

Functional Programming

As is typical in functional programming languages, a common theme in R programming is avoidance of explicit iteration. Instead of coding loops, you exploit R's functional features, which let you express iterative behavior implicitly. This can lead to code that executes much more efficiently, and it can make a huge timing difference when running R on large data sets.

As you will see, the functional programming nature of the R language offers many advantages:

- Clearer, more compact code
- Potentially much faster execution speed
- Less debugging, because the code is simpler
- Easier transition to parallel programming

Whom Is This Book For?

Many use R mainly in an ad hoc way—to plot a histogram here, perform a regression analysis there, and carry out other discrete tasks involving statistical operations. But this book is for those who wish to develop *software* in R. The programming skills of our intended readers may range anywhere from those of a professional software developer to "I took a programming course in college," but their key goal is to write R code for specific purposes. (Statistical knowledge will generally not be needed.)

Here are some examples of people who may benefit from this book:

- Analysts employed by, say, a hospital or government agency who produce statistical reports on a regular basis and need to develop production programs for this purpose
- Academic researchers developing statistical methodology that is either new or combines existing methods into integrated procedures who need to codify this methodology so that it can be used by the general research community
- Specialists in marketing, litigation support, journalism, publishing, and so on who need to develop code to produce sophisticated graphical presentations of data
- Professional programmers with experience in software development who have been assigned by their employers to projects involving statistical analysis
- Students in statistical computing courses

Accordingly, this book is not a compendium of the myriad types of statistical methods that are available in the wonderful R package. It really is about programming and covers programming-related topics missing from most other books on R. I place a programming spin on even the basic subjects. Here are some examples of this approach in action:

- Throughout the book, you'll find "Extended Example" sections. These usually present complete, general-purpose functions rather than isolated code fragments based on specific data. Indeed, you may find some of these functions useful for your own daily R work. By studying these examples, you learn not only how individual R constructs work but also how to put them together into a useful program. In many cases, I've included a discussion of design alternatives, answering the question "Why did we do it this way?"

- The material is approached with a programmer's sensibilities in mind. For instance, in the discussion of data frames, I not only state that a data frame is an R list but also point out the programming implications of that fact. Comparisons of R to other languages are also brought in when useful, for those who happen to know other languages.

- Debugging plays a key role when programming in any language, yet it is not emphasized in most R books. In this book, I devote an entire chapter to debugging techniques, using the "extended example" approach to present fully worked-out demonstrations of how actual programs are debugged.

- Today, multicore computers are common even in the home, and graphics processing unit (GPU) programming is waging a quiet revolution in scientific computing. An increasing number of R applications involve very large amounts of computation, and parallel processing has become a major issue for R programmers. Thus, there is a chapter on this topic, which again presents not just the mechanics but also extended examples.

- There is a separate chapter on how to take advantage of the knowledge of R's internal behavior and other facilities to speed up R code.

- A chapter discusses the interface of R to other languages, such as C and Python, again with emphasis on extended examples as well as tips on debugging.

My Own Background

I come to the R party through a somewhat unusual route.

After writing a dissertation in abstract probability theory, I spent the early years of my career as a statistics professor—teaching, doing research, and consulting in statistical methodology. I was one of about a dozen professors at the University of California, Davis who founded the Department of Statistics at that university.

Later I moved to the Department of Computer Science at the same institution, where I have since spent most of my career. I do research in parallel programming, web traffic, data mining, disk system performance, and various other areas. Much of my computer science teaching and research involves statistics.

Thus, I have the points of view of both a "hard-core" computer scientist and of a statistician and statistics researcher. I hope this blend enables this book to fill a gap in the literature and enhances its value for you, the reader.

1

GETTING STARTED

 As detailed in the introduction, R is an extremely versatile open source programming language for statistics and data science. It is widely used in every field where there is data—business, industry, government, medicine, academia, and so on.

In this chapter, you'll get a quick introduction to R—how to invoke it, what it can do, and what files it uses. We'll cover just enough to give you the basics you need to work through the examples in the next few chapters, where the details will be presented.

R may already be installed on your system, if your employer or university has made it available to users. If not, see Appendix A for installation instructions.

1.1   How to Run R

R operates in two modes: *interactive* and *batch*. The one typically used is interactive mode. In this mode, you type in commands, R displays results, you type in more commands, and so on. On the other hand, batch mode does not require interaction with the user. It's useful for production jobs, such as when a program must be run periodically, say once per day, because you can automate the process.

1.1.1 Interactive Mode

On a Linux or Mac system, start an R session by typing R on the command line in a terminal window. On a Windows machine, start R by clicking the R icon.

The result is a greeting and the R prompt, which is the > sign. The screen will look something like this:

```
R version 2.10.0 (2009-10-26)
Copyright (C) 2009 The R Foundation for Statistical Computing
ISBN 3-900051-07-0
...
Type 'demo()' for some demos, 'help()' for on-line help, or
'help.start()' for an HTML browser interface to help.
Type 'q()' to quit R.


>
```

You can then execute R commands. The window in which all this appears is called the R *console*.

As a quick example, consider a standard normal distribution—that is, with mean 0 and variance 1. If a random variable X has that distribution, then its values are centered around 0, some negative, some positive, averaging in the end to 0. Now form a new random variable $Y = |X|$. Since we've taken the absolute value, the values of Y will *not* be centered around 0, and the mean of Y will be positive.

Let's find the mean of Y. Our approach is based on a simulated example of $N(0,1)$ variates.

```
> mean(abs(rnorm(100)))
[1] 0.7194236
```

This code generates the 100 random variates, finds their absolute values, and then finds the mean of the absolute values.

The [1] you see means that the first item in this line of output is item 1. In this case, our output consists of only one line (and one item), so this is redundant. This notation becomes helpful when you need to read voluminous output that consists of a lot of items spread over many lines. For example, if there were two rows of output with six items per row, the second row would be labeled [7].

```
> rnorm(10)
 [1] -0.6427784 -1.0416696 -1.4020476 -0.6718250 -0.9590894 -0.8684650
 [7] -0.5974668  0.6877001  1.3577618 -2.2794378
```

Here, there are 10 values in the output, and the label [7] in the second row lets you quickly see that 0.6877001, for instance, is the eighth output item.

You can also store R commands in a file. By convention, R code files have the suffix *.R* or *.r*. If you create a code file called *z.R*, you can execute the contents of that file by issuing the following command:

```
> source("z.R")
```

1.1.2   Batch Mode

Sometimes it's convenient to automate R sessions. For example, you may wish to run an R script that generates a graph without needing to bother with manually launching R and executing the script yourself. Here you would run R in batch mode.

As an example, let's put our graph-making code into a file named *z.R* with the following contents:

```
pdf("xh.pdf")  # set graphical output file
hist(rnorm(100))  # generate 100 N(0,1) variates and plot their histogram
dev.off()  # close the graphical output file
```

The items marked with # are *comments*. They're ignored by the R interpreter. Comments serve as notes to remind us and others what the code is doing, in a human-readable format.

Here's a step-by-step breakdown of what we're doing in the preceding code:

- We call the pdf() function to inform R that we want the graph we create to be saved in the PDF file *xh.pdf.*

- We call rnorm() (for *random normal*) to generate 100 $N(0,1)$ random variates.

- We call hist() on those variates to draw a histogram of these values.

- We call dev.off() to close the graphical "device" we are using, which is the file *xh.pdf* in this case. This is the mechanism that actually causes the file to be written to disk.

We could run this code automatically, without entering R's interactive mode, by invoking R with an operating system shell command (such as at the $ prompt commonly used in Linux systems):

```
$ R CMD BATCH z.R
```

You can confirm that this worked by using your PDF viewer to display the saved histogram. (It will just be a plain-vanilla histogram, but R is capable of producing quite sophisticated variations.)

1.2 A First R Session

Let's make a simple data set (in R parlance, a *vector*) consisting of the numbers 1, 2, and 4, and name it x:

```
> x <- c(1,2,4)
```

The standard assignment operator in R is <-. You can also use =, but this is discouraged, as it does not work in some special situations. Note that there are no fixed types associated with variables. Here, we've assigned a vector to x, but later we might assign something of a different type to it. We'll look at vectors and the other types in Section 1.4.

The c stands for *concatenate*. Here, we are concatenating the numbers 1, 2, and 4. More precisely, we are concatenating three one-element vectors that consist of those numbers. This is because any number is also considered to be a one-element vector.

Now we can also do the following:

```
> q <- c(x,x,8)
```

which sets q to (1,2,4,1,2,4,8) (yes, including the duplicates).

Now let's confirm that the data is really in x. To print the vector to the screen, simply type its name. If you type any variable name (or, more generally, any expression) while in interactive mode, R will print out the value of that variable (or expression). Programmers familiar with other languages such as Python will find this feature familiar. For our example, enter this:

```
> x
[1] 1 2 4
```

Yep, sure enough, x consists of the numbers 1, 2, and 4.

Individual elements of a vector are accessed via [ ]. Here's how we can print out the third element of x:

```
> x[3]
[1] 4
```

As in other languages, the selector (here, 3) is called the *index* or *subscript*. Those familiar with ALGOL-family languages, such as C and C++, should note that elements of R vectors are indexed starting from 1, not 0.

Subsetting is a very important operation on vectors. Here's an example:

```
> x <- c(1,2,4)
> x[2:3]
[1] 2 4
```

The expression x[2:3] refers to the subvector of x consisting of elements 2 through 3, which are 2 and 4 here.

We can easily find the mean and standard deviation of our data set, as follows:

```
> mean(x)
[1] 2.333333
> sd(x)
[1] 1.527525
```

This again demonstrates typing an expression at the prompt in order to print it. In the first line, our expression is the function call mean(x). The return value from that call is printed automatically, without requiring a call to R's print() function.

If we want to save the computed mean in a variable instead of just printing it to the screen, we could execute this code:

```
> y <- mean(x)
```

Again, let's confirm that y really does contain the mean of x:

```
> y
[1] 2.333333
```

As noted earlier, we use # to write comments, like this:

```
> y  # print out y
[1] 2.333333
```

Comments are especially valuable for documenting program code, but they are useful in interactive sessions, too, since R records the command history (as discussed in Section 1.6). If you save your session and resume it later, the comments can help you remember what you were doing.

Finally, let's do something with one of R's internal data sets (these are used for demos). You can get a list of these data sets by typing the following:

```
> data()
```

One of the data sets is called Nile and contains data on the flow of the Nile River. Let's find the mean and standard deviation of this data set:

```
> mean(Nile)
[1] 919.35
> sd(Nile)
[1] 169.2275
```

We can also plot a histogram of the data:

```
> hist(Nile)
```

A window pops up with the histogram in it, as shown in Figure 1-1. This graph is bare-bones simple, but R has all kinds of optional bells and whistles for plotting. For instance, you can change the number of bins by specifying the breaks variable. The call hist(z,breaks=12) would draw a histogram of the data set z with 12 bins. You can also create nicer labels, make use of color, and make many other changes to create a more informative and eye-appealing graph. When you become more familiar with R, you'll be able to construct complex, rich color graphics of striking beauty.

Histogram of Nile

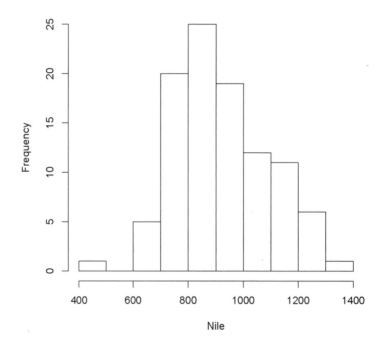

Figure 1-1: Nile data, plain presentation

Well, that's the end of our first, five-minute introduction to R. Quit R by calling the q() function (or alternatively by pressing CTRL-D in Linux or CMD-D on a Mac):

```
> q()
Save workspace image? [y/n/c]: n
```

That last prompt asks whether you want to save your variables so that you can resume work later. If you answer y, then all those objects will be loaded automatically the next time you run R. This is a very important feature, especially when working with large or numerous data sets. Answering y here also saves the session's command history. We'll talk more about saving your workspace and the command history in Section 1.6.

1.3   Introduction to Functions

As in most programming languages, the heart of R programming consists of writing *functions*. A function is a group of instructions that takes inputs, uses them to compute other values, and returns a result.

As a simple introduction, let's define a function named oddcount(), whose purpose is to count the odd numbers in a vector of integers. Normally, we would compose the function code using a text editor and save it in a file, but in this quick-and-dirty example, we'll enter it line by line in R's interactive mode. We'll then call the function on a couple of test cases.

```
# counts the number of odd integers in x
> oddcount <- function(x)  {
+    k <- 0  # assign 0 to k
+    for (n in x)  {
+       if (n %% 2 == 1) k <- k+1  # %% is the modulo operator
+    }
+    return(k)
+ }
> oddcount(c(1,3,5))
[1] 3
> oddcount(c(1,2,3,7,9))
[1] 4
```

First, we told R that we wanted to define a function named oddcount with one argument, x. The left brace demarcates the start of the body of the function. We wrote one R statement per line.

Until the body of the function is finished, R reminds you that you're still in the definition by using + as its prompt, instead of the usual >. (Actually, + is a line-continuation character, not a prompt for a new input.) R resumes the > prompt after you finally enter a right brace to conclude the function body.

After defining the function, we evaluated two calls to oddcount(). Since there are three odd numbers in the vector (1,3,5), the call oddcount(c(1,3,5)) returns the value 3. There are four odd numbers in (1,2,3,7,9), so the second call returns 4.

Notice that the modulo operator for remainder arithmetic is %% in R, as indicated by the comment. For example, 38 divided by 7 leaves a remainder of 3:

```
> 38 %% 7
[1] 3
```

For instance, let's see what happens with the following code:

```
for (n in x)  {
    if (n %% 2 == 1) k <- k+1
}
```

First, it sets n to x[1], and then it tests that value for being odd or even. If the value is odd, which is the case here, the count variable k is incremented. Then n is set to x[2], tested for being odd or even, and so on.

By the way, C/C++ programmers might be tempted to write the preceding loop like this:

```
for (i in 1:length(x)) {
    if (x[i] %% 2 == 1) k <- k+1
}
```

Here, length(x) is the number of elements in x. Suppose there are 25 elements. Then 1:length(x) means 1:25, which in turn means 1,2,3,...,25. This code would also work (unless x were to have length 0), but one of the major themes of R programming is to avoid loops if possible; if not, keep loops simple. Look again at our original formulation:

```
for (n in x)  {
    if (n %% 2 == 1) k <- k+1
}
```

It's simpler and cleaner, as we do not need to resort to using the length() function and array indexing.

At the end of the code, we use the return statement:

```
return(k)
```

This has the function return the computed value of k to the code that called it. However, simply writing the following also works:

```
k
```

R functions will return the last value computed if there is no explicit return() call. However, this approach must be used with care, as we will discuss in Section 7.4.1.

In programming language terminology, x is the *formal argument* (or *formal parameter*) of the function oddcount(). In the first function call in the preceding example, c(1,3,5) is referred to as the *actual argument*. These terms allude to the fact that x in the function definition is just a placeholder, whereas c(1,3,5) is the value actually used in the computation. Similarly, in the second function call, c(1,2,3,7,9) is the actual argument.

1.3.1 Variable Scope

A variable that is visible only within a function body is said to be *local* to that function. In oddcount(), k and n are local variables. They disappear after the function returns:

```
> oddcount(c(1,2,3,7,9))
[1] 4
> n
Error: object 'n' not found
```

It's very important to note that the formal parameters in an R function are local variables. Suppose we make the following function call:

```
> z <- c(2,6,7)
> oddcount(z)
```

Now suppose that the code of oddcount() changes x. Then z would *not* change. After the call to oddcount(), z would have the same value as before. To evaluate a function call, R copies each actual argument to the corresponding local parameter variable, and changes to that variable are not visible outside the function. *Scoping rules* such as these will be discussed in detail in Chapter 7.

Variables created outside functions are *global* and are available within functions as well. Here's an example:

```
> f <- function(x) return(x+y)
> y <- 3
> f(5)
[1] 8
```

Here y is a global variable.

A global variable can be written to from within a function by using R's *superassignment operator*, <<-. This is also discussed in Chapter 7.

1.3.2 Default Arguments

R also makes frequent use of *default arguments*. Consider a function definition like this:

```
> g <- function(x,y=2,z=T) { ... }
```

Here y will be initialized to 2 if the programmer does not specify y in the call. Similarly, z will have the default value TRUE.

Now consider this call:

```
> g(12,z=FALSE)
```

Here, the value 12 is the actual argument for x, and we accept the default value of 2 for y, but we override the default for z, setting its value to FALSE.

The preceding example also demonstrates that, like many programming languages, R has a *Boolean* type; that is, it has the logical values TRUE and FALSE.

NOTE   *R allows TRUE and FALSE to be abbreviated to T and F. However, you may choose not to abbreviate these values to avoid trouble if you have a variable named T or F.*

1.4   Preview of Some Important R Data Structures

R has a variety of data structures. Here, we will sketch some of the most frequently used structures to give you an overview of R before we dive into the details. This way, you can at least get started with some meaningful examples, even if the full story behind them must wait.

1.4.1   Vectors, the R Workhorse

The vector type is really the heart of R. It's hard to imagine R code, or even an interactive R session, that doesn't involve vectors.

The elements of a vector must all have the same *mode*, or data type. You can have a vector consisting of three character strings (of mode character) or three integer elements (of mode integer), but not a vector with one integer element and two character string elements.

We'll talk more about vectors in Chapter 2.

1.4.1.1   Scalars

Scalars, or individual numbers, do not really exist in R. As mentioned earlier, what appear to be individual numbers are actually one-element vectors. Consider the following:

```
> x <- 8
> x
[1] 8
```

Recall that the [1] here signifies that the following row of numbers begins with element 1 of a vector—in this case, x[1]. So you can see that R was indeed treating x as a vector, albeit a vector with just one element.

1.4.2 Character Strings

Character strings are actually single-element vectors of mode character, (rather than mode numeric):

```
> x <- c(5,12,13)
> x
[1]  5 12 13
> length(x)
[1] 3
> mode(x)
[1] "numeric"
> y <- "abc"
> y
[1] "abc"
> length(y)
[1] 1
> mode(y)
[1] "character"
> z <- c("abc","29 88")
> length(z)
[1] 2
> mode(z)
[1] "character"
```

In the first example, we create a vector x of numbers, thus of mode numeric. Then we create two vectors of mode character: y is a one-element (that is, one-string) vector, and z consists of two strings.

R has various string-manipulation functions. Many deal with putting strings together or taking them apart, such as the two shown here:

```
> u <- paste("abc","de","f")  # concatenate the strings
> u
[1] "abc de f"
> v <- strsplit(u," ")  # split the string according to blanks
> v
[[1]]
[1] "abc" "de"  "f"
```

Strings will be covered in detail in Chapter 11.

1.4.3 Matrices

An R matrix corresponds to the mathematical concept of the same name: a rectangular array of numbers. Technically, a matrix is a vector, but with two additional attributes: the number of rows and the number of columns. Here is some sample matrix code:

```
> m <- rbind(c(1,4),c(2,2))
> m
     [,1] [,2]
[1,]   1    4
[2,]   2    2
> m %*% c(1,1)
     [,1]
[1,]   5
[2,]   4
```

First, we use the rbind() (for *row bind*) function to build a matrix from two vectors that will serve as its rows, storing the result in m. (A corresponding function, cbind(), combines several columns into a matrix.) Then entering the variable name alone, which we know will print the variable, confirms that the intended matrix was produced. Finally, we compute the matrix product of the vector (1,1) and m. The matrix-multiplication operator, which you may know from linear algebra courses, is %*% in R.

Matrices are indexed using double subscripting, much as in C/C++, although subscripts start at 1 instead of 0.

```
> m[1,2]
[1] 4
> m[2,2]
[1] 2
```

An extremely useful feature of R is that you can extract submatrices from a matrix, much as you extract subvectors from vectors. Here's an example:

```
> m[1,]   # row 1
[1] 1 4
> m[,2]   # column 2
[1] 4 2
```

We'll talk more about matrices in Chapter 3.

1.4.4   Lists

Like an R vector, an R list is a container for values, but its contents can be items of different data types. (C/C++ programmers will note the analogy to a C struct.) List elements are accessed using two-part names, which are indicated with the dollar sign $ in R. Here's a quick example:

```
> x <- list(u=2, v="abc")
> x
```

```
$u
[1] 2

$v
[1] "abc"

> x$u
[1] 2
```

The expression x$u refers to the u component in the list x. The latter contains one other component, denoted by v.

A common use of lists is to combine multiple values into a single package that can be returned by a function. This is especially useful for statistical functions, which can have elaborate results. As an example, consider R's basic histogram function, hist(), introduced in Section 1.2. We called the function on R's built-in Nile River data set:

```
> hist(Nile)
```

This produced a graph, but hist() also returns a value, which we can save:

```
> hn <- hist(Nile)
```

What's in hn? Let's take a look:

```
> print(hn)
$breaks
 [1]  400  500  600  700  800  900 1000 1100 1200 1300 1400

$counts
 [1]  1  0  5 20 25 19 12 11  6  1

$intensities
 [1] 9.999998e-05 0.000000e+00 5.000000e-04 2.000000e-03 2.500000e-03
 [6] 1.900000e-03 1.200000e-03 1.100000e-03 6.000000e-04 1.000000e-04

$density
 [1] 9.999998e-05 0.000000e+00 5.000000e-04 2.000000e-03 2.500000e-03
 [6] 1.900000e-03 1.200000e-03 1.100000e-03 6.000000e-04 1.000000e-04

$mids
 [1]  450  550  650  750  850  950 1050 1150 1250 1350

$xname
[1] "Nile"

$equidist
[1] TRUE
```

```
attr(,"class")
[1] "histogram"
```

Don't try to understand all of that right away. For now, the point is that, besides making a graph, hist() returns a list with a number of components. Here, these components describe the characteristics of the histogram. For instance, the breaks component tells us where the bins in the histogram start and end, and the counts component is the numbers of observations in each bin.

The designers of R decided to package all of the information returned by hist() into an R list, which can be accessed and manipulated by further R commands via the dollar sign.

Remember that we could also print hn simply by typing its name:

```
> hn
```

But a more compact alternative for printing lists like this is str():

```
> str(hn)
List of 7
 $ breaks     : num [1:11] 400 500 600 700 800 900 1000 1100 1200 1300 ...
 $ counts     : int [1:10] 1 0 5 20 25 19 12 11 6 1
 $ intensities: num [1:10] 0.0001 0 0.0005 0.002 0.0025 ...
 $ density    : num [1:10] 0.0001 0 0.0005 0.002 0.0025 ...
 $ mids       : num [1:10] 450 550 650 750 850 950 1050 1150 1250 1350
 $ xname      : chr "Nile"
 $ equidist   : logi TRUE
 - attr(*, "class")= chr "histogram"
```

Here str stands for *structure*. This function shows the internal structure of any R object, not just lists.

1.4.5   Data Frames

A typical data set contains data of different modes. In an employee data set, for example, we might have character string data, such as employee names, and numeric data, such as salaries. So, although a data set of (say) 50 employees with 4 variables per worker has the look and feel of a 50-by-4 matrix, it does not qualify as such in R, because it mixes types.

Instead of a matrix, we use a *data frame*. A data frame in R is a list, with each component of the list being a vector corresponding to a column in our "matrix" of data. Indeed, you can create data frames in just this way:

```
> d <- data.frame(list(kids=c("Jack","Jill"),ages=c(12,10)))
> d
  kids ages
1 Jack   12
```

```
2 Jill   10
> d$ages
[1] 12 10
```

Typically, though, data frames are created by reading in a data set from a file or database.

We'll talk more about data frames in Chapter 5.

1.4.6   Classes

R is an object-oriented language. *Objects* are instances of *classes*. Classes are a bit more abstract than the data types you've met so far. Here, we'll look briefly at the concept using R's S3 classes. (The name stems from their use in the old S language, version 3, which was the inspiration for R.) Most of R is based on these classes, and they are exceedingly simple. Their instances are simply R lists but with an extra attribute: the class name.

For example, we noted earlier that the (nongraphical) output of the hist() histogram function is a list with various components, such as break and count components. There was also an *attribute*, which specified the class of the list, namely histogram.

```
> print(hn)
$breaks
 [1]   400   500   600   700   800   900 1000 1100 1200 1300 1400

$counts
 [1]   1   0   5  20  25  19  12  11   6   1
...
...
attr(,"class")
[1] "histogram"
```

At this point, you might be wondering, "If S3 class objects are just lists, why do we need them?" The answer is that the classes are used by *generic* functions. A generic function stands for a family of functions, all serving a similar purpose but each appropriate to a specific class.

A commonly used generic function is summary(). An R user who wants to use a statistical function, like hist(), but is unsure of how to deal with its output (which can be voluminous), can simply call summary() on the output, which is not just a list but an instance of an S3 class.

The summary() function, in turn, is actually a family of summary-making functions, each handling objects of a particular class. When you call summary() on some output, R searches for a summary function appropriate to the class at hand and uses it to give a friendlier representation of the list. Thus, calling summary() on the output of hist() produces a summary tailored to that function, and calling summary() on the output of the lm() regression function produces a summary appropriate for that function.

The plot() function is another generic function. You can use plot() on just about any R object. R will find an appropriate plotting function based on the object's class.

Classes are used to organize objects. Together with generic functions, they allow flexible code to be developed for handling a variety of different but related tasks. Chapter 9 covers classes in depth.

1.5   Extended Example: Regression Analysis of Exam Grades

For our next example, we'll walk through a brief statistical regression analysis. There isn't much actual programming in this example, but it illustrates how some of the data types we just discussed are used, including R's S3 objects. Also, it will serve as the basis for several of our programming examples in subsequent chapters.

I have a file, *ExamsQuiz.txt*, containing grades from a class I taught. Here are its first few lines:

```
2    3.3   4
3.3  2     3.7
4    4.3   4
2.3  0     3.3
...
```

The numbers correspond to letter grades on a four-point scale; 3.3 is a B+, for instance. Each line contains the data for one student, consisting of the midterm examination grade, final examination grade, and average quiz grade. It might be interesting to see how well the midterm and quiz grades predict the student's grade on the final examination.

Let's first read in the data file:

```
> examsquiz <- read.table("ExamsQuiz.txt",header=FALSE)
```

Our file does not include a header line naming the variables in each student record, so we specified header=FALSE in the function call. This is an example of a default argument, which we talked about earlier. Actually, the default value of the header argument is FALSE already (which you can check by consulting R's online help for read.table()), so we didn't need to specify this setting, but it's clearer if we do.

Our data is now in examsquiz, which is an R object of class data.frame.

```
> class(examsquiz)
[1] "data.frame"
```

Just to check that the file was read in correctly, let's take a look at the first few rows:

```
> head(examsquiz)
   V1  V2  V3
```

```
1 2.0 3.3 4.0
2 3.3 2.0 3.7
3 4.0 4.3 4.0
4 2.3 0.0 3.3
5 2.3 1.0 3.3
6 3.3 3.7 4.0
```

Lacking a header for the data, R named the columns V1, V2, and V3. Row numbers appear on the left. As you might be thinking, it would be better to have a header in our data file, with meaningful names like Exam1. In later examples, we will usually specify names.

Let's try to predict the exam 2 score (given in the second column of examsquiz) from exam 1 (first column):

```
lma <- lm(examsquiz[,2] ~ examsquiz[,1])
```

The lm() (for *linear model*) function call here instructs R to fit this prediction equation:

$$\text{predicted Exam 2} = \beta_0 + \beta_1 \text{ Exam 1}$$

Here, β_0 and β_1 are constants to be estimated from our data. In other words, we are fitting a straight line to the (exam 1, exam 2) pairs in our data. This is done through a classic least-squares method. (Don't worry if you don't have background in this.)

Note that the exam 1 scores, which are stored in the first column of our data frame, are collectively referred to as examsquiz[,1]. Omission of the first subscript (the row number) means that we are referring to an entire column of the frame. The exam 2 scores are similarly referenced. So, our call to lm() above predicts the second column of examsquiz from the first.

We also could have written

```
lma <- lm(examsquiz$V2 ~ examsquiz$V1)
```

recalling that a data frame is just a list whose elements are vectors. Here, the columns are the V1, V2, and V3 components of the list.

The results returned by lm() are now in an object that we've stored in the variable lma. It is an instance of the class lm. We can list its components by calling attributes():

```
> attributes(lma)
$names
 [1] "coefficients"  "residuals"    "effects"    "rank"
 [5] "fitted.values" "assign"       "qr"         "df.residual"
 [9] "xlevels"       "call"         "terms"      "model"

$class
[1] "lm"
```

As usual, a more detailed accounting can be obtained via the call str(lma). The estimated values of β_i are stored in lma$coefficients. You can display them by typing the name at the prompt.

You can also save some typing by abbreviating component names, as long as you don't shorten a component's name to the point of being ambiguous. For example, if a list consists of the components xyz, xywa, and xbcde, then the second and third components can be abbreviated to xyw and xb, respectively. So here we could type the following:

```
> lma$coef
 (Intercept) examsquiz[, 1]
   1.1205209      0.5899803
```

Since lma$coefficients is a vector, printing it is simple. But consider what happens when you print the object lma itself:

```
> lma

Call:
lm(formula = examsquiz[, 2] ~ examsquiz[, 1])

Coefficients:
 (Intercept)   examsquiz[, 1]
       1.121            0.590
```

Why did R print only these items and not the other components of lma? The answer is that here R is using the print() function, which is another example of generic functions. As a generic function, print() actually hands off the work to another function whose job is to print objects of class lm—the print.lm() function—and this is what that function displays.

We can get a more detailed printout of the contents of lma by calling summary(), the generic function discussed earlier. It triggers a call to summary.lm() behind the scenes, and we get a regression-specific summary:

```
> summary(lma)

Call:
lm(formula = examsquiz[, 2] ~ examsquiz[, 1])

Residuals:
    Min      1Q  Median      3Q     Max
-3.4804 -0.1239  0.3426  0.7261  1.2225

Coefficients:
              Estimate Std. Error t value Pr(>|t|)
(Intercept)     1.1205     0.6375   1.758  0.08709 .
examsquiz[, 1]  0.5900     0.2030   2.907  0.00614 **
...
```

A number of other generic functions are defined for this class. See the online help for lm() for details. (Using R's online documentation is discussed in Section 1.7.)

To estimate a prediction equation for exam 2 from both the exam 1 and the quiz scores, we would use the + notation:

```
> lmb <- lm(examsquiz[,2] ~ examsquiz[,1] + examsquiz[,3])
```

Note that the + doesn't mean that we compute the sum of the two quantities. It is merely a delimiter in our list of predictor variables.

1.6   Startup and Shutdown

Like that of many sophisticated software applications, R's behavior can be customized using startup files. In addition, R can save all or part of a session, such as a record of what you did, to an output file. If there are R commands that you would like to execute at the beginning of every R session, you can place them in a file called *.Rprofile* located either in your home directory or in the directory from which you are running R. The latter directory is searched for this file first, which allows you to have custom profiles for particular projects.

For example, to set the text editor that R invokes if you call edit(), you can use a line in *.Rprofile* like this (if you're on a Linux system):

```
options(editor="/usr/bin/vim")
```

R's options() function is used for configuration, that is, to tweak various settings. You can specify the full path to your own editor, using the notation (slashes or backslashes) appropriate to your operating system.

As another example, in *.Rprofile* on my Linux machine at home, I have the following line:

```
.libPaths("/home/nm/R")
```

This automatically adds a directory that contains all my auxiliary packages to my R search path.

Like most programs, R has the notion of your *current working directory*. Upon startup, this will be the directory from which you launched R, if you're using Linux or a Mac. In Windows, it will probably be your *Documents* folder. If you then reference files during your R session, they will be assumed to be in that directory. You can always check your current directory by typing the following:

```
> getwd()
```

You can change your working directory by calling setwd() with the desired directory as a quoted argument. For example,

```
> setwd("q")
```

would set the working directory to *q*.

As you proceed through an interactive R session, R records the commands you submit. If you answer yes to the question "Save workspace image?" when you quit, R will save all the objects you created in that session and restore them in your next session. This means you do not need to redo the work from scratch to continue where you left off.

The saved workspace is in a file named *.Rdata*, which is located either in the directory from which you invoked the R session (Linux) or in the R installation directory (Windows). You can consult the *.Rhistory* file, which records your commands, to remind yourself how that workspace was created.

If you want speedier startup/shutdown, you can skip loading all those files and the saving of your session at the end by running R with the vanilla option:

```
R --vanilla
```

Other options fall between vanilla and "load everything." You can find more information about startup files by querying R's online help facility, as follows:

```
> ?Startup
```

1.7 Getting Help

A plethora of resources are available to help you learn more about R. These include several facilities within R itself and, of course, on the Web.

Much work has gone into making R self-documenting. We'll look at some of R's built-in help facilities and then at those available on the Internet.

1.7.1 The help() Function

To get online help, invoke help(). For example, to get information on the seq() function, type this:

```
> help(seq)
```

The shortcut to help() is a question mark (?):

```
> ?seq
```

Special characters and some reserved words must be quoted when used with the help() function. For instance, you need to type the following to get help on the < operator:

```
> ?"<"
```

And to see what the online manual has to say about for loops, enter this:

```
> ?"for"
```

1.7.2   The example() Function

Each of the help entries comes with examples. One really nice feature of R is that the example() function will actually run those examples for you. Here's an illustration:

```
> example(seq)

seq> seq(0, 1, length.out=11)
 [1] 0.0 0.1 0.2 0.3 0.4 0.5 0.6 0.7 0.8 0.9 1.0

seq> seq(stats::rnorm(20))
 [1]  1  2  3  4  5  6  7  8  9 10 11 12 13 14 15 16 17 18 19 20

seq> seq(1, 9, by = 2) # match
[1] 1 3 5 7 9

seq> seq(1, 9, by = pi)# stay below
[1] 1.000000 4.141593 7.283185

seq> seq(1, 6, by = 3)
[1] 1 4

seq> seq(1.575, 5.125, by=0.05)
 [1] 1.575 1.625 1.675 1.725 1.775 1.825 1.875 1.925 1.975 2.025 2.075 2.125
[13] 2.175 2.225 2.275 2.325 2.375 2.425 2.475 2.525 2.575 2.625 2.675 2.725
[25] 2.775 2.825 2.875 2.925 2.975 3.025 3.075 3.125 3.175 3.225 3.275 3.325
[37] 3.375 3.425 3.475 3.525 3.575 3.625 3.675 3.725 3.775 3.825 3.875 3.925
[49] 3.975 4.025 4.075 4.125 4.175 4.225 4.275 4.325 4.375 4.425 4.475 4.525
[61] 4.575 4.625 4.675 4.725 4.775 4.825 4.875 4.925 4.975 5.025 5.075 5.125

seq> seq(17) # same as 1:17
 [1]  1  2  3  4  5  6  7  8  9 10 11 12 13 14 15 16 17
```

The seq() function generates various kinds of numeric sequences in arithmetic progression. Running example(seq) resulted in R's running some examples of seq() before our very eyes.

Imagine how useful this can be for graphics! If you are interested in seeing what one of R's excellent graphics functions does, the example() function will give you a "graphic" illustration.

To see a quick and very nice example, try running the following command:

```
> example(persp)
```

This displays a series of sample graphs for the persp() function. One of these is shown in Figure 1-2. Press ENTER in the R console when you are ready to go to the next one. Note that the code for each example is shown in the console, so you can experiment by tweaking the arguments.

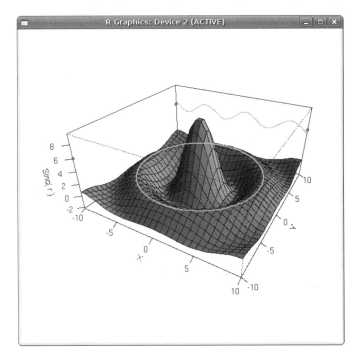

Figure 1-2: One of the persp() examples

1.7.3   If You Don't Know Quite What You're Looking For

You can use the function help.search() to do a Google-style search through R's documentation. For instance, say you need a function to generate random variates from multivariate normal distributions. To determine which function, if any, does this, you could try something like this:

```
> help.search("multivariate normal")
```

This produces a response containing this excerpt:

mvrnorm(MASS)	Simulate from a Multivariate Normal Distribution

You can see that the function mvrnorm() will do the job, and it is in the package MASS.

There is also a question-mark shortcut to help.search():

```
> ??"multivariate normal"
```

1.7.4   Help for Other Topics

R's internal help files include more than just pages for specific functions. For example, the previous section mentioned that the function mvrnorm() is in the package MASS. You can get information about the function by entering this:

```
> ?mvrnorm
```

And you can also learn about the entire package by typing this:

```
> help(package=MASS)
```

Help is available for general topics, too. For instance, if you're interested in learning about files, type the following:

```
> ?files
```

This gives you information about a number of file-manipulation functions, such as file.create().

Here are some other topics:

```
Arithmetic
Comparison
Control
Dates
Extract
Math
Memory
NA
NULL
NumericaConstants
Paren
Quotes
Startup
Syntax
```

You may find it helpful to browse through these topics, even without a specific goal in mind.

1.7.5 Help for Batch Mode

Recall that R has batch commands that allow you to run a command directly from your operating system's shell. To get help on a particular batch command, you can type:

```
R CMD command --help
```

For example, to learn all the options associated with the INSTALL command (discussed in Appendix B), you can type this:

```
R CMD INSTALL --help
```

1.7.6 Help on the Internet

There are many excellent resources on R on the Internet. Here are a few:

- The R Project's own manuals are available from the R home page, *http://www.r-project.org/*. Click Manuals.
- Various R search engines are listed on the R home page. Click Search.
- The sos package offers highly sophisticated searching of R materials. See Appendix B for instructions on how to install R packages.
- I use the RSeek search engine quite often: *http://www.rseek.org/*.
- You can post your R questions to *r*-help, the R list server. You can obtain information about this and other R list servers at *http://www.r-project.org/ mail.html*. You can use various interfaces. I like Gmane (*http://www .gmane.org/*).

Because of its single-letter name, R is difficult to search for using general-purpose search engines such as Google. But there are tricks you can employ. One approach is to use Google's filetype criterion. To search for R scripts (files having a .R suffix) pertaining to, say, permutations, enter this:

```
filetype:R permutations -rebol
```

The -rebol asks Google to exclude pages with the word "rebol," as the REBOL programming language uses the same suffix.

The Comprehensive R Archive Network (CRAN), at *http://cran.r-project .org/*, is a repository of user-contributed R code and thus makes for a good Google search term. Searching for "lm CRAN," for instance, will help you find material on R's lm() function.

2

VECTORS

The fundamental data type in R is the *vector*. You saw a few examples in Chapter 1, and now you'll learn the details. We'll start by examining how vectors relate to some other data types in R. You'll see that unlike in languages in the C family, individual numbers (scalars) do not have separate data types but instead are special cases of vectors. On the other hand, as in C family languages, matrices are special cases of vectors.

We'll spend a considerable amount of time on the following topics:

Recycling   The automatic lengthening of vectors in certain settings

Filtering   The extraction of subsets of vectors

Vectorization   Where functions are applied element-wise to vectors

All of these operations are central to R programming, and you will see them referred to often in the remainder of the book.

2.1 Scalars, Vectors, Arrays, and Matrices

In many programming languages, vector variables are considered different from *scalars*, which are single-number variables. Consider the following C code, for example:

```
int x;
int y[3];
```

This requests the compiler to allocate space for a single integer named x and a three-element integer array (C terminology analogous to R's vector type) named y. But in R, numbers are actually considered one-element vectors, and there is really no such thing as a scalar.

R variable types are called *modes*. Recall from Chapter 1 that all elements in a vector must have the same mode, which can be integer, numeric (floating-point number), character (string), logical (Boolean), complex, and so on. If you need your program code to check the mode of a variable x, you can query it by the call typeof(x).

Unlike vector indices in ALGOL-family languages, such as C and Python, vector indices in R begin at 1.

2.1.1 Adding and Deleting Vector Elements

Vectors are stored like arrays in C, contiguously, and thus you cannot insert or delete elements—something you may be used to if you are a Python programmer. The size of a vector is determined at its creation, so if you wish to add or delete elements, you'll need to reassign the vector.

For example, let's add an element to the middle of a four-element vector:

```
> x <- c(88,5,12,13)
> x <- c(x[1:3],168,x[4])   # insert 168 before the 13
> x
[1]   88   5  12 168  13
```

Here, we created a four-element vector and assigned it to x. To insert a new number 168 between the third and fourth elements, we strung together the first three elements of x, then the 168, then the fourth element of x. This creates a *new* five-element vector, leaving x intact for the time being. We then assigned that new vector to x.

In the result, it appears as if we had actually changed the vector stored in x, but really we created a new vector and stored *that* vector in x. This difference may seem subtle, but it has implications. For instance, in some cases, it may restrict the potential for fast performance in R, as discussed in Chapter 14.

NOTE   *For readers with a background in C, internally, x is really a pointer, and the reassignment is implemented by pointing x to the newly created vector.*

2.1.2 Obtaining the Length of a Vector

You can obtain the length of a vector by using the length() function:

```
> x <- c(1,2,4)
> length(x)
[1] 3
```

In this example, we already know the length of x, so there really is no need to query it. But in writing general function code, you'll often need to know the lengths of vector arguments.

For instance, suppose that we wish to have a function that determines the index of the first 1 value in the function's vector argument (assuming we are sure there is such a value). Here is one (not necessarily efficient) way we could write the code:

```
first1 <- function(x) {
    for (i in 1:length(x)) {
        if (x[i] == 1) break  # break out of loop
    }
    return(i)
}
```

Without the length() function, we would have needed to add a second argument to first1(), say naming it n, to specify the length of x.

Note that in this case, writing the loop as follows *won't* work:

```
for (n in x)
```

The problem with this approach is that it doesn't allow us to retrieve the index of the desired element. Thus, we need an explicit loop, which in turn requires calculating the length of x.

One more point about that loop: For careful coding, you should worry that length(x) might be 0. In such a case, look what happens to the expression 1:length(x) in our for loop:

```
> x <- c()
> x
NULL
> length(x)
[1] 0
> 1:length(x)
[1] 1 0
```

Our variable i in this loop takes on the value 1, then 0, which is certainly not what we want if the vector x is empty.

A safe alternative is to use the more advanced R function seq(), as we'll discuss in Section 2.4.4.

2.1.3 Matrices and Arrays as Vectors

Arrays and matrices (and even lists, in a sense) are actually vectors too, as you'll see. They merely have extra class attributes. For example, matrices have the number of rows and columns. We'll discuss them in detail in the next chapter, but it's worth noting now that arrays and matrices are vectors, and that means that everything we say about vectors applies to them, too.

Consider the following example:

```
> m
     [,1] [,2]
[1,]    1    2
[2,]    3    4
> m + 10:13
     [,1] [,2]
[1,]   11   14
[2,]   14   17
```

The 2-by-2 matrix m is stored as a four-element vector, column-wise, as (1,3,2,4). We then added (10,11,12,13) to it, yielding (11,14,14,17), but R remembered that we were working with matrices and thus gave the 2-by-2 result you see in the example.

2.2 Declarations

Typically, compiled languages require that you *declare* variables; that is, warn the interpreter/compiler of the variables' existence before using them. This is the case in our earlier C example:

```
int x;
int y[3];
```

As with most scripting languages (such as Python and Perl), you do not declare variables in R. For instance, consider this code:

```
z <- 3
```

This code, with *no* previous reference to z, is perfectly legal (and commonplace).

However, if you reference specific elements of a vector, you must warn R. For instance, say we wish y to be a two-component vector with values 5 and 12. The following will *not* work:

```
> y[1] <- 5
> y[2] <- 12
```

Instead, you must create y first, for instance this way:

```
> y <- vector(length=2)
> y[1] <- 5
> y[2] <- 12
```

The following will also work:

```
> y <- c(5,12)
```

This approach is all right because on the right-hand side we are creating a new vector, to which we then bind y.

The reason we cannot suddenly spring an expression like y[2] on R stems from R's functional language nature. The reading and writing of individual vector elements are actually handled by functions. If R doesn't already know that y is a vector, these functions have nothing on which to act.

Speaking of binding, just as variables are not declared, they are not constrained in terms of mode. The following sequence of events is perfectly valid:

```
> x <- c(1,5)
> x
[1] 1 5
> x <- "abc"
```

First, x is associated with a numeric vector, then with a string. (Again, for C/C++ programmers: x is nothing more than a pointer, which can point to different types of objects at different times.)

2.3 Recycling

When applying an operation to two vectors that requires them to be the same length, R automatically *recycles*, or repeats, the shorter one, until it is long enough to match the longer one. Here is an example:

```
> c(1,2,4) + c(6,0,9,20,22)
[1]  7  2 13 21 24
Warning message:
longer object length
  is not a multiple of shorter object length in: c(1, 2, 4) + c(6,
  0, 9, 20, 22)
```

The shorter vector was recycled, so the operation was taken to be as follows:

```
> c(1,2,4,1,2) + c(6,0,9,20,22)
```

Here's a more subtle example:

```
> x
     [,1] [,2]
[1,]    1    4
[2,]    2    5
[3,]    3    6
> x+c(1,2)
     [,1] [,2]
[1,]    2    6
[2,]    4    6
[3,]    4    8
```

Again, keep in mind that matrices are actually long vectors. Here, x, as a 3-by-2 matrix, is also a six-element vector, which in R is stored column by column. In other words, in terms of storage, x is the same as c(1,2,3,4,5,6). We added a two-element vector to this six-element one, so our added vector needed to be repeated twice to make six elements. In other words, we were essentially doing this:

```
x + c(1,2,1,2,1,2)
```

Not only that, but c(1,2,1,2,1,2) was also changed from a vector to a matrix having the same shape as x before the addition took place:

```
1 2
2 1
1 2
```

Thus, the net result was to compute the following:

$$\begin{pmatrix} 1 & 4 \\ 2 & 5 \\ 3 & 6 \end{pmatrix} + \begin{pmatrix} 1 & 2 \\ 2 & 1 \\ 1 & 2 \end{pmatrix}$$

2.4   Common Vector Operations

Now let's look at some common operations related to vectors. We'll cover arithmetic and logical operations, vector indexing, and some useful ways to create vectors. Then we'll look at two extended examples of using these operations.

2.4.1   Vector Arithmetic and Logical Operations

Remember that R is a functional language. Every operator, including + in the following example, is actually a function.

```
> 2+3
[1] 5
> "+"(2,3)
[1] 5
```

Recall further that scalars are actually one-element vectors. So, we can add vectors, and the + operation will be applied element-wise.

```
> x <- c(1,2,4)
> x + c(5,0,-1)
[1] 6 2 3
```

If you are familiar with linear algebra, you may be surprised at what happens when we multiply two vectors.

```
> x * c(5,0,-1)
[1]  5  0 -4
```

But remember, because of the way the * function is applied, the multiplication is done element by element. The first element of the product (5) is the result of the first element of x (1) being multiplied by the first element of c(5,0,1) (5), and so on.

The same principle applies to other numeric operators. Here's an example:

```
> x <- c(1,2,4)
> x / c(5,4,-1)
[1]  0.2  0.5 -4.0
> x %% c(5,4,-1)
[1] 1 2 0
```

2.4.2   Vector Indexing

One of the most important and frequently used operations in R is that of *indexing* vectors, in which we form a subvector by picking elements of the given vector for specific indices. The format is vector1[vector2], with the result that we select those elements of vector1 whose indices are given in vector2.

```
> y <- c(1.2,3.9,0.4,0.12)
> y[c(1,3)]  # extract elements 1 and 3 of y
[1] 1.2 0.4
> y[2:3]
[1] 3.9 0.4
> v <- 3:4
> y[v]
[1] 0.40 0.12
```

Note that duplicates are allowed.

```
> x <- c(4,2,17,5)
> y <- x[c(1,1,3)]
> y
[1]  4  4 17
```

Negative subscripts mean that we want to exclude the given elements in our output.

```
> z <- c(5,12,13)
> z[-1]   # exclude element 1
[1] 12 13
> z[-1:-2]   # exclude elements 1 through 2
[1] 13
```

In such contexts, it is often useful to use the length() function. For instance, suppose we wish to pick up all elements of a vector z except for the last. The following code will do just that:

```
> z <- c(5,12,13)
> z[1:(length(z)-1)]
[1]  5 12
```

Or more simply:

```
> z[-length(z)]
[1]  5 12
```

This is more general than using z[1:2]. Our program may need to work for more than just vectors of length 2, and the second approach would give us that generality.

2.4.3   Generating Useful Vectors with the : Operator

There are a few R operators that are especially useful for creating vectors. Let's start with the colon operator :, which was introduced in Chapter 1. It produces a vector consisting of a range of numbers.

```
> 5:8
[1] 5 6 7 8
> 5:1
[1] 5 4 3 2 1
```

You may recall that it was used earlier in this chapter in a loop context, as follows:

```
for (i in 1:length(x)) {
```

Beware of operator precedence issues.

```
> i <- 2
> 1:i-1  # this means (1:i) - 1, not 1:(i-1)
[1] 0 1
> 1:(i-1)
[1] 1
```

In the expression 1:i-1, the colon operator takes precedence over the subtraction. So, the expression 1:i is evaluated first, returning 1:2. R then subtracts 1 from that expression. That means subtracting a one-element vector from a two-element one, which is done via recycling. The one-element vector (1) will be extended to (1,1) to be of compatible length with 1:2. Element-wise subtraction then yields the vector (0,1).

In the expression 1:(i-1), on the other hand, the parentheses have higher precedence than the colon. Thus, 1 is subtracted from i, resulting in 1:1, as seen in the preceding example.

NOTE *You can obtain complete details of operator precedence in R through the included help. Just type ?Syntax at the command prompt.*

2.4.4 Generating Vector Sequences with seq()

A generalization of : is the seq() (or *sequence*) function, which generates a sequence in arithmetic progression. For instance, whereas 3:8 yields the vector (3,4,5,6,7,8), with the elements spaced one unit apart ($4 - 3 = 1, 5 - 4 = 1$, and so on), we can make them, say, three units apart, as follows:

```
> seq(from=12,to=30,by=3)
[1] 12 15 18 21 24 27 30
```

The spacing can be a noninteger value, too, say 0.1.

```
> seq(from=1.1,to=2,length=10)
[1] 1.1 1.2 1.3 1.4 1.5 1.6 1.7 1.8 1.9 2.0
```

One handy use for seq() is to deal with the empty-vector problem we mentioned earlier in Section 2.1.2. There, we were dealing with a loop that began with this:

```
for (i in 1:length(x))
```

If x is empty, this loop should not have any iterations, but it actually has two, since 1:length(x) evaluates to (1,0). We could fix this by writing the statement as follows:

```
for (i in seq(x))
```

To see why this works, let's do a quick test of seq():

```
> x <- c(5,12,13)
> x
[1]  5 12 13
> seq(x)
[1] 1 2 3
> x <- NULL
> x
NULL
> seq(x)
integer(0)
```

You can see that seq(x) gives us the same result as 1:length(x) if x is not empty, but it correctly evaluates to NULL if x is empty, resulting in zero iterations in the above loop.

2.4.5   Repeating Vector Constants with rep()

The rep() (or *repeat*) function allows us to conveniently put the same constant into long vectors. The call form is rep(x,times), which creates a vector of *times*length(x)* elements—that is, times copies of x. Here is an example:

```
> x <- rep(8,4)
> x
[1] 8 8 8 8
> rep(c(5,12,13),3)
[1]  5 12 13  5 12 13  5 12 13
> rep(1:3,2)
[1] 1 2 3 1 2 3
```

There is also a named argument each, with very different behavior, which interleaves the copies of x.

```
> rep(c(5,12,13),each=2)
[1]  5  5 12 12 13 13
```

2.5 Using all() and any()

The any() and all() functions are handy shortcuts. They report whether any or all of their arguments are TRUE.

```
> x <- 1:10
> any(x > 8)
[1] TRUE
> any(x > 88)
[1] FALSE
> all(x > 88)
[1] FALSE
> all(x > 0)
[1] TRUE
```

For example, suppose that R executes the following:

```
> any(x > 8)
```

It first evaluates x > 8, yielding this:

```
(FALSE,FALSE,FALSE,FALSE,FALSE,FALSE,FALSE,FALSE,TRUE,TRUE)
```

The any() function then reports whether any of those values is TRUE. The all() function works similarly and reports if *all* of the values are TRUE.

2.5.1 Extended Example: Finding Runs of Consecutive Ones

Suppose that we are interested in finding runs of consecutive 1s in vectors that consist just of 1s and 0s. In the vector (1,0,0,1,1,1,0,1,1), for instance, there is a run of length 3 starting at index 4, and runs of length 2 beginning at indices 4, 5, and 8. So the call findruns(c(1,0,0,1,1,1,0,1,1),2) to our function to be shown below returns (4,5,8). Here is the code:

```
1  findruns <- function(x,k) {
2     n <- length(x)
3     runs <- NULL
4     for (i in 1:(n-k+1)) {
5        if (all(x[i:(i+k-1)]==1)) runs <- c(runs,i)
6     }
7     return(runs)
8  }
```

In line 5, we need to determine whether all of the k values starting at x[i]—that is, all of the values in x[i],x[i+1],...,x[i+k-1]—are 1s. The expression x[i:(i+k-1)] gives us this range in x, and then applying all() tells us whether there is a run there.

Let's test it.

```
> y <- c(1,0,0,1,1,1,0,1,1)
> findruns(y,3)
[1] 4
> findruns(y,2)
[1] 4 5 8
> findruns(y,6)
NULL
```

Although the use of all() is good in the preceding code, the buildup of the vector runs is not so good. Vector allocation is time consuming. Each execution of the following slows down our code, as it allocates a new vector in the call c(runs,i). (The fact that new vector is assigned to runs is irrelevant; we still have done a vector memory space allocation.)

```
runs <- c(runs,i)
```

In a short loop, this probably will be no problem, but when application performance is an issue, there are better ways.

One alternative is to preallocate the memory space, like this:

```
1   findruns1 <- function(x,k) {
2       n <- length(x)
3       runs <- vector(length=n)
4       count <- 0
5       for (i in 1:(n-k+1)) {
6           if (all(x[i:(i+k-1)]==1)) {
7               count <- count + 1
8               runs[count] <- i
9           }
10      }
11      if (count > 0) {
12          runs <- runs[1:count]
13      } else runs <- NULL
14      return(runs)
15  }
```

In line 3, we set up space of a vector of length n. This means we avoid new allocations during execution of the loop. We merely fill runs, in line 8. Just before exiting the function, we redefine runs in line 12 to remove the unused portion of the vector.

This is better, as we've reduced the number of memory allocations to just two, down from possibly many in the first version of the code.

If we really need the speed, we might consider recoding this in C, as discussed in Chapter 14.

2.5.2   Extended Example: Predicting Discrete-Valued Time Series

Suppose we observe 0- and 1-valued data, one per time period. To make things concrete, say it's daily weather data: 1 for rain and 0 for no rain. Suppose we wish to predict whether it will rain tomorrow, knowing whether it rained or not in recent days. Specifically, for some number k, we will predict tomorrow's weather based on the weather record of the last k days. We'll use majority rule: If the number of 1s in the previous k time periods is at least k/2, we'll predict the next value to be 1; otherwise, our prediction is 0. For instance, if k = 3 and the data for the last three periods is 1,0,1, we'll predict the next period to be a 1.

But how should we choose k? Clearly, if we choose too small a value, it may give us too small a sample from which to predict. Too large a value will cause us to rely on data from the distant past that may have little or no predictive value.

A common solution to this problem is to take known data, called a *training set*, and then ask how well various values of k would have performed on that data.

In the weather case, suppose we have 500 days of data and suppose we are considering using k = 3. To assess the predictive ability of that value for k, we "predict" each day in our data from the previous three days and then compare the predictions with the known values. After doing this throughout our data, we have an error rate for k = 3. We do the same for k = 1, k = 2, k = 4, and so on, up to some maximum value of k that we feel is enough. We then use whichever value of k worked best in our training data for future predictions.

So how would we code that in R? Here's a naive approach:

```
1   preda <- function(x,k) {
2      n <- length(x)
3      k2 <- k/2
4      # the vector pred will contain our predicted values
5      pred <- vector(length=n-k)
6      for (i in 1:(n-k)) {
7         if (sum(x[i:(i+(k-1))]) >= k2) pred[i] <- 1 else pred[i] <- 0
8      }
9      return(mean(abs(pred-x[(k+1):n])))
10  }
```

The heart of the code is line 7. There, we're predicting day i+k (prediction to be stored in pred[i]) from the k days previous to it—that is, days i,...,i+k-1. Thus, we need to count the 1s among those days. Since we're working with 0 and 1 data, the number of 1s is simply the sum of x[j] among those days, which we can conveniently obtain as follows:

```
sum(x[i:(i+(k-1))])
```

The use of sum() and vector indexing allow us to do this computation compactly, avoiding the need to write a loop, so it's simpler and faster. This is typical R.

The same is true for this expression, on line 9:

```
mean(abs(pred-x[(k+1):n]))
```

Here, pred contains the predicted values, while x[(k+1):n] has the actual values for the days in question. Subtracting the second from the first gives us values of either 0, 1, or -1. Here, 1 or -1 correspond to prediction errors in one direction or the other, predicting 0 when the true value was 1 or vice versa. Taking absolute values with abs(), we have 0s and 1s, the latter corresponding to errors.

So we now know where days gave us errors. It remains to calculate the proportion of errors. We do this by applying mean(), where we are exploiting the mathematical fact that the mean of 0 and 1 data is the proportion of 1s. This is a common R trick.

The above coding of our preda() function is fairly straightforward, and it has the advantage of simplicity and compactness. However, it is probably slow. We could try to speed it up by vectorizing the loop, as discussed in Section 2.6. However, that would not address the major obstacle to speed here, which is all of the duplicate computation that the code does. For successive values of i in the loop, sum() is being called on vectors that differ by only two elements. Except for cases in which k is very small, this could really slow things down.

So, let's rewrite the code to take advantage of previous computation. In each iteration of the loop, we will update the previous sum we found, rather than compute the new sum from scratch.

```
1  predb <- function(x,k) {
2      n <- length(x)
3      k2 <- k/2
4      pred <- vector(length=n-k)
5      sm <- sum(x[1:k])
6      if (sm >= k2) pred[1] <- 1 else pred[1] <- 0
7      if (n-k >= 2) {
8          for (i in 2:(n-k)) {
9              sm <- sm + x[i+k-1] - x[i-1]
10             if (sm >= k2) pred[i] <- 1 else pred[i] <- 0
11         }
12     }
13     return(mean(abs(pred-x[(k+1):n])))
14 }
```

The key is line 9. Here, we are updating sm, by subtracting the oldest element making up the sum (x[i-1]) and adding the new one (x[i+k-1]).

Yet another approach to this problem is to use the R function cumsum(), which forms cumulative sums from a vector. Here is an example:

```
> y <- c(5,2,-3,8)
> cumsum(y)
[1]  5  7  4 12
```

Here, the cumulative sums of y are $5 = 5$, $5 + 2 = 7$, $5 + 2 + (-3) = 4$, and $5 + 2 + (-3) + 8 = 12$, the values returned by cumsum().

The expression sum(x[i:(i+(k-1)) in preda() in the example suggests using differences of cumsum() instead:

```
predc <- function(x,k) {
    n <- length(x)
    k2 <- k/2
    # the vector red will contain our predicted values
    pred <- vector(length=n-k)
    csx <- c(0,cumsum(x))
    for (i in 1:(n-k)) {
        if (csx[i+k] - csx[i] >= k2) pred[i] <- 1 else pred[i] <- 0
    }
    return(mean(abs(pred-x[(k+1):n])))
}
```

Instead of applying sum() to a window of k consecutive elements in x, like this:

```
sum(x[i:(i+(k-1))
```

we compute that same sum by finding the difference between the cumulative sums at the end and beginning of that window, like this:

```
csx[i+k] - csx[i]
```

Note the prepending of a 0 in the vector of cumulative sums:

```
csx <- c(0,cumsum(x))
```

This is needed in order to handle the case i = 1 correctly.

This approach in predc() requires just one subtraction operation per iteration of the loop, compared to two in predb().

2.6 Vectorized Operations

Suppose we have a function f() that we wish to apply to all elements of a vector x. In many cases, we can accomplish this by simply calling f() on x itself.

This can really simplify our code and, moreover, give us a dramatic performance increase of hundredsfold or more.

One of the most effective ways to achieve speed in R code is to use operations that are *vectorized*, meaning that a function applied to a vector is actually applied individually to each element.

2.6.1   Vector In, Vector Out

You saw examples of vectorized functions earlier in the chapter, with the + and * operators. Another example is >.

```
> u <- c(5,2,8)
> v <- c(1,3,9)
> u > v
[1]  TRUE FALSE FALSE
```

Here, the > function was applied to u[1] and v[1], resulting in TRUE, then to u[2] and v[2], resulting in FALSE, and so on.

A key point is that if an R function uses vectorized operations, it, too, is vectorized, thus enabling a potential speedup. Here is an example:

```
> w <- function(x) return(x+1)
> w(u)
[1] 6 3 9
```

Here, w() uses +, which is vectorized, so w() is vectorized as well. As you can see, there is an unlimited number of vectorized functions, as complex ones are built up from simpler ones.

Note that even the transcendental functions—square roots, logs, trig functions, and so on—are vectorized.

```
> sqrt(1:9)
[1] 1.000000 1.414214 1.732051 2.000000 2.236068 2.449490 2.645751 2.828427
[9] 3.000000
```

This applies to many other built-in R functions. For instance, let's apply the function for rounding to the nearest integer to an example vector y:

```
> y <- c(1.2,3.9,0.4)
> z <- round(y)
> z
[1] 1 4 0
```

The point is that the round() function is applied individually to each element in the vector y. And remember that scalars are really single-element vectors, so the "ordinary" use of round() on just one number is merely a special case.

```
> round(1.2)
[1] 1
```

Here, we used the built-in function round(), but you can do the same thing with functions that you write yourself.

As mentioned earlier, even operators such as + are really functions. For example, consider this code:

```
> y <- c(12,5,13)
> y+4
[1] 16  9 17
```

The reason element-wise addition of 4 works here is that the + is actually a function! Here it is explicitly:

```
> '+'(y,4)
[1] 16  9 17
```

Note, too, that recycling played a key role here, with the 4 recycled into (4,4,4).

Since we know that R has no scalars, let's consider vectorized functions that appear to have scalar arguments.

```
> f
function(x,c) return((x+c)^2)
> f(1:3,0)
[1] 1 4 9
> f(1:3,1)
[1]  4  9 16
```

In our definition of f() here, we clearly intend c to be a scalar, but, of course, it is actually a vector of length 1. Even if we use a single number for c in our call to f(), it will be extended through recycling to a vector for our computation of x+c within f(). So in our call f(1:3,1) in the example, the quantity x+c becomes as follows:

$$\begin{pmatrix} 1 \\ 2 \\ 3 \end{pmatrix} + \begin{pmatrix} 1 \\ 1 \\ 1 \end{pmatrix}$$

This brings up a question of code safety. There is nothing in f() that keeps us from using an explicit vector for c, such as in this example:

```
> f(1:3,1:3)
[1]  4 16 36
```

You should work through the computation to confirm that (4,16,36) is indeed the expected output.

If you really want to restrict c to scalars, you should insert some kind of check, say this one:

```
> f
function(x,c) {
if (length(c) != 1) stop("vector c not allowed")
   return((x+c)^2)
}
```

2.6.2 Vector In, Matrix Out

The vectorized functions we've been working with so far have scalar return values. Calling sqrt() on a number gives us a number. If we apply this function to an eight-element vector, we get eight numbers, thus another eight-element vector, as output.

But what if our function itself is vector-valued, as z12() is here:

```
z12 <- function(z) return(c(z,z^2))
```

Applying z12() to 5, say, gives us the two-element vector (5,25). If we apply this function to an eight-element vector, it produces 16 numbers:

```
x <- 1:8
> z12(x)
 [1]  1  2  3  4  5  6  7  8  1  4  9 16 25 36 49 64
```

It might be more natural to have these arranged as an 8-by-2 matrix, which we can do with the matrix function:

```
> matrix(z12(x),ncol=2)
     [,1] [,2]
[1,]    1    1
[2,]    2    4
[3,]    3    9
[4,]    4   16
[5,]    5   25
[6,]    6   36
[7,]    7   49
[8,]    8   64
```

But we can streamline things using sapply() (or *simplify apply*). The call sapply(x,f) applies the function f() to each element of x and then converts the result to a matrix. Here is an example:

```
> z12 <- function(z) return(c(z,z^2))
> sapply(1:8,z12)
     [,1] [,2] [,3] [,4] [,5] [,6] [,7] [,8]
```

```
[1,]   1   2   3    4    5    6    7    8
[2,]   1   4   9   16   25   36   49   64
```

We do get a 2-by-8 matrix, not an 8-by-2 one, but it's just as useful this way. We'll discuss sapply() further in Chapter 4.

2.7   NA and NULL Values

Readers with a background in other scripting languages may be aware of "no such animal" values, such as None in Python and undefined in Perl. R actually has two such values: NA and NULL.

In statistical data sets, we often encounter missing data, which we represent in R with the value NA. NULL, on the other hand, represents that the value in question simply doesn't exist, rather than being existent but unknown. Let's see how this comes into play in concrete terms.

2.7.1   Using NA

In many of R's statistical functions, we can instruct the function to skip over any missing values, or NAs. Here is an example:

```
> x <- c(88,NA,12,168,13)
> x
[1]  88  NA  12 168  13
> mean(x)
[1] NA
> mean(x,na.rm=T)
[1] 70.25
> x <- c(88,NULL,12,168,13)
> mean(x)
[1] 70.25
```

In the first call, mean() refused to calculate, as one value in x was NA. But by setting the optional argument na.rm (*NA remove*) to true (T), we calculated the mean of the remaining elements. But R automatically skipped over the NULL value, which we'll look at in the next section.

There are multiple NA values, one for each mode:

```
> x <- c(5,NA,12)
> mode(x[1])
[1] "numeric"
> mode(x[2])
[1] "numeric"
> y <- c("abc","def",NA)
> mode(y[2])
[1] "character"
> mode(y[3])
[1] "character"
```

2.7.2 Using NULL

One use of NULL is to build up vectors in loops, in which each iteration adds another element to the vector. In this simple example, we build up a vector of even numbers:

```
# build up a vector of the even numbers in 1:10
> z <- NULL
> for (i in 1:10) if (i %%2 == 0) z <- c(z,i)
> z
[1]  2  4  6  8 10
```

Recall from Chapter 1 that %% is the modulo operator, giving remainders upon division. For example, 13 %% 4 is 1, as the remainder of dividing 13 by 4 is 1. (See Section 7.2 for a list of arithmetic and logic operators.) Thus the example loop starts with a NULL vector and then adds the element 2 to it, then 4, and so on.

This is a very artificial example, of course, and there are much better ways to do this particular task. Here are two more ways another way to find even numbers in 1:10:

```
> seq(2,10,2)
[1]  2  4  6  8 10
> 2*1:5
[1]  2  4  6  8 10
```

But the point here is to demonstrate the difference between NA and NULL. If we were to use NA instead of NULL in the preceding example, we would pick up an unwanted NA:

```
> z <- NA
> for (i in 1:10) if (i %%2 == 0) z <- c(z,i)
> z
[1] NA  2  4  6  8 10
```

NULL values really are counted as nonexistent, as you can see here:

```
> u <- NULL
> length(u)
[1] 0
> v <- NA
> length(v)
[1] 1
```

NULL is a special R object with no mode.

2.8 Filtering

Another feature reflecting the functional language nature of R is *filtering*. This allows us to extract a vector's elements that satisfy certain conditions. Filtering is one of the most common operations in R, as statistical analyses often focus on data that satisfies conditions of interest.

2.8.1 Generating Filtering Indices

Let's start with a simple example:

```
> z <- c(5,2,-3,8)
> w <- z[z*z > 8]
> w
[1] 5  -3  8
```

Looking at this code in an intuitive, "What is our intent?" manner, we see that we asked R to extract from z all its elements whose squares were greater than 8 and then assign that subvector to w.

But filtering is such a key operation in R that it's worthwhile to examine the technical details of how R achieves our intent above. Let's look at it done piece by piece:

```
> z <- c(5,2,-3,8)
> z
[1]  5  2 -3  8
> z*z > 8
[1]  TRUE FALSE  TRUE  TRUE
```

Evaluation of the expression z*z > 8 gives us a vector of Boolean values! It's very important that you understand exactly how this comes about.

First, in the expression z*z > 8, note that *everything* is a vector or vector operator:

- Since z is a vector, that means z*z will also be a vector (of the same length as z).

- Due to recycling, the number 8 (or vector of length 1) becomes the vector (8,8,8,8) here.

- The operator >, like +, is actually a function.

Let's look at an example of that last point:

```
> ">"(2,1)
[1] TRUE
> ">"(2,5)
[1] FALSE
```

Thus, the following:

```
z*z > 8
```

is really this:

```
">"(z*z,8)
```

In other words, we are applying a function to vectors—yet another case of vectorization, no different from the others you've seen. And thus the result is a vector—in this case, a vector of Booleans. Then the resulting Boolean values are used to cull out the desired elements of z:

```
> z[c(TRUE,FALSE,TRUE,TRUE)]
[1]  5 -3  8
```

This next example will place things into even sharper focus. Here, we will again define our extraction condition in terms of z, but then we will use the results to extract from another vector, y, instead of extracting from z:

```
> z <- c(5,2,-3,8)
> j <- z*z > 8
> j
[1]  TRUE FALSE  TRUE  TRUE
> y <- c(1,2,30,5)
> y[j]
[1]  1 30  5
```

Or, more compactly, we could write the following:

```
> z <- c(5,2,-3,8)
> y <- c(1,2,30,5)
> y[z*z > 8]
[1]  1 30  5
```

Again, the point is that in this example, we are using one vector, z, to determine indices to use in filtering *another* vector, y. In contrast, our earlier example used z to filter itself.

Here's another example, this one involving assignment. Say we have a vector x in which we wish to replace all elements larger than a 3 with a 0. We can do that very compactly—in fact, in just one line:

```
> x[x > 3] <- 0
```

Let's check:

```
> x <- c(1,3,8,2,20)
> x[x > 3] <- 0
> x
[1] 1 3 0 2 0
```

2.8.2   Filtering with the subset() Function

Filtering can also be done with the subset() function. When applied to vectors, the difference between using this function and ordinary filtering lies in the manner in which NA values are handled.

```
> x <- c(6,1:3,NA,12)
> x
[1]  6  1  2  3 NA 12
> x[x > 5]
[1]  6 NA 12
> subset(x,x > 5)
[1]  6 12
```

When we did ordinary filtering in the previous section, R basically said, "Well, x[5] is unknown, so it's also unknown whether its square is greater than 5." But you may not want NAs in your results. When you wish to exclude NA values, using subset() saves you the trouble of removing the NA values yourself.

2.8.3   The Selection Function which()

As you've seen, filtering consists of extracting elements of a vector z that satisfy a certain condition. In some cases, though, we may just want to find the positions within z at which the condition occurs. We can do this using which(), as follows:

```
> z <- c(5,2,-3,8)
> which(z*z > 8)
[1] 1 3 4
```

The result says that elements 1, 3, and 4 of z have squares greater than 8.

As with filtering, it is important to understand exactly what occurred in the preceding code. The expression

```
z*z > 8
```

is evaluated to (TRUE,FALSE,TRUE,TRUE). The which() function then simply reports which elements of the latter expression are TRUE.

One handy (though somewhat wasteful) use of `which()` is for determining the location within a vector at which the first occurrence of some condition holds. For example, recall our code on page 27 to find the first 1 value within a vector x:

```
first1 <- function(x) {
   for (i in 1:length(x)) {
      if (x[i] == 1) break  # break out of loop
   }
   return(i)
}
```

Here is an alternative way of coding this task:

```
first1a <- function(x) return(which(x == 1)[1])
```

The call to `which()` yields the indices of the 1s in x. These indices will be given in the form of a vector, and we ask for element index 1 in that vector, which is the index of the first 1.

That is much more compact. On the other hand, it's wasteful, as it actually finds *all* instances of 1s in x, when we need only the first. So, although it is a vectorized approach and thus possibly faster, if the first 1 comes early in x, this approach may actually be slower.

2.9   A Vectorized if-then-else: The ifelse() Function

In addition to the usual if-then-else construct found in most languages, R also includes a vectorized version, the `ifelse()` function. The form is as follows:

```
ifelse(b,u,v)
```

where b is a Boolean vector, and u and v are vectors.

The return value is itself a vector; element i is u[i] if b[i] is true, or v[i] if b[i] is false. The concept is pretty abstract, so let's go right to an example:

```
> x <- 1:10
> y <- ifelse(x %% 2 == 0,5,12)  # %% is the mod operator
> y
 [1] 12  5 12  5 12  5 12  5 12  5
```

Here, we wish to produce a vector in which there is a 5 wherever x is even or a 12 wherever x is odd. So, the actual argument corresponding to the formal argument b is (F,T,F,T,F,T,F,T,F,T). The second actual argument, 5, corresponding to u, is treated as (5,5,...) (ten 5s) by recycling. The third argument, 12, is also recycled, to (12,12,...).

Here is another example:

```
> x <- c(5,2,9,12)
> ifelse(x > 6,2*x,3*x)
[1] 15  6 18 24
```

We return a vector consisting of the elements of x, either multiplied by 2 or 3, depending on whether the element is greater than 6.

Again, it helps to think through what is really occurring here. The expression x > 6 is a vector of Booleans. If the ith component is true, then the ith element of the return value will be set to the ith element of 2*x; otherwise, it will be set to 3*x[i], and so on.

The advantage of ifelse() over the standard if-then-else construct is that it is vectorized, thus potentially much faster.

2.9.1   Extended Example: A Measure of Association

In assessing the statistical relation of two variables, there are many alternatives to the standard correlation measure (Pearson product-moment correlation). Some readers may have heard of the Spearman rank correlation, for example. These alternative measures have various motivations, such as robustness to *outliers*, which are extreme and possibly erroneous data items.

Here, let's propose a new such measure, not necessarily for novel statistical merits (actually it is related to one in broad use, Kendall's τ), but to illustrate some of the R programming techniques introduced in this chapter, especially ifelse().

Consider vectors x and y, which are time series, say for measurements of air temperature and pressure collected once each hour. We'll define our measure of association between them to be the fraction of the time x and y increase or decrease together—that is, the proportion of i for which y[i+1]-y[i] has the same sign as x[i+1]-x[i]. Here is the code:

```
1   # findud() converts vector v to 1s, 0s, representing an element
2   # increasing or not, relative to the previous one; output length is 1
3   # less than input
4   findud <- function(v) {
5       vud <- v[-1] - v[-length(v)]
6       return(ifelse(vud > 0,1,-1))
7   }
8
9   udcorr <- function(x,y) {
10      ud <- lapply(list(x,y),findud)
11      return(mean(ud[[1]] == ud[[2]]))
12  }
```

Here's an example:

```
> x
[1]   5 12 13  3  6  0  1 15 16  8 88
> y
[1]   4  2  3 23  6 10 11 12  6  3  2
> udcorr(x,y)
[1] 0.4
```

In this example, x and y increased together in 3 of the 10 opportunities (the first time being the increases from 12 to 13 and 2 to 3) and decreased together once. That gives an association measure of 4/10 = 0.4.

Let's see how this works. The first order of business is to recode x and y to sequences of 1s and −1s, with a value of 1 meaning an increase of the current observation over the last. We've done that in lines 5 and 6.

For example, think what happens in line 5 when we call findud() with v having a length of, say, 16 elements. Then v[-1] will be a vector of 15 elements, starting with the second element in v. Similarly, v[-length(v)] will again be a vector of 15 elements, this time starting from the first element in v. The result is that we are subtracting the original series from the series obtained by shifting rightward by one time period. The difference gives us the sequence of increase/decrease statuses for each time period—exactly what we need.

We then need to change those differences to 1 and −1s, according to whether a difference is positive or negative. The ifelse() call does this easily, compactly, and with smaller execution time than a loop version of the code would have.

We could have then written two calls to findud(): one for x and the other for y. But by putting x and y into a list and then using lapply(), we can do this without duplicating code. If we were applying the same operation to many vectors instead of only two, especially in the case of a variable number of vectors, using lapply() like this would be a big help in compacting and clarifying the code, and it might be slightly faster as well.

We then find the fraction of matches, as follows:

```
return(mean(ud[[1]] == ud[[2]]))
```

Note that lapply() returns a list. The components are our 1/−1–coded vectors. The expression ud[[1]] == ud[[2]] returns a vector of TRUE and FALSE values, which are treated as 1 and 0 values by mean(). That gives us the desired fraction.

A more advanced version would make use of R's diff() function, which does *lag* operations for vectors. We might, for instance, compare each element with the element three spots behind it, termed a *lag of 3*. The default lag value is one time period, just what we need here.

```
> u
[1] 1 6 7 2 3 5
> diff(u)
[1]  5  1 -5  1  2
```

Then line 5 in the preceding example would become this:

```
vud <- diff(v)
```

We can make the code really compact by using another advanced R function, sign(), which converts the numbers in its argument vector to 1, 0, or −1, depending on whether they are positive, zero, or negative. Here is an example:

```
> u
[1] 1 6 7 2 3 5
> diff(u)
[1]  5  1 -5  1  2
> sign(diff(u))
[1]  1  1 -1  1  1
```

Using sign() then allows us to turn this udcorr()function into a one-liner, as follows:

```
> udcorr <- function(x,y) mean(sign(diff(x)) == sign(diff(y)))
```

This is certainly a lot shorter than the original version. But is it better? For most people, it probably would take longer to write. And although the code is short, it is arguably harder to understand.

All R programmers must find their own "happy medium" in trading brevity for clarity.

2.9.2 Extended Example: Recoding an Abalone Data Set

Due to the vector nature of the arguments, you can nest ifelse() operations. In the following example, which involves an abalone data set, gender is coded as M, F, or I (for infant). We wish to recode those characters as 1, 2, or 3. The real data set consists of more than 4,000 observations, but for our example, we'll say we have just a few, stored in g:

```
> g
[1] "M" "F" "F" "I" "M" "M" "F"
> ifelse(g == "M",1,ifelse(g == "F",2,3))
[1] 1 2 2 3 1 1 2
```

What actually happens in that nested ifelse()? Let's take a careful look. First, for the sake of concreteness, let's find what the formal argument names are in the function ifelse():

```
> args(ifelse)
function (test, yes, no)
NULL
```

Remember, for each element of test that is true, the function evaluates to the corresponding element in yes. Similarly, if test[i] is false, the function evaluates to no[i]. All values so generated are returned together in a vector.

In our case here, R will execute the outer ifelse() call first, in which test is g == "M", and yes is 1 (recycled); no will (later) be the result of executing ifelse(g=="F",2,3). Now since test[1] is true, we generate yes[1], which is 1. So, the first element of the return value of our outer call will be 1.

Next R will evaluate test[2]. That is false, so R needs to find no[2]. R now needs to execute the inner ifelse() call. It hasn't done so before, because it hasn't needed it until now. R uses the principle of *lazy evaluation*, meaning that an expression is not computed until it is needed.

R will now evaluate ifelse(g=="F",2,3), yielding (3,2,2,3,3,3,2); this is no for the outer ifelse() call, so the latter's second return element will be the second element of (3,2,2,3,3,3,2), which is 2.

When the outer ifelse() call gets to test[4], it will see that value to be false and thus will return no[4]. Since R had already computed no, it has the value needed, which is 3.

Remember that the vectors involved could be columns in matrices, which is a very common scenario. Say our abalone data is stored in the matrix ab, with gender in the first column. Then if we wish to recode as in the preceding example, we could do it this way:

```
> ab[,1] <- ifelse(ab[,1] == "M",1,ifelse(ab[,1] == "F",2,3))
```

Suppose we wish to form subgroups according to gender. We could use which() to find the element numbers corresponding to M, F, and I:

```
> m <- which(g == "M")
> f <- which(g == "F")
> i <- which(g == "I")
> m
[1] 1 5 6
> f
[1] 2 3 7
> i
[1] 4
```

Going one step further, we could save these groups in a list, like this:

```
> grps <- list()
> for (gen in c("M","F","I")) grps[[gen]] <- which(g==gen)
> grps
$M
[1] 1 5 6

$F
[1] 2 3 7

$I
[1] 4
```

Note that we take advantage of the fact that R's for() loop has the ability to loop through a vector of strings. (You'll see a more efficient approach in Section 4.4.)

We might use our recoded data to draw some graphs, exploring the various variables in the abalone data set. Let's summarize the nature of the variables by adding the following header to the file:

```
Gender,Length,Diameter,Height,WholeWt,ShuckedWt,ViscWt,ShellWt,Rings
```

We could, for instance, plot diameter versus length, with a separate plot for males and females, using the following code:

```
aba <- read.csv("abalone.data",header=T,as.is=T)
grps <- list()
for (gen in c("M","F")) grps[[gen]] <- which(aba[,1]==gen)
abam <- aba[grps$M,]
abaf <- aba[grps$F,]
plot(abam$Length,abam$Diameter)
plot(abaf$Length,abaf$Diameter,pch="x",new=FALSE)
```

First, we read in the data set, assigning it to the variable aba (to remind us that it's abalone data). The call to read.csv() is similar to the read.table() call we used in Chapter 1, as we'll discuss in Chapters 6 and 10. We then form abam and abaf, the submatrices of aba corresponding to males and females, respectively.

Next, we create the plots. The first call does a scatter plot of diameter against length for the males. The second call is for the females. Since we want this plot to be superimposed on the same graph as the males, we set the argument new=FALSE, instructing R to *not* create a new graph. The argument pch="x" means that we want the plot characters for the female graph to consist of *x* characters, rather than the default *o* characters.

The graph (for the entire data set) is shown in Figure 2-1. By the way, it is not completely satisfactory. Apparently, there is such a strong correlation between diameter and length that the points densely fill up a section of the graph, and the male and female plots pretty much coincide. (It does appear that males have more variability, though.) This is a common issue in statistical graphics. A finer graphical analysis may be more illuminating, but at least here we see evidence of the strong correlation and that the relation does not vary much across genders.

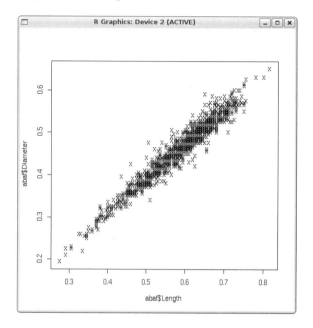

Figure 2-1: Abalone diameter vs. length by gender

We can compact the plotting code in the previous example by yet another use of ifelse. This exploits the fact that the plot parameter pch is allowed to be a vector rather than a single character. In other words, R allows us to specify a different plot character for each point.

```
pchvec <- ifelse(aba$Gender == "M","o","x")
plot(aba$Length,aba$Diameter,pch=pchvec)
```

(Here, we've omitted the recoding to 1, 2, and 3, but you may wish to retain it for various reasons.)

2.10   Testing Vector Equality

Suppose we wish to test whether two vectors are equal. The naive approach, using ==, won't work.

```
> x <- 1:3
> y <- c(1,3,4)
> x == y
[1]  TRUE FALSE FALSE
```

What happened? The key point is that we are dealing with vectorization. Just like almost anything else in R, == is a function.

```
> "=="(3,2)
[1] FALSE
> i <- 2
> "=="(i,2)
[1] TRUE
```

In fact, == is a vectorized function. The expression x == y applies the function ==() to the elements of x and y. yielding a vector of Boolean values.

What can be done instead? One option is to work with the vectorized nature of ==, applying the function all():

```
> x <- 1:3
> y <- c(1,3,4)
> x == y
[1]  TRUE FALSE FALSE
> all(x == y)
[1] FALSE
```

Applying all() to the result of == asks whether all of the elements of the latter are true, which is the same as asking whether x and y are identical.

Or even better, we can simply use the identical function, like this:

```
> identical(x,y)
[1] FALSE
```

Be careful, though because the word *identical* really means what it says. Consider this little R session:

```
> x <- 1:2
> y <- c(1,2)
> x
[1] 1 2
> y
[1] 1 2
> identical(x,y)
[1] FALSE
> typeof(x)
[1] "integer"
> typeof(y)
[1] "double"
```

So, : produces integers while c() produces floating-point numbers. Who knew?

2.11 Vector Element Names

The elements of a vector can optionally be given names. For example, say we have a 50-element vector showing the population of each state in the United States. We could name each element according to its state name, such as "Montana" and "New Jersey". This in turn might lead to naming points in plots, and so on.

We can assign or query vector element names via the names() function:

```
> x <- c(1,2,4)
> names(x)
NULL
> names(x) <- c("a","b","ab")
> names(x)
[1] "a"  "b"  "ab"
> x
 a  b ab
 1  2  4
```

We can remove the names from a vector by assigning NULL:

```
> names(x) <- NULL
> x
[1] 1 2 4
```

We can even reference elements of the vector by name:

```
> x <- c(1,2,4)
> names(x) <- c("a","b","ab")
> x["b"]
b
2
```

2.12 More on c()

In this section, we'll discuss a couple of miscellaneous facts related to the concatenate function, c(), that often come in handy.

If the arguments you pass to c() are of differing modes, they will be reduced to a type that is the lowest common denominator, as follows:

```
> c(5,2,"abc")
[1] "5"   "2"   "abc"
> c(5,2,list(a=1,b=4))
[[1]]
[1] 5

[[2]]
[1] 2
```

```
$a
[1] 1

$b
[1] 4
```

In the first example, we are mixing integer and character modes, a combination that R chooses to reduce to the latter mode. In the second example, R considers the list mode to be of lower precedence in mixed expressions. We'll discuss this further in Section 4.3.

You probably will not wish to write code that makes such combinations, but you may encounter code in which this occurs, so it's important to understand the effect.

Another point to keep in mind is that c() has a flattening effect for vectors, as in this example:

```
> c(5,2,c(1.5,6))
[1] 5.0 2.0 1.5 6.0
```

Those familiar with other languages, such as Python, may have expected the preceding code to produce a two-level object. That doesn't occur with R vectors though you can have two-level lists, as you'll see in Chapter 4.

In the next chapter, we move on to a very important special case of vectors, that of matrices and arrays.

3

MATRICES AND ARRAYS

 A *matrix* is a vector with two additional attributes: the number of rows and the number of columns. Since matrices are vectors, they also have modes, such as numeric and character. (On the other hand, vectors are *not* one-column or one-row matrices.)

Matrices are special cases of a more general R type of object: *arrays.* Arrays can be multidimensional. For example, a three-dimensional array would consist of rows, columns, and layers, not just rows and columns as in the matrix case. Most of this chapter will concern matrices, but we will briefly discuss higher-dimensional arrays in the final section.

Much of R's power comes from the various operations you can perform on matrices. We'll cover these operations in this chapter, especially those analogous to vector subsetting and vectorization.

3.1   Creating Matrices

Matrix row and column subscripts begin with 1. For example, the upper-left corner of the matrix a is denoted a[1,1]. The internal storage of a matrix is in *column-major order*, meaning that first all of column 1 is stored, then all of column 2, and so on, as you saw in Section 2.1.3.

One way to create a matrix is by using the matrix() function:

```
> y <- matrix(c(1,2,3,4),nrow=2,ncol=2)
> y
  [,1] [,2]
[1,] 1    3
[2,] 2    4
```

Here, we concatenate what we intend as the first column, the numbers 1 and 2, with what we intend as the second column, 3 and 4. So, our data is (1,2,3,4). Next, we specify the number of rows and columns. The fact that R uses column-major order then determines where these four numbers are put within the matrix.

Since we specified the matrix entries in the preceding example, and there were four of them, we did not need to specify both ncol and nrow; just nrow or ncol would have been enough. Having four elements in all, in two rows, implies two columns:

```
> y <- matrix(c(1,2,3,4),nrow=2)
> y
  [,1] [,2]
[1,] 1    3
[2,] 2    4
```

Note that when we then print out y, R shows us its notation for rows and columns. For instance, [,2] means the entirety of column 2, as can be seen in this check:

```
> y[,2]
[1] 3 4
```

Another way to build y is to specify elements individually:

```
> y <- matrix(nrow=2,ncol=2)
> y[1,1] <- 1
> y[2,1] <- 2
> y[1,2] <- 3
> y[2,2] <- 4
> y
  [,1] [,2]
[1,] 1    3
[2,] 2    4
```

Note that we do need to warn R ahead of time that y will be a matrix and give the number of rows and columns.

Though internal storage of a matrix is in column-major order, you can set the `byrow` argument in `matrix()` to true to indicate that the data is coming in row-major order. Here's an example of using `byrow`:

```
> m <- matrix(c(1,2,3,4,5,6),nrow=2,byrow=T)
> m
     [,1] [,2] [,3]
[1,]   1    2    3
[2,]   4    5    6
```

Note that the matrix is still stored in column-major order. The `byrow` argument enabled only our *input* to come in row-major form. This may be more convenient if you are reading from a data file organized that way, for example.

3.2 General Matrix Operations

Now that we've covered the basics of creating a matrix, we'll look at some common operations performed with matrices. These include performing linear algebra operations, matrix indexing, and matrix filtering.

3.2.1 Performing Linear Algebra Operations on Matrices

You can perform various linear algebra operations on matrices, such as matrix multiplication, matrix scalar multiplication, and matrix addition. Using y from the preceding example, here is how to perform those three operations:

```
> y %*% y  # mathematical matrix multiplication
     [,1] [,2]
[1,] 7    15
[2,]10    22
> 3*y  # mathematical multiplication of matrix by scalar
     [,1] [,2]
[1,] 3     9
[2,] 6    12
> y+y  # mathematical matrix addition
     [,1] [,2]
[1,] 2     6
[2,] 4     8
```

For more on linear algebra operations on matrices, see Section 8.4.

3.2.2 Matrix Indexing

The same operations we discussed for vectors in Section 2.4.2 apply to matrices as well. Here's an example:

```
> z
  [,1] [,2] [,3]
[1,] 1    1    1
[2,] 2    1    0
[3,] 3    0    1
[4,] 4    0    0
> z[,2:3]
  [,1] [,2]
[1,] 1    1
[2,] 1    0
[3,] 0    1
[4,] 0    0
```

Here, we requested the submatrix of z consisting of all elements with column numbers 2 and 3 and any row number. This extracts the second and third columns.

Here's an example of extracting rows instead of columns:

```
> y
  [,1] [,2]
[1,]11   12
[2,]21   22
[3,]31   32
> y[2:3,]
  [,1] [,2]
[1,]21   22
[2,]31   32
> y[2:3,2]
[1] 22 32
```

You can also assign values to submatrices:

```
> y
    [,1] [,2]
[1,]  1    4
[2,]  2    5
[3,]  3    6
> y[c(1,3),] <- matrix(c(1,1,8,12),nrow=2)
> y
    [,1] [,2]
[1,]  1    8
[2,]  2    5
[3,]  1   12
```

Here, we assigned new values to the first and third rows of y.

And here's another example of assignment to submatrices:

```
> x <- matrix(nrow=3,ncol=3)
> y <- matrix(c(4,5,2,3),nrow=2)
> y
     [,1] [,2]
[1,]    4    2
[2,]    5    3
> x[2:3,2:3] <- y
> x
     [,1] [,2] [,3]
[1,]   NA   NA   NA
[2,]   NA    4    2
[3,]   NA    5    3
```

Negative subscripts, used with vectors to exclude certain elements, work the same way with matrices:

```
> y
     [,1] [,2]
[1,]    1    4
[2,]    2    5
[3,]    3    6
> y[-2,]
     [,1] [,2]
[1,]    1    4
[2,]    3    6
```

In the second command, we requested all rows of y except the second.

3.2.3 Extended Example: Image Manipulation

Image files are inherently matrices, since the pixels are arranged in rows and columns. If we have a grayscale image, for each pixel, we store the *intensity*—the brightness–of the image at that pixel. So, the intensity of a pixel in, say, row 28 and column 88 of the image is stored in row 28, column 88 of the matrix. For a color image, three matrices are stored, with intensities for red, green, and blue components, but we'll stick to grayscale here.

For our example, let's consider an image of the Mount Rushmore National Memorial in the United States. Let's read it in, using the pixmap library. (Appendix B describes how to download and install libraries.)

```
> library(pixmap)
> mtrush1 <- read.pnm("mtrush1.pgm")
> mtrush1
Pixmap image
  Type          : pixmapGrey
```

```
  Size         : 194x259
  Resolution   : 1x1
  Bounding box : 0 0 259 194
> plot(mtrush1)
```

We read in the file named *mtrush1.pgm*, returning an object of class
pixmap. We then plot it, as seen in Figure 3-1.

Figure 3-1: Reading in Mount Rushmore

Now, let's see what this class consists of:

```
> str(mtrush1)
Formal class 'pixmapGrey' [package "pixmap"] with 6 slots
  ..@ grey    : num [1:194, 1:259] 0.278 0.263 0.239 0.212 0.192 ...
  ..@ channels: chr "grey"
  ..@ size    : int [1:2] 194 259
...
```

The class here is of the S4 type, whose components are designated by @,
rather than $. S3 and S4 classes will be discussed in Chapter 9, but the key
item here is the intensity matrix, mtrush1@grey. In the example, this matrix
has 194 rows and 259 columns.

The intensities in this class are stored as numbers ranging from 0.0
(black) to 1.0 (white), with intermediate values literally being shades of
gray. For instance, the pixel at row 28, column 88 is pretty bright.

```
> mtrush1@grey[28,88]
[1] 0.7960784
```

To demonstrate matrix operations, let's blot out President Roosevelt.
(Sorry, Teddy, nothing personal.) To determine the relevant rows and columns, you can use R's locator() function. When you call this function, it

waits for the user to click a point within a graph and returns the exact coordinates of that point. In this manner, I found that Roosevelt's portion of the picture is in rows 84 through 163 and columns 135 through 177. (Note that row numbers in pixmap objects increase from the top of the picture to the bottom, the opposite of the numbering used by locator().) So, to blot out that part of the image, we set all the pixels in that range to 1.0.

```
> mtrush2 <- mtrush1
> mtrush2@grey[84:163,135:177] <- 1
> plot(mtrush2)
```

The result is shown in Figure 3-2.

Figure 3-2: Mount Rushmore, with President Roosevelt removed

What if we merely wanted to disguise President Roosevelt's identity? We could do this by adding random noise to the picture. Here's code to do that:

```
# adds random noise to img, at the range rows,cols of img; img and the
# return value are both objects of class pixmap; the parameter q
# controls the weight of the noise, with the result being 1-q times the
# original image plus q times the random noise
blurpart <- function(img,rows,cols,q) {
   lrows <- length(rows)
   lcols <- length(cols)
   newimg <- img
   randomnoise <- matrix(nrow=lrows,ncol=lcols,runif(lrows*lcols))
   newimg@grey[rows,cols] <- (1-q) * img@grey[rows,cols] + q * randomnoise
   return(newimg)
}
```

As the comments indicate, we generate random noise and then take a weighted average of the target pixels and the noise. The parameter q controls the weight of the noise, with larger q values producing more blurring. The random noise itself is a sample from U(0,1), the uniform distribution on the interval (0,1). Note that the following is a matrix operation:

```
newimg@grey[rows,cols] <- (1-q) * img@grey[rows,cols] + q * randomnoise
```

So, let's give it a try:

```
> mtrush3 <- blurpart(mtrush1,84:163,135:177,0.65)
> plot(mtrush3)
```

The result is shown in Figure 3-3.

Figure 3-3: Mount Rushmore, with President Roosevelt blurred

3.2.4   Filtering on Matrices

Filtering can be done with matrices, just as with vectors. You must be careful with the syntax, though. Let's start with a simple example:

```
> x
     x
[1,] 1 2
[2,] 2 3
[3,] 3 4
> x[x[,2] >= 3,]
     x
[1,] 2 3
[2,] 3 4
```

Again, let's dissect this, just as we did when we first looked at filtering in Chapter 2:

```
> j <- x[,2] >= 3
> j
[1] FALSE  TRUE  TRUE
```

Here, we look at the vector x[,2], which is the second column of x, and determine which of its elements are greater than or equal to 3. The result, assigned to j, is a Boolean vector.

Now, use j in x:

```
> x[j,]
     x
[1,] 2 3
[2,] 3 4
```

Here, we compute x[j,]—that is, the rows of x specified by the true elements of j—getting the rows corresponding to the elements in column 2 that were at least equal to 3. Hence, the behavior shown earlier when this example was introduced:

```
> x
     x
[1,] 1 2
[2,] 2 3
[3,] 3 4
> x[x[,2] >= 3,]
     x
[1,] 2 3
[2,] 3 4
```

For performance purposes, it's worth noting again that the computation of j here is a completely vectorized operation, since all of the following are true:

- The object x[,2] is a vector.
- The operator >= compares two vectors.
- The number 3 was recycled to a vector of 3s.

Also note that even though j was defined in terms of x and then was used to extract from x, it did not need to be that way. The filtering criterion can be based on a variable separate from the one to which the filtering will be applied. Here's an example with the same x as above:

```
> x[z %% 2 == 1,]
     [,1] [,2]
```

```
[1,]   1    2
[2,]   3    4
```

Here, the expression z %% 2 == 1 tests each element of z for being an odd number, thus yielding (TRUE,FALSE,TRUE). As a result, we extracted the first and third rows of x.

Here is another example:

```
> m
     [,1] [,2]
[1,]   1    4
[2,]   2    5
[3,]   3    6
> m[m[,1] > 1 & m[,2] > 5,]
[1] 3 6
```

We're using the same principle here, but with a slightly more complex set of conditions for row extraction. (Column extraction, or more generally, extraction of any submatrix, is similar.) First, the expression m[,1] > 1 compares each element of the first column of m to 1 and returns (FALSE,TRUE,TRUE). The second expression, m[,2] > 5, similarly returns (FALSE,FALSE,TRUE). We then take the logical AND of (FALSE,TRUE,TRUE) and (FALSE,FALSE,TRUE), yielding (FALSE,FALSE,TRUE). Using the latter in the row indices of m, we get the third row of m.

Note that we needed to use &, the vector Boolean AND operator, rather than the scalar one that we would use in an if statement, &&. A complete list of such operators is given in Section 7.2.

The alert reader may have noticed an anomaly in the preceding example. Our filtering should have given us a submatrix of size 1 by 2, but instead it gave us a two-element vector. The elements were correct, but the data type was not. This would cause trouble if we were to then input it to some other matrix function. The solution is to use the drop argument, which tells R to retain the two-dimensional nature of our data. We'll discuss drop in detail in Section 3.6 when we examine unintended dimension reduction.

Since matrices are vectors, you can also apply vector operations to them. Here's an example:

```
> m
     [,1] [,2]
[1,]   5   -1
[2,]   2   10
[3,]   9   11
> which(m > 2)
[1] 1 3 5 6
```

R informed us here that, from a vector-indexing point of view, elements 1, 3, 5, and 6 of m are larger than 2. For example, element 5 is the element in row 2, column 2 of m, which we see has the value 10, which is indeed greater than 2.

3.2.5   Extended Example: Generating a Covariance Matrix

This example demonstrates R's row() and col() functions, whose arguments are matrices. For example, for a matrix a, row(a[2,8]) will return the row number of that element of a, which is 2. Well, we knew row(a[2,8]) is in row 2, didn't we? So why would this function be useful?

Let's consider an example. When writing simulation code for multi-variate normal distributions—for instance, using mvrnorm() from the MASS library—we need to specify a covariance matrix. The key point for our purposes here is that the matrix is symmetric; for example, the element in row 1, column 2 is equal to the element in row 2, column 1.

Suppose that we are working with an n-variate normal distribution. Our matrix will have n rows and n columns, and we wish each of the n variables to have variance 1, with correlation rho between pairs of variables. For n = 3 and rho = 0.2, for example, the desired matrix is as follows:

$$\begin{pmatrix} 1 & 0.2 & 0.2 \\ 0.2 & 1 & 0.2 \\ 0.2 & 0.2 & 1 \end{pmatrix}$$

Here is code to generate this kind of matrix:

```
makecov <- function(rho,n) {
    m <- matrix(nrow=n,ncol=n)
    m <- ifelse(row(m) == col(m),1,rho)
    return(m)
}
```

Let's see how this works. First, as you probably guessed, col() returns the column number of its argument, just as row() does for the row number. Then the expression row(m) in line 3 returns a matrix of integer values, each one showing the row number of the corresponding element of m. For instance,

```
> z
     [,1] [,2]
[1,]   3    6
[2,]   4    7
[3,]   5    8
> row(z)
     [,1] [,2]
[1,]   1    1
[2,]   2    2
[3,]   3    3
```

Thus the expression row(m) == col(m) in the same line returns a matrix of TRUE and FALSE values, TRUE values on the diagonal of the matrix and FALSE values elsewhere. Once again, keep in mind that binary operators—in this case, ==—are functions. Of course, row() and col() are functions too, so this expression:

```
row(m) == col(m)
```

applies that function to each element of the matrix m, and it returns a TRUE/FALSE matrix of the same size as m. The ifelse() expression is another function call.

```
ifelse(row(m) == col(m),1,rho)
```

In this case, with the argument being the TRUE/FALSE matrix just discussed, the result is to place the values 1 and rho in the proper places in our output matrix.

3.3 Applying Functions to Matrix Rows and Columns

One of the most famous and most used features of R is the *apply() family of functions, such as apply(), tapply(), and lapply(). Here, we'll look at apply(), which instructs R to call a user-specified function on each of the rows or each of the columns of a matrix.

3.3.1 Using the apply() Function

This is the general form of apply for matrices:

```
apply(m,dimcode,f,fargs)
```

where the arguments are as follows:

- m is the matrix.
- dimcode is the dimension, equal to 1 if the function applies to rows or 2 for columns.
- f is the function to be applied.
- fargs is an optional set of arguments to be supplied to f.

For example, here we apply the R function mean() to each column of a matrix z:

```
> z
     [,1] [,2]
[1,]    1    4
[2,]    2    5
[3,]    3    6
```

```
> apply(z,2,mean)
[1] 2 5
```

In this case, we could have used the colMeans() function, but this provides a simple example of using apply().

A function you write yourself is just as legitimate for use in apply() as any R built-in function such as mean(). Here's an example using our own function f:

```
> z
     [,1] [,2]
[1,]   1    4
[2,]   2    5
[3,]   3    6
> f <- function(x) x/c(2,8)
> y <- apply(z,1,f)
> y
     [,1]  [,2] [,3]
[1,]  0.5 1.000 1.50
[2,]  0.5 0.625 0.75
```

Our f() function divides a two-element vector by the vector (2,8). (Recycling would be used if x had a length longer than 2.) The call to apply() asks R to call f() on each of the rows of z. The first such row is (1,4), so in the call to f(), the actual argument corresponding to the formal argument x is (1,4). Thus, R computes the value of (1,4)/(2,8), which in R's element-wise vector arithmetic is (0.5,0.5). The computations for the other two rows are similar.

You may have been surprised that the size of the result here is 2 by 3 rather than 3 by 2. That first computation, (0.5,0.5), ends up at the first column in the output of apply(), not the first row. But this is the behavior of apply(). If the function to be applied returns a vector of k components, then the result of apply() will have k rows. You can use the matrix transpose function t() to change it if necessary, as follows:

```
> t(apply(z,1,f))
     [,1]  [,2]
[1,]  0.5 0.500
[2,]  1.0 0.625
[3,]  1.5 0.750
```

If the function returns a scalar (which we know is just a one-element vector), the final result will be a vector, not a matrix.

As you can see, the function to be applied needs to take at least one argument. The formal argument here will correspond to an actual argument of one row or column in the matrix, as described previously. In some cases, you will need additional arguments for this function, which you can place following the function name in your call to apply().

For instance, suppose we have a matrix of 1s and 0s and want to create a vector as follows: For each row of the matrix, the corresponding element of the vector will be either 1 or 0, depending on whether the majority of the first d elements in that row is 1 or 0. Here, d will be a parameter that we may wish to vary. We could do this:

```
> copymaj
function(rw,d) {
    maj <- sum(rw[1:d]) / d
    return(if(maj > 0.5) 1 else 0)
}
> x
     [,1] [,2] [,3] [,4] [,5]
[1,]   1    0    1    1    0
[2,]   1    1    1    1    0
[3,]   1    0    0    1    1
[4,]   0    1    1    1    0
> apply(x,1,copymaj,3)
[1] 1 1 0 1
> apply(x,1,copymaj,2)
[1] 0 1 0 0
```

Here, the values 3 and 2 form the actual arguments for the formal argument d in copymaj(). Let's look at what happened in the case of row 1 of x. That row consisted of (1,0,1,1,0), the first d elements of which were (1,0,1). A majority of those three elements were 1s, so copymaj() returned a 1, and thus the first element of the output of apply() was a 1.

Contrary to common opinion, using apply() will generally not speed up your code. The benefits are that it makes for very compact code, which may be easier to read and modify, and you avoid possible bugs in writing code for looping. Moreover, as R moves closer and closer to parallel processing, functions like apply() will become more and more important. For example, the clusterApply() function in the snow package gives R some parallel-processing capability by distributing the submatrix data to various network nodes, with each node basically applying the given function on its submatrix.

3.3.2   Extended Example: Finding Outliers

In statistics, *outliers* are data points that differ greatly from most of the other observations. As such, they are treated either as suspect (they might be erroneous) or unrepresentative (such as Bill Gates's income among the incomes of the citizens of the state of Washington). Many methods have been devised to identify outliers. We'll build a very simple one here.

Say we have retail sales data in a matrix rs. Each row of data is for a different store, and observations within a row are daily sales figures. As a simple (undoubtedly overly simple) approach, let's write code to identify the most deviant observation for each store. We'll define that as the observation further from the median value for that store. Here's the code:

```
1  findols <- function(x) {
2      findol <- function(xrow) {
3          mdn <- median(xrow)
4          devs <- abs(xrow-mdn)
5          return(which.max(devs))
6      }
7      return(apply(x,1,findol))
8  }
```

Our call will be as follows:

```
findols(rs)
```

How will this work? First, we need a function to specify in our apply() call.

Since this function will be applied to each row of our sales matrix, our description implies that it needs to report the index of the most deviant observation in a given row. Our function findol() does that, in lines 4 and 5. (Note that we've defined one function within another here, a common practice if the inner function is short.) In the expression xrow-mdn, we are subtracting a number that is a one-element vector from a vector that generally will have a length greater than 1. Thus, recycling is used to extend mdn to conform with xrow before the subtraction.

Then in line 5, we use the R function which.max(). Instead of finding the maximum value in a vector, which the max() function does, which.max() tells us *where* that maximum value occurs—that is, the *index* where it occurs. This is just what we need.

Finally, in line 7, we ask R to apply findol() to each row of x, thus producing the indices of the most deviant observation in each row.

3.4 Adding and Deleting Matrix Rows and Columns

Technically, matrices are of fixed length and dimensions, so we cannot add or delete rows or columns. However, matrices can be *reassigned*, and thus we can achieve the same effect as if we had directly done additions or deletions.

3.4.1 Changing the Size of a Matrix

Recall how we reassign vectors to change their size:

```
> x
[1] 12  5 13 16  8
> x <- c(x,20)  # append 20
> x
[1] 12  5 13 16  8 20
```

```
> x <- c(x[1:3],20,x[4:6])  # insert 20
> x
[1] 12  5 13 20 16  8 20
> x <- x[-2:-4]  # delete elements 2 through 4
> x
[1] 12 16  8 20
```

In the first case, x is originally of length 5, which we extend to 6 via concatenation and then reassignment. We didn't literally change the length of x but instead created a new vector from x and then assigned x to that new vector.

NOTE *Reassignment occurs even when you don't see it, as you'll see in Chapter 14. For instance, even the innocuous-looking assignment x[2] <- 12 is actually a reassignment.*

Analogous operations can be used to change the size of a matrix. For instance, the rbind() (*row bind*) and cbind() (*column bind*) functions let you add rows or columns to a matrix.

```
> one
[1] 1 1 1 1
> z
  [,1] [,2] [,3]
[1,] 1    1    1
[2,] 2    1    0
[3,] 3    0    1
[4,] 4    0    0
> cbind(one,z)
[1,]1 1 1 1
[2,]1 2 1 0
[3,]1 3 0 1
[4,]1 4 0 0
```

Here, cbind() creates a new matrix by combining a column of 1s with the columns of z. We choose to get a quick printout, but we could have assigned the result to z (or another variable), as follows:

```
z <- cbind(one,z)
```

Note, too, that we could have relied on recycling:

```
> cbind(1,z)
    [,1] [,2] [,3] [,4]
[1,]  1    1    1    1
[2,]  1    2    1    0
[3,]  1    3    0    1
[4,]  1    4    0    0
```

Here, the 1 value was recycled into a vector of four 1 values.

You can also use the rbind() and cbind() functions as a quick way to create small matrices. Here's an example:

```
> q <- cbind(c(1,2),c(3,4))
> q
     [,1] [,2]
[1,]    1    3
[2,]    2    4
```

Be careful with rbind and cbin(), though. Like creating a vector, creating a matrix is time consuming (matrices are vectors, after all). In the following code, cbind() creates a new matrix:

```
z <- cbind(one,z)
```

The new matrix happens to be reassigned to z; that is, we gave it the name z—the same name as the original matrix, which is now gone. But the point is that we did incur a time penalty in creating the matrix. If we did this repeatedly inside a loop, the cumulative penalty would be large.

So, if you are adding rows or columns one at a time within a loop, and the matrix will eventually become large, it's better to allocate a large matrix in the first place. It will be empty at first, but you fill in the rows or columns one at a time, rather than doing a time-consuming matrix memory allocation each time.

You can delete rows or columns by reassignment, too:

```
> m <- matrix(1:6,nrow=3)
> m
     [,1] [,2]
[1,]    1    4
[2,]    2    5
[3,]    3    6
> m <- m[c(1,3),]
> m
     [,1] [,2]
[1,]    1    4
[2,]    3    6
```

3.4.2   Extended Example: Finding the Closest Pair of Vertices in a Graph

Finding the distances between vertices on a graph is a common example used in computer science courses and is used in statistics/data sciences too. This kind of problem arises in some clustering algorithms, for instance, and in genomics applications.

Here, we'll look at the common example of finding distances between cities, as it is easier to describe than, say, finding distances between DNA strands.

Suppose we need a function that inputs a distance matrix, where the element in row i, column j gives the distance between city i and city j and outputs the minimum one-hop distance between cities and the pair of cities that achieves that minimum. Here's the code for the solution:

```
1   # returns the minimum value of d[i,j], i != j, and the row/col attaining
2   # that minimum, for square symmetric matrix d; no special policy on ties
3   mind <- function(d) {
4       n <- nrow(d)
5       # add a column to identify row number for apply()
6       dd <- cbind(d,1:n)
7       wmins <- apply(dd[-n,],1,imin)
8       # wmins will be 2xn, 1st row being indices and 2nd being values
9       i <- which.min(wmins[2,])
10      j <- wmins[1,i]
11      return(c(d[i,j],i,j))
12  }
13
14  # finds the location, value of the minimum in a row x
15  imin <- function(x) {
16      lx <- length(x)
17      i <- x[lx]  # original row number
18      j <- which.min(x[(i+1):(lx-1)])
19      k <- i+j
20      return(c(k,x[k]))
21  }
```

And here's an example of putting our new function to use:

```
> q
     [,1] [,2] [,3] [,4] [,5]
[1,]    0   12   13    8   20
[2,]   12    0   15   28   88
[3,]   13   15    0    6    9
[4,]    8   28    6    0   33
[5,]   20   88    9   33    0
> mind(q)
[1] 6 3 4
```

The minimum value was 6, located in row 3, column 4. As you can see, a call to apply() plays a prominent role.

Our task is fairly simple: We need to find the minimum nonzero element in the matrix. We find the minimum in each row—a single call to apply() accomplishes this for all the rows—and then find the smallest value among those minima. But as you'll see, the code logic becomes rather intricate.

One key point is that the matrix is *symmetric*, because the distance from city i to city j is the same as from j to i. So in finding the minimum value in the ith row, we need look at only elements i+1, i+2,..., *n*, where *n* is the number of rows and columns in the matrix. Note too that this means we can skip the last row of d in our call to apply() in line 7.

Since the matrix could be large—a thousand cities would mean a million entries in the matrix—we should exploit that symmetry and save work. That, however, presents a problem. In order to go through the basic computation, the function called by apply() needs to know the number of the row in the original matrix—knowledge that apply() does not provide to the function. So, in line 6, we augment the matrix with an extra column, consisting of the row numbers, so that the function called by apply() can take row numbers into account.

The function called by apply() is imin(), beginning in line 15, which finds the mininum in the row specified in the formal argument x. It returns not only the mininum in the given row but also the index at which that minimum occurs. When imin() is called on row 1 of our example matrix q above, the minimum value is 8, which occurs in index 4. For this latter purpose, the R function which.min(), used in line 18, is very handy.

Line 19 is noteworthy. Recall that due to the symmetry of the matrix, we skip the early part of each row, as is seen in the expression (i+1):(lx-1) in line 18. But that means that the call to which.min() in that line will return the minimum's index *relative* to the range (i+1):(lx-1). In row 3 of our example matrix q, we would get an index of 1 instead of 4. Thus, we must adjust by adding i, which we do in line 19.

Finally, making proper use of the output of apply() here is a bit tricky. Think again of the example matrix q above. The call to apply() will return the matrix wmins:

$$\begin{pmatrix} 4 & 3 & 4 & 5 \\ 8 & 15 & 6 & 33 \end{pmatrix}$$

As noted in the comments, the second row of that matrix contains the upper-diagonal minima from the various rows of d, while the first row contains the indices of those values. For instance, the first column of wmins gives the information for the first row of q, reporting that the smallest value in that row is 8, occurring at index 4 of the row.

Thus line 9 will pick up the number i of the row containing the smallest value in the entire matrix, 6 in our q example. Line 10 will give us the position j in that row where the minimum occurs, 4 in the case of q. In other words, the overall minimum is in row i and column j, information that we then use in line 11.

Meanwhile, row 1 of apply()'s output shows the indices within those rows at which the row minima occur. That's great, because we can now find which other city was in the best pair. We know that city 3 is one of them, so we go to entry 3 in row 1 of the output, finding 4. So, the pair of cities closest to each other is city 3 and city 4. Lines 9 and 10 then generalize this reasoning.

If the minimal element in our matrix is unique, there is an alternate approach that is far simpler:

```
minda <- function(d) {
    smallest <- min(d)
    ij <- which(d == smallest,arr.ind=TRUE)
    return(c(smallest,ij))
}
```

This works, but it does have some possible drawbacks. Here's the key line in this new code:

```
ij <- which(d == smallest,arr.ind=TRUE)
```

It determines the index of the element of d that achieves the minimum. The argument arr.ind=TRUE specifies that the returned index will be a matrix index—that is, a row and a column, rather than a single vector subscript. Without this argument, d would be treated as a vector.

As noted, this new code works only if the minimum is unique. If that is not the case, which() will return multiple row/column number pairs, contrary to our basic goal. And if we used the original code and d had multiple minimal elements, just one of them would be returned.

Another problem is performance. This new code is essentially making two (behind-the-scenes) loops through our matrix: one to compute smallest and the other in the call to which(). This will likely be slower than our original code.

Of these two approaches, you might choose the original code if execution speed is an issue or if there may be multiple minima, but otherwise opt for the alternate code; the simplicity of the latter will make the code easier to read and maintain.

3.5   More on the Vector/Matrix Distinction

At the beginning of the chapter, I said that a matrix is just a vector but with two additional attributes: the number of rows and the number of columns. Here, we'll take a closer look at the vector nature of matrices. Consider this example:

```
> z <- matrix(1:8,nrow=4)
> z
     [,1] [,2]
[1,]    1    5
[2,]    2    6
[3,]    3    7
[4,]    4    8
```

As z is still a vector, we can query its length:

```
> length(z)
[1] 8
```

But as a matrix, z is a bit more than a vector:

```
> class(z)
[1] "matrix"
> attributes(z)
$dim
[1] 4 2
```

In other words, there actually is a matrix *class*, in the object-oriented programming sense. As noted in Chapter 1, most of R consists of S3 classes, whose components are denoted by dollar signs. The matrix class has one attribute, named dim, which is a vector containing the numbers of rows and columns in the matrix. Classes will be covered in detail in Chapter 9.

You can also obtain dim via the dim() function:

```
> dim(z)
[1] 4 2
```

The numbers of rows and columns are obtainable individually via the nrow() and ncol() functions:

```
> nrow(z)
[1] 4
> ncol(z)
[1] 2
```

These just piggyback on dim(), as you can see by inspecting the code. Recall once again that objects can be printed in interactive mode by simply typing their names:

```
> nrow
function (x)
dim(x)[1]
```

These functions are useful when you are writing a general-purpose library function whose argument is a matrix. By being able to determine the number of rows and columns in your code, you alleviate the caller of the burden of supplying that information as two additional arguments. This is one of the benefits of object-oriented programming.

3.6 Avoiding Unintended Dimension Reduction

In the world of statistics, dimension reduction is a good thing, with many statistical procedures aimed to do it well. If we are working with, say, 10 variables and can reduce that number to 3 that still capture the essence of our data, we're happy.

However, in R, something else might merit the name *dimension reduction* that we may sometimes wish to avoid. Say we have a four-row matrix and extract a row from it:

```
> z
     [,1] [,2]
[1,]    1    5
[2,]    2    6
[3,]    3    7
[4,]    4    8
> r <- z[2,]
> r
[1] 2 6
```

This seems innocuous, but note the format in which R has displayed r. It's a vector format, not a matrix format. In other words, r is a vector of length 2, rather than a 1-by-2 matrix. We can confirm this in a couple of ways:

```
> attributes(z)
$dim
[1] 4 2
> attributes(r)
NULL
> str(z)
 int [1:4, 1:2] 1 2 3 4 5 6 7 8
> str(r)
 int [1:2] 2 6
```

Here, R informs us that z has row and column numbers, while r does not. Similarly, str() tells us that z has indices ranging in 1:4 and 1:2, for rows and columns, while r's indices simply range in 1:2. No doubt about it—r is a vector, not a matrix.

This seems natural, but in many cases, it will cause trouble in programs that do a lot of matrix operations. You may find that your code works fine in general but fails in a special case. For instance, suppose that your code extracts a submatrix from a given matrix and then does some matrix operations on the submatrix. If the submatrix has only one row, R will make it a vector, which could ruin your computation.

Fortunately, R has a way to suppress this dimension reduction: the drop argument. Here's an example, using the matrix z from above:

```
> r <- z[2,, drop=FALSE]
> r
     [,1] [,2]
[1,]    2    6
> dim(r)
[1] 1 2
```

Now r is a 1-by-2 matrix, not a two-element vector.

For these reasons, you may find it useful to routinely include the drop=FALSE argument in all your matrix code.

Why can we speak of drop as an argument? Because that [is actually a function, just as is the case for operators like +. Consider the following code:

```
> z[3,2]
[1] 7
> "["(z,3,2)
[1] 7
```

If you have a vector that you wish to be treated as a matrix, you can use the as.matrix() function, as follows:

```
> u
[1] 1 2 3
> v <- as.matrix(u)
> attributes(u)
NULL
> attributes(v)
$dim
[1] 3 1
```

3.7   Naming Matrix Rows and Columns

The natural way to refer to rows and columns in a matrix is via the row and column numbers. However, you can also give names to these entities. Here's an example:

```
> z
     [,1] [,2]
[1,] 1 3
[2,] 2 4
> colnames(z)
NULL
> colnames(z) <- c("a","b")
```

```
> z
    a b
[1,] 1 3
[2,] 2 4
> colnames(z)
[1] "a" "b"
> z[,"a"]
[1] 1 2
```

As you see here, these names can then be used to reference specific columns. The function `rownames()` works similarly.

Naming rows and columns is usually less important when writing R code for general applications, but it can be useful when analyzing a specific data set.

3.8   Higher-Dimensional Arrays

In a statistical context, a typical matrix in R has rows corresponding to observations, say on various people, and columns corresponding to variables, such as weight and blood pressure. The matrix is then a two-dimensional data structure. But suppose we also have data taken at different times, one data point per person per variable per time. Time then becomes the third dimension, in addition to rows and columns. In R, such data sets are called *arrays*.

As a simple example, consider students and test scores. Say each test consists of two parts, so we record two scores for a student for each test. Now suppose that we have two tests, and to keep the example small, assume we have only three students. Here's the data for the first test:

```
> firsttest
     [,1] [,2]
[1,]   46   30
[2,]   21   25
[3,]   50   50
```

Student 1 had scores of 46 and 30 on the first test, student 2 scored 21 and 25, and so on. Here are the scores for the same students on the second test:

```
> secondtest
     [,1] [,2]
[1,]   46   43
[2,]   41   35
[3,]   50   50
```

Now let's put both tests into one data structure, which we'll name tests. We'll arrange it to have two "layers"—one layer per test—with three rows and two columns within each layer. We'll store firsttest in the first layer and secondtest in the second.

In layer 1, there will be three rows for the three students' scores on the first test, with two columns per row for the two portions of a test. We use R's array function to create the data structure:

```
> tests <- array(data=c(firsttest,secondtest),dim=c(3,2,2))
```

In the argument dim=c(3,2,2), we are specifying two layers (this is the second 2), each consisting of three rows and two columns. This then becomes an attribute of the data structure:

```
> attributes(tests)
$dim
[1] 3 2 2
```

Each element of tests now has three subscripts, rather than two as in the matrix case. The first subscript corresponds to the first element in the $dim vector, the second subscript corresponds to the second element in the vector, and so on. For instance, the score on the second portion of test 1 for student 3 is retrieved as follows:

```
> tests[3,2,1]
[1] 48
```

R's print function for arrays displays the data layer by layer:

```
> tests
, , 1

     [,1] [,2]
[1,]   46   30
[2,]   21   25
[3,]   50   48

, , 2

     [,1] [,2]
[1,]   46   43
[2,]   41   35
[3,]   50   49
```

Just as we built our three-dimensional array by combining two matrices, we can build four-dimensional arrays by combining two or more three-dimensional arrays, and so on.

One of the most common uses of arrays is in calculating tables. See Section 6.3 for an example of a three-dimensional table.

4

LISTS

In contrast to a vector, in which all elements must be of the same mode, R's list structure can combine objects of different types. For those familiar with Python, an R list is similar to a Python dictionary or, for that matter, a Perl hash. C programmers may find it similar to a C struct. The list plays a central role in R, forming the basis for data frames, object-oriented programming, and so on.

In this chapter, we'll cover how to create lists and how to work with them. As with vectors and matrices, one common operation with lists is indexing. List indexing is similar to vector and matrix indexing but with some major differences. And like matrices, lists have an analog for the apply() function. We'll discuss these and other list topics, including ways to take lists apart, which often comes in handy.

4.1 Creating Lists

Technically, a list is a vector. Ordinary vectors—those of the type we've been using so far in this book—are termed *atomic* vectors, since their components cannot be broken down into smaller components. In contrast, lists are referred to as *recursive* vectors.

For our first look at lists, let's consider an employee database. For each employee, we wish to store the name, salary, and a Boolean indicating union membership. Since we have three different modes here—character, numeric, and logical—it's a perfect place for using lists. Our entire database might then be a list of lists, or some other kind of list such as a data frame, though we won't pursue that here.

We could create a list to represent our employee, Joe, this way:

```
j <- list(name="Joe", salary=55000, union=T)
```

We could print out j, either in full or by component:

```
> j
$name
[1] "Joe"

$salary
[1] 55000

$union
[1] TRUE
```

Actually, the component names—called *tags* in the R literature—such as salary are optional. We could alternatively do this:

```
> jalt <- list("Joe", 55000, T)
> jalt
[[1]]
[1] "Joe"

[[2]]
[1] 55000

[[3]]
[1] TRUE
```

However, it is generally considered clearer and less error-prone to use names instead of numeric indices.

Names of list components can be abbreviated to whatever extent is possible without causing ambiguity:

```
> j$sal
[1] 55000
```

Since lists are vectors, they can be created via vector():

```
> z <- vector(mode="list")
> z[["abc"]] <- 3
> z
$abc
[1] 3
```

4.2   General List Operations

Now that you've seen a simple example of creating a list, let's look at how to access and work with lists.

4.2.1   List Indexing

You can access a list component in several different ways:

```
> j$salary
[1] 55000
> j[["salary"]]
[1] 55000
> j[[2]]
[1] 55000
```

We can refer to list components by their numerical indices, treating the list as a vector. However, note that in this case, we use double brackets instead of single ones.

So, there are three ways to access an individual component c of a list lst and return it in the data type of c:

- lst$c

- lst[["c"]]

- lst[[i]], where i is the index of c within lst

Each of these is useful in different contexts, as you will see in subsequent examples. But note the qualifying phrase, "return it in the data type of c." An alternative to the second and third techniques listed is to use single brackets rather than double brackets:

- lst["c"]

- lst[i], where i is the index of c within lst

Both single-bracket and double-bracket indexing access list elements in vector-index fashion. But there is an important difference from ordinary (atomic) vector indexing. If single brackets [ ] are used, the result is another list—a sublist of the original. For instance, continuing the preceding example, we have this:

```
> j[1:2]
$name
[1] "Joe"

$salary
[1] 55000
> j2 <- j[2]
> j2
$salary
[1] 55000
> class(j2)
[1] "list"
> str(j2)
List of 1
 $ salary: num 55000
```

The subsetting operation returned another list consisting of the first two components of the original list j. Note that the word *returned* makes sense here, since index brackets are functions. This is similar to other cases you've seen for operators that do not at first appear to be functions, such as +.

By contrast, you can use double brackets [[ ]] for referencing only a single component, with the result having the type of that component.

```
> j[[1:2]]
Error in j[[1:2]] : subscript out of bounds
> j2a <- j[[2]]
> j2a
[1] 55000
> class(j2a)
[1] "numeric"
```

4.2.2   Adding and Deleting List Elements

The operations of adding and deleting list elements arise in a surprising number of contexts. This is especially true for data structures in which lists form the foundation, such as data frames and R classes.

New components can be added *after* a list is created.

```
> z <- list(a="abc",b=12)
> z
$a
[1] "abc"
```

```
$b
[1] 12

> z$c <- "sailing" # add a c component
> # did c really get added?
> z
$a
[1] "abc"

$b
[1] 12

$c
[1] "sailing"
```

Adding components can also be done via a vector index:

```
> z[[4]] <- 28
> z[5:7] <- c(FALSE,TRUE,TRUE)
> z
$a
[1] "abc"

$b
[1] 12

$c
[1] "sailing"

[[4]]
[1] 28

[[5]]
[1] FALSE

[[6]]
[1] TRUE

[[7]]
[1] TRUE
```

You can delete a list component by setting it to NULL.

```
> z$b <- NULL
> z
$a
[1] "abc"
```

```
$c
[1] "sailing"

[[3]]
[1] 28

[[4]]
[1] FALSE

[[5]]
[1] TRUE

[[6]]
[1] TRUE
```

Note that upon deleting z$b, the indices of the elements after it moved up by 1. For instance, the former z[[4]] became z[[3]].

You can also concatenate lists.

```
> c(list("Joe", 55000, T),list(5))
[[1]]
[1] "Joe"

[[2]]
[1] 55000

[[3]]
[1] TRUE

[[4]]
[1] 5
```

4.2.3   Getting the Size of a List

Since a list is a vector, you can obtain the number of components in a list via length().

```
> length(j)
[1] 3
```

4.2.4   Extended Example: Text Concordance

Web search and other types of textual data mining are of great interest today. Let's use this area for an example of R list code.

We'll write a function called findwords() that will determine which words are in a text file and compile a list of the locations of each word's occurrences in the text. This would be useful for contextual analysis, for example.

Suppose our input file, *testconcord.txt*, has the following contents (taken from this book!):

```
The [1] here means that the first item in this line of output is
item 1. In this case, our output consists of only one line (and one
item), so this is redundant, but this notation helps to read
voluminous output that consists of many items spread over many
lines.  For example, if there were two rows of output with six items
per row, the second row would be labeled [7].
```

In order to identify words, we replace all nonletter characters with blanks and get rid of capitalization. We could use the string functions presented in Chapter 11 to do this, but to keep matters simple, such code is not shown here. The new file, *testconcorda.txt*, looks like this:

```
the       here means that the first item in this line of output is
item      in this case  our output consists of only one line  and one
item    so this is redundant  but this notation helps to read
voluminous output that consists of many items spread over many
lines    for example  if there were two rows of output with six items
per row   the second row would be labeled
```

Then, for instance, the word *item* has locations 7, 14, and 27, which means that it occupies the seventh, fourteenth, and twenty-seventh word positions in the file.

Here is an excerpt from the list that is returned when our function findwords() is called on this file:

```
> findwords("testconcorda.txt")
Read 68 items
$the
[1]  1   5 63

$here
[1] 2

$means
[1] 3

$that
[1]  4 40

$first
[1] 6

$item
[1]  7 14 27
...
```

The list consists of one component per word in the file, with a word's component showing the positions within the file where that word occurs. Sure enough, the word *item* is shown as occurring at positions 7, 14, and 27.

Before looking at the code, let's talk a bit about our choice of a list structure here. One alternative would be to use a matrix, with one row per word in the text. We could use rownames() to name the rows, with the entries within a row showing the positions of that word. For instance, row item would consist of 7, 14, 27, and then 0s in the remainder of the row. But the matrix approach has a couple of major drawbacks:

- There is a problem in terms of the columns to allocate for our matrix. If the maximum frequency with which a word appears in our text is, say, 10, then we would need 10 columns. But we would not know that ahead of time. We could add a new column each time we encountered a new word, using cbind() (in addition to using rbind() to add a row for the word itself). Or we could write code to do a preliminary run through the input file to determine the maximum word frequency. Either of these would come at the expense of increased code complexity and possibly increased runtime.

- Such a storage scheme would be quite wasteful of memory, since most rows would probably consist of a lot of zeros. In other words, the matrix would be *sparse*—a situation that also often occurs in numerical analysis contexts.

Thus, the list structure really makes sense. Let's see how to code it.

```
1  findwords <- function(tf) {
2     # read in the words from the file, into a vector of mode character
3     txt <- scan(tf,"")
4     wl <- list()
5     for (i in 1:length(txt)) {
6        wrd <- txt[i]  # ith word in input file
7        wl[[wrd]] <- c(wl[[wrd]],i)
8     }
9     return(wl)
10 }
```

We read in the words of the file (*words* simply meaning any groups of letters separated by spaces) by calling scan(). The details of reading and writing files are covered in Chapter 10, but the important point here is that txt will now be a vector of strings: one string per instance of a word in the file. Here is what txt looks like after the read:

```
> txt
 [1] "the"    "here"    "means"   "that"    "the"
 [6] "first"  "item"    "in"      "this"    "line"
[11] "of"     "output"  "is"      "item"    "in"
[16] "this"   "case"    "our"     "output"  "consists"
```

```
[21] "of"        "only"    "one"        "line"      "and"
[26] "one"       "item"    "so"         "this"      "is"
[31] "redundant" "but"     "this"       "notation"  "helps"
[36] "to"        "read"    "voluminous" "output"    "that"
[41] "consists"  "of"      "many"       "items"     "spread"
[46] "over"      "many"    "lines"      "for"       "example"
[51] "if"        "there"   "were"       "two"       "rows"
[56] "of"        "output"  "with"       "six"       "items"
[61] "per"       "row"     "the"        "second"    "row"
[66] "would"     "be"      "labeled"
```

The list operations in lines 4 through 8 build up our main variable, a list wl (for *word list*). We loop through all the words from our long line, with wrd being the current one.

Let's see what happens with the code in line 7 when i = 4, so that wrd = "that" in our example file *testconcorda.txt*. At this point, wl[["that"]] will not yet exist. As mentioned, R is set up so that in such a case, wl[["that"]] = NULL, which means in line 7, we can concatenate it! Thus wl[["that"]] will become the one-element vector (4). Later, when i = 40, wl[["that"]] will become (4,40), representing the fact that words 4 and 40 in the file are both "that". Note how convenient it is that list indexing can be done through quoted strings, such as in wl[["that"]].

An advanced, more elegant version of this code uses R's split() function, as you'll see in Section 6.2.2.

4.3   Accessing List Components and Values

If the components in a list do have tags, as is the case with name, salary, and union for j in Section 4.1, you can obtain them via names():

```
> names(j)
[1] "name"   "salary" "union"
```

To obtain the values, use unlist():

```
> ulj <- unlist(j)
> ulj
  name  salary   union
 "Joe" "55000"  "TRUE"
> class(ulj)
[1] "character"
```

The return value of unlist() is a vector—in this case, a vector of character strings. Note that the element names in this vector come from the components in the original list.

On the other hand, if we were to start with numbers, we would get numbers.

```
> z <- list(a=5,b=12,c=13)
> y <- unlist(z)
> class(y)
[1] "numeric"
> y
 a  b  c
 5 12 13
```

So the output of unlist() in this case was a numeric vector. What about a mixed case?

```
> w <- list(a=5,b="xyz")
> wu <- unlist(w)
> class(wu)
[1] "character"
> wu
    a     b
  "5" "xyz"
```

Here, R chose the least common denominator: character strings. This sounds like some kind of precedence structure, and it is. As R's help for unlist() states:

> Where possible the list components are coerced to a common mode during the unlisting, and so the result often ends up as a character vector. Vectors will be coerced to the highest type of the components in the hierarchy NULL < raw < logical < integer < real < complex < character < list < expression: pairlists are treated as lists.

But there is something else to deal with here. Though wu is a vector and not a list, R did give each of the elements a name. We can remove them by setting their names to NULL, as you saw in Section 2.11.

```
> names(wu) <- NULL
> wu
[1] "5"   "xyz"
```

We can also remove the elements' names directly with unname(), as follows:

```
> wun <- unname(wu)
> wun
[1] "5"   "xyz"
```

This also has the advantage of not destroying the names in wu, in case they are needed later. If they will not be needed later, we could simply assign back to wu instead of to wun in the preceding statement.

4.4 Applying Functions to Lists

Two functions are handy for applying functions to lists: lapply and sapply.

4.4.1 Using the lapply() and sapply() Functions

The function lapply() (for *list apply*) works like the matrix apply() function, calling the specified function on each component of a list (or vector coerced to a list) and returning another list. Here's an example:

```
> lapply(list(1:3,25:29),median)
[[1]]
[1] 2

[[2]]
[1] 27
```

R applied median() to 1:3 and to 25:29, returning a list consisting of 2 and 27.

In some cases, such as the example here, the list returned by lapply() could be simplified to a vector or matrix. This is exactly what sapply() (for *simplified [l]apply*) does.

```
> sapply(list(1:3,25:29),median)
[1]  2 27
```

You saw an example of matrix output in Section 2.6.2. There, we applied a vectorized, vector-valued function—a function whose return value is a vector, each of whose components is vectorized— to a vector input. Using sapply(), rather than applying the function directly, gave us the desired matrix form in the output.

4.4.2 Extended Example: Text Concordance, Continued

The text concordance creator, findwords(), which we developed in Section 4.2.4, returns a list of word locations, indexed by word. It would be nice to be able to sort this list in various ways.

Recall that for the input file *testconcorda.txt*, we got this output:

```
$the
[1]  1  5 63

$here
[1] 2
```

```
$means
[1] 3

$that
[1]  4 40
...
```

Here's code to present the list in alphabetical order by word:

```
1  # sorts wrdlst, the output of findwords() alphabetically by word
2  alphawl <- function(wrdlst) {
3      nms <- names(wrdlst) # the words
4      sn <- sort(nms)  # same words in alpha order
5      return(wrdlst[sn])  # return rearranged version
6  }
```

Since our words are the names of the list components, we can extract the words by simply calling names(). We sort these alphabetically, and then in line 5, we use the sorted version as input to list indexing, giving us a sorted version of the list. Note the use of single brackets, rather than double, as the former are required for subsetting lists. (You might also consider using order() instead of sort(), which we'll look at in Section 8.3.)

Let's try it out.

```
> alphawl(wl)
$and
[1] 25

$be
[1] 67

$but
[1] 32

$case
[1] 17

$consists
[1] 20 41

$example
[1] 50
...
```

It works fine. The entry for *and* was displayed first, then *be*, and so on.

We can sort by word frequency in a similar manner.

```
1  # orders the output of findwords() by word frequency
2  freqwl <- function(wrdlst) {
3     freqs <- sapply(wrdlst,length)  # get word frequencies
4     return(wrdlst[order(freqs)])
5  }
```

In line 3, we are using the fact that each element in wrdlst is a vector
of numbers representing the positions in our input file at which the given
word is found. Calling length() on that vector gives us the number of times
the given word appears in that file. The result of calling sapply() will be the
vector of word frequencies.

We could use sort() here again, but order() is more direct. This latter
function returns the indices of a sorted vector with respect to the original
vector. Here's an example:

```
> x <- c(12,5,13,8)
> order(x)
[1] 2 4 1 3
```

The output here indicates that x[2] is the smallest element in x, x[4]
is the second smallest, and so on. In our case, we use order() to determine
which word is least frequent, second least frequent, and so on. Plugging
these indices into our word list gives us the same word list but in order of
frequency.

Let's check it.

```
> freqwl(wl)
$here
[1] 2

$means
[1] 3

$first
[1] 6
...
$that
[1]   4 40

$`in`
[1]   8 15

$line
[1] 10 24
...
$this
```

```
[1]   9 16 29 33

$of
[1] 11 21 42 56

$output
[1] 12 19 39 57
```

Yep, ordered from least to most frequent.

We can also do a plot of the most frequent words. I ran the following code on an article on R in the *New York Times*, "Data Analysts Captivated by R's Power," from January 6, 2009.

```
> nyt <- findwords("nyt.txt")
Read 1011 items
> snyt <- freqwl(nyt)
> nwords <- length(ssnyt)
> freqs9 <- sapply(ssnyt[round(0.9*nwords):nwords],length)
> barplot(freqs9)
```

My goal was to plot the frequencies of the top 10 percent of the words in the article. The results are shown in Figure 4-1.

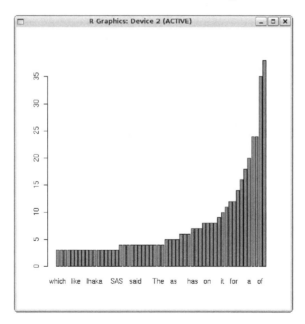

Figure 4-1: Top word frequencies in an article about R

4.4.3   Extended Example: Back to the Abalone Data

Let's use the lapply() function in our abalone gender example in Section 2.9.2. Recall that at one point in that example, we wished to know the indices of the observations that were male, female, and infant. For an easy demonstration, let's use the same test case: a vector of genders.

```
g <- c("M","F","F","I","M","M","F")
```

A more compact way of accomplishing our goal is as follows:

```
> lapply(c("M","F","I"),function(gender) which(g==gender))
[[1]]
[1] 1 5 6

[[2]]
[1] 2 3 7

[[3]]
[1] 4
```

The lapply() function expects its first argument to be a list. Here it was a vector, but lapply() will *coerce* that vector to a list form. Also, lapply() expects its second argument to be a function. This could be the name of a function, as you saw before, or the actual code, as we have here. This is an *anonymous* function, which you'll learn more about in Section 7.13.

Then lapply() calls that anonymous function on "M", then on "F", and then on "I". In that first case, the function calculates which(g=="M"), giving us the vector of indices in g of the males. After determining the indices for the females and infants, lapply() will return the three vectors in a list.

Note that even though the object of our main attention is the vector g of genders, it is not the first argument in the lapply() call in the example. Instead, that argument is an innocuous-looking vector of the three possible gender encodings. By contrast, g is mentioned only briefly in the function, as the second actual argument. This is a common situation in R. An even better way to do this will be presented in Section 6.2.2.

4.5   Recursive Lists

Lists can be recursive, meaning that you can have lists within lists. Here's an example:

```
> b <- list(u = 5, v = 12)
> c <- list(w = 13)
> a <- list(b,c)
> a
[[1]]
[[1]]$u
```

```
[1] 5

[[1]]$v
[1] 12


[[2]]
[[2]]$w
[1] 13


> length(a)
[1] 2
```

This code makes a into a two-component list, with each component itself also being a list.

The concatenate function c() has an optional argument recursive, which controls whether *flattening* occurs when recursive lists are combined.

```
> c(list(a=1,b=2,c=list(d=5,e=9)))
$a
[1] 1

$b
[1] 2

$c
$c$d
[1] 5

$c$e
[1] 9
> c(list(a=1,b=2,c=list(d=5,e=9)),recursive=T)
  a   b c.d c.e
  1   2   5   9
```

In the first case, we accepted the default value of recursive, which is FALSE, and obtained a recursive list, with the c component of the main list itself being another list. In the second call, with recursive set to TRUE, we got a single list as a result; only the names look recursive. (It's odd that setting recursive to TRUE gives a *nonrecursive* list.)

Recall that our first example of lists consisted of an employee database. I mentioned that since each employee was represented as a list, the entire database would be a list of lists. That is a concrete example of recursive lists.

5

DATA FRAMES

On an intuitive level, a *data frame* is like a matrix, with a two-dimensional rows-and-columns structure. However, it differs from a matrix in that each column may have a different mode. For instance, one column may consist of numbers, and another column might have character strings. In this sense, just as lists are the heterogeneous analogs of vectors in one dimension, data frames are the heterogeneous analogs of matrices for two-dimensional data.

On a technical level, a data frame is a list, with the components of that list being equal-length vectors. Actually, R does allow the components to be other types of objects, including other data frames. This gives us heterogeneous–data analogs of arrays in our analogy. But this use of data frames is rare in practice, and in this book, we will assume all components of a data frame are vectors.

In this chapter, we'll present quite a few data frame examples, so you can become familiar with their variety of uses in R.

5.1 Creating Data Frames

To begin, let's take another look at our simple data frame example from Section 1.4.5:

```
> kids <- c("Jack","Jill")
> ages <- c(12,10)
> d <- data.frame(kids,ages,stringsAsFactors=FALSE)
> d  # matrix-like viewpoint
  kids ages
1 Jack   12
2 Jill   10
```

The first two arguments in the call to data.frame() are clear: We wish to produce a data frame from our two vectors: kids and ages. However, that third argument, stringsAsFactors=FALSE requires more comment.

If the named argument stringsAsFactors is not specified, then by default, stringsAsFactors will be TRUE. (You can also use options() to arrange the opposite default.) This means that if we create a data frame from a character vector—in this case, kids—R will convert that vector to a *factor*. Because our work with character data will typically be with vectors rather than factors, we'll set stringsAsFactors to FALSE. We'll cover factors in Chapter 6.

5.1.1 Accessing Data Frames

Now that we have a data frame, let's explore a bit. Since d is a list, we can access it as such via component index values or component names:

```
> d[[1]]
[1] "Jack" "Jill"
> d$kids
[1] "Jack" "Jill"
```

But we can treat it in a matrix-like fashion as well. For example, we can view column 1:

```
> d[,1]
[1] "Jack" "Jill"
```

This matrix-like quality is also seen when we take d apart using str():

```
> str(d)
'data.frame':   2 obs. of  2 variables:
 $ kids: chr  "Jack" "Jill"
 $ ages: num  12 10
```

R tells us here that d consists of two observations—our two rows—that store data on two variables—our two columns.

Consider three ways to access the first column of our data frame above: d[[1]], d[,1], and d$kids. Of these, the third would generally considered to be clearer and, more importantly, safer than the first two. This better identifies the column and makes it less likely that you will reference the wrong column. But in writing general code—say writing R packages—matrix-like notation d[,1] is needed, and it is especially handy if you are extracting subdata frames (as you'll see when we talk about extracting subdata frames in Section 5.2).

5.1.2   Extended Example: Regression Analysis of Exam Grades Continued

Recall our course examination data set in Section 1.5. There, we didn't have a header, but for this example we do, and the first few records in the file now are as follows:

```
"Exam 1" "Exam 2" Quiz
2.0      3.3      4.0
3.3      2.0      3.7
4.0      4.0      4.0
2.3      0.0      3.3
2.3      1.0      3.3
3.3      3.7      4.0
```

As you can see, each line contains the three test scores for one student. This is the classic two-dimensional file notion, like that alluded to in the preceding output of str(). Here, each line in our file contains the data for one observation in a statistical data set. The idea of a data frame is to encapsulate such data, along with variable names, into one object.

Notice that we have separated the fields here by spaces. Other delimiters may be specified, notably commas for comma-separated value (CSV) files (as you'll see in Section 5.2.5). The variable names specified in the first record must be separated by the same delimiter as used for the data, which is spaces in this case. If the names themselves contain embedded spaces, as we have here, they must be quoted.

We read in the file as before, but in this case we state that there is a header record:

```
examsquiz <- read.table("exams",header=TRUE)
```

The column names now appear, with periods replacing blanks:

```
> head(examsquiz)
  Exam.1 Exam.2 Quiz
1    2.0    3.3  4.0
2    3.3    2.0  3.7
3    4.0    4.0  4.0
4    2.3    0.0  3.3
```

```
5   2.3   1.0  3.3
6   3.3   3.7  4.0
```

5.2   Other Matrix-Like Operations

Various matrix operations also apply to data frames. Most notably and usefully, we can do filtering to extract various subdata frames of interest.

5.2.1   Extracting Subdata Frames

As mentioned, a data frame can be viewed in row-and-column terms. In particular, we can extract subdata frames by rows or columns. Here's an example:

```
> examsquiz[2:5,]
  Exam.1 Exam.2 Quiz
2   3.3      2  3.7
3   4.0      4  4.0
4   2.3      0  3.3
5   2.3      1  3.3
> examsquiz[2:5,2]
[1] 2 4 0 1
> class(examsquiz[2:5,2])
[1] "numeric"
> examsquiz[2:5,2,drop=FALSE]
  Exam.2
2      2
3      4
4      0
5      1
> class(examsquiz[2:5,2,drop=FALSE])
[1] "data.frame"
```

Note that in that second call, since examsquiz[2:5,2] is a vector, R created a vector instead of another data frame. By specifying drop=FALSE, as described for the matrix case in Section 3.6, we can keep it as a (one-column) data frame.

We can also do filtering. Here's how to extract the subframe of all students whose first exam score was at least 3.8:

```
> examsquiz[examsquiz$Exam.1 >= 3.8,]
   Exam.1 Exam.2 Quiz
3       4    4.0  4.0
9       4    3.3  4.0
11      4    4.0  4.0
14      4    0.0  4.0
16      4    3.7  4.0
```

19	4	4.0	4.0
22	4	4.0	4.0
25	4	4.0	3.3
29	4	3.0	3.7

5.2.2 More on Treatment of NA Values

Suppose the second exam score for the first student had been missing. Then we would have typed the following into that line when we were preparing the data file:

```
2.0 NA 4.0
```

In any subsequent statistical analyses, R would do its best to cope with the missing data. However, in some situations, we need to set the option na.rm=TRUE, explicitly telling R to ignore NA values. For instance, with the missing exam score, calculating the mean score on exam 2 by calling R's mean() function would skip that first student in finding the mean. Otherwise, R would just report NA for the mean.

Here's a little example:

```
> x <- c(2,NA,4)
> mean(x)
[1] NA
> mean(x,na.rm=TRUE)
[1] 3
```

In Section 2.8.2, you were introduced to the subset() function, which saves you the trouble of specifying na.rm=TRUE. You can apply it in data frames for row selection. The column names are taken in the context of the given data frame. In our example, instead of typing this:

```
> examsquiz[examsquiz$Exam.1 >= 3.8,]
```

we could run this:

```
> subset(examsquiz,Exam.1 >= 3.8)
```

Note that we do not need to write this:

```
> subset(examsquiz,examsquiz$Exam.1 >= 3.8)
```

In some cases, we may wish to rid our data frame of any observation that has at least one NA value. A handy function for this purpose is complete.cases().

```
> d4
    kids states
1   Jack    CA
2   <NA>    MA
3 Jillian   MA
4   John   <NA>
> complete.cases(d4)
[1]  TRUE FALSE  TRUE FALSE
> d5 <- d4[complete.cases(d4),]
> d5
    kids states
1   Jack    CA
3 Jillian   MA
```

Cases 2 and 4 were incomplete; hence the FALSE values in the output of complete.cases(d4). We then use that output to select the intact rows.

5.2.3   Using the rbind() and cbind() Functions and Alternatives

The rbind() and cbind() matrix functions introduced in Section 3.4 work with data frames, too, providing that you have compatible sizes, of course. For instance, you can use cbind() to add a new column that has the same length as the existing columns.

In using rbind() to add a row, the added row is typically in the form of another data frame or list.

```
> d
  kids ages
1 Jack   12
2 Jill   10
> rbind(d,list("Laura",19))
   kids ages
1  Jack   12
2  Jill   10
3 Laura   19
```

You can also create new columns from old ones. For instance, we can add a variable that is the difference between exams 1 and 2:

```
> eq <- cbind(examsquiz,examsquiz$Exam.2-examsquiz$Exam.1)
> class(eq)
[1] "data.frame"
> head(eq)
  Exam.1 Exam.2 Quiz examsquiz$Exam.2 - examsquiz$Exam.1
1 2.0 3.3 4.0 1.3
2 3.3 2.0 3.7 -1.3
```

```
3 4.0 4.0 4.0 0.0
4 2.3 0.0 3.3 -2.3
5 2.3 1.0 3.3 -1.3
6 3.3 3.7 4.0 0.4
```

The new name is rather unwieldy: It's long, and it has embedded blanks. We could change it, using the names() function, but it would be better to exploit the list basis of data frames and add a column (of the same length) to the data frame for this result:

```
> examsquiz$ExamDiff <- examsquiz$Exam.2 - examsquiz$Exam.1
> head(examsquiz)
  Exam.1 Exam.2 Quiz ExamDiff
1    2.0    3.3  4.0      1.3
2    3.3    2.0  3.7     -1.3
3    4.0    4.0  4.0      0.0
4    2.3    0.0  3.3     -2.3
5    2.3    1.0  3.3     -1.3
6    3.3    3.7  4.0      0.4
```

What happened here? Since one can add a new component to an already existing list at any time, we did so: We added a component ExamDiff to the list/data frame examsquiz.

We can even exploit recycling to add a column that is of a different length than those in the data frame:

```
> d
  kids ages
1 Jack   12
2 Jill   10
> d$one <- 1
> d
  kids ages one
1 Jack   12   1
2 Jill   10   1
```

5.2.4 Applying apply()

You can use apply() on data frames, if the columns are all of the same type. For instance, we can find the maximum grade for each student, as follows:

```
> apply(examsquiz,1,max)
 [1] 4.0 3.7 4.0 3.3 3.3 4.0 3.7 3.3 4.0 4.0 4.0 3.3 4.0 4.0 3.7 4.0 3.3 3.7 4.0
[20] 3.7 4.0 4.0 3.3 3.3 4.0 4.0 3.3 3.3 4.0 3.7 3.3 3.3 3.7 2.7 3.3 4.0 3.7 3.7
[39] 3.7
```

5.2.5 Extended Example: A Salary Study

In a study of engineers and programmers, I considered the question, "How many of these workers are the best and the brightest—that is, people of extraordinary ability?" (Some of the details have been changed here.)

The government data I had available was limited. One (admittedly imperfect) way to determine whether a worker is of extraordinary ability is to look at the ratio of actual salary to the government prevailing wage for that job and location. If that ratio is substantially higher than 1.0, you can reasonably assume that this worker has a high level of talent.

I used R to prepare and analyze the data and will present excerpts of my preparation code here. First, I read in the data file:

```
all2006 <- read.csv("2006.csv",header=TRUE,as.is=TRUE)
```

The function read.csv() is essentially identical to read.table() except that the input data is in the CSV format exported by spreadsheets, which is the way the data set was prepared by the US Department of Labor (DOL). The as.is argument is the negation of stringsAsFactors, which you saw earlier in Section 5.1. So, setting as.is to TRUE here is simply an alternate way to achieve stringsAsFactors=FALSE.

At this point, I had a data frame, all2006, consisting of all the data for the year 2006. I then did some filtering:

```
all2006 <- all2006[all2006$Wage_Per=="Year",] # exclude hourly-wagers
all2006 <- all2006[all2006$Wage_Offered_From > 20000,] # exclude weird cases
all2006 <- all2006[all2006$Prevailing_Wage_Amount > 200,] # exclude hrly prv wg
```

These operations are typical data cleaning. Most large data sets contain some outlandish values—some are obvious errors, others use different measurement systems, and so on. I needed to remedy this situation before doing any analysis.

I also needed to create a new column for the ratio between actual wage and prevailing wage:

```
all2006$rat <- all2006$Wage_Offered_From / all2006$Prevailing_Wage_Amount
```

Since I knew I would be calculating the median in this new column for many subsets of the data, I defined a function to do the work:

```
medrat <- function(dataframe) {
    return(median(dataframe$rat,na.rm=TRUE))
}
```

Note the need to exclude NA values, which are common in government data sets.

I was particularly interested in three occupations and thus extracted subdata frames for them to make their analyses more convenient:

```
se2006 <- all2006[grep("Software Engineer",all2006),]
prg2006 <- all2006[grep("Programmer",all2006),]
ee2006 <- all2006[grep("Electronics Engineer",all2006),]
```

Here, I used R's grep() function to identify the rows containing the given job title. Details on this function are in Chapter 11.

Another aspect of interest was analysis by firm. I wrote this function to extract the subdata frame for a given firm:

```
makecorp <- function(corpname) {
   t <- all2006[all2006$Employer_Name == corpname,]
   return(t)
}
```

I then created subdata frames for a number of firms (only some are shown here).

```
corplist <- c("MICROSOFT CORPORATION","ms","INTEL CORPORATION","intel","
   SUN MICROSYSTEMS, INC.","sun","GOOGLE INC.","google")

for (i in 1:(length(corplist)/2)) {
   corp <- corplist[2*i-1]
   newdtf <- paste(corplist[2*i],"2006",sep="")
   assign(newdtf,makecorp(corp),pos=.GlobalEnv)
}
```

There's quite a bit to discuss in the above code. First, note that I want the variables I'm creating to be at the top (that is, global) level, which is the usual place one does interactive analysis. Also, I'm creating my new variable names from character strings, such as "intel2006." For these reasons, the assign() function is wonderful. It allows me to assign a variable by its name as a string and enables me to specify top level (as discussed in Section 7.8.2).

The paste() function allows me to concatenate strings, with sep="" specifying that I don't want any characters between strings in my concatenation.

5.3 Merging Data Frames

In the relational database world, one of the most important operations is that of a *join*, in which two tables can be combined according to the values of a common variable. In R, two data frames can be similarly combined using the merge() function.

The simplest form is as follows:

```
merge(x,y)
```

This merges data frames x and y. It assumes that the two data frames have one or more columns with names in common. Here's an example:

```
> d1
    kids states
1   Jack     CA
2   Jill     MA
3 Jillian    MA
4   John     HI
> d2
  ages    kids
1  10     Jill
2   7  Lillian
3  12     Jack
> d <- merge(d1,d2)
> d
  kids states ages
1 Jack     CA   12
2 Jill     MA   10
```

Here, the two data frames have the variable kids in common. R found the rows in which this variable had the same value of kids in both data frames (the ones for Jack and Jill). It then created a data frame with corresponding rows and with columns taken from data frames (kids, states, and ages).

The merge() function has named arguments by.x and by.y, which handle cases in which variables have similar information but different names in the two data frames. Here's an example:

```
> d3
  ages    pals
1  12     Jack
2  10     Jill
3   7  Lillian
> merge(d1,d3,by.x="kids",by.y="pals")
  kids states ages
1 Jack     CA   12
2 Jill     MA   10
```

Even though our variable was called kids in one data frame and pals in the other, it was meant to store the same information, and thus the merge made sense.

Duplicate matches will appear in full in the result, possibly in undesirable ways.

```
> d1
    kids states
1   Jack     CA
2   Jill     MA
```

```
3 Jillian    MA
4    John    HI
> d2a <- rbind(d2,list(15,"Jill"))
> d2a
  ages   kids
1   12   Jack
2   10   Jill
3    7 Lillian
4   15   Jill
> merge(d1,d2a)
  kids states ages
1 Jack     CA   12
2 Jill     MA   10
3 Jill     MA   15
```

There are two Jills in d2a. There is a Jill in d1 who lives in Massachusetts and another Jill with unknown residence. In our previous example, merge(d1,d2), there was only one Jill, who was presumed to be the same person in both data frames. But here, in the call merge(d1,d2a), it may have been the case that only one of the Jills was a Massachusetts resident. It is clear from this little example that you must choose matching variables with great care.

5.3.1   Extended Example: An Employee Database

The following is an adaptation of one of my consulting projects. At issue was whether older workers were faring as well as younger ones. I had data on several variables, such as age and performance ratings, which I used in my comparison of the older and younger employees. I also had employee ID numbers, which were crucial in being able to connect the two data files: *DA* and *DB*.

The *DA* file had this header:

```
"EmpID","Perf 1","Perf 2","Perf 3","Job Title"
```

These are names for the employee ID, three performance ratings, and the job title. *DB* had no header. The variables again began with the ID, followed by start and end dates of employment.

Both files were in CSV format. Part of my data-cleaning phase consisted of checking that each record contained the proper number of fields. *DA*, for example, should have five fields per record. Here is the check:

```
> count.fields("DA",sep=",")
 [1] 5 5 5 5 5 5 5 5 5 5 5 5 5 5 5 5 5 5 5 5 5 5 5 5 5 5 5 5 5 5 5 5 5 5 5
5 5 5 5
...
```

Here, I specified that the file *DA* had fields separated by commas. The function then reported the number of fields in each record of the file, which fortunately were all 5s.

I could have used all() to check this, rather than checking it visually, via this call:

```
all(count.fields("DA",sep=",") >= 5)
```

A return value of TRUE would mean everything is fine. Alternatively, I could have used this form:

```
table(count.fields("DA",sep=","))
```

I would then get counts of the numbers of records with five fields, four fields, six fields, and so on.

After this check, I then read in the files as data frames:

```
da <- read.csv("DA",header=TRUE,stringsAsFactors=FALSE)
db <- read.csv("DB",header=FALSE,stringsAsFactors=FALSE)
```

I wanted to check for possible spelling errors in the various fields, so I ran the following code:

```
for (col in 1:6)
   print(unique(sort(da[,col])))
```

This gave me a list of the distinct values in each column so that I could visually scan for incorrect spellings.

I needed to merge the two data frames, matching by employee ID, so I ran the following code:

```
mrg <- merge(da,db,by.x=1,by.y=1)
```

I specified that the first column would be the merge variable in both cases. (As remarked earlier, I could also have used field names rather than numbers here.)

5.4   Applying Functions to Data Frames

As with lists, you can use the lapply and sapply functions with data frames.

5.4.1   Using lapply() and sapply() on Data Frames

Keep in mind that data frames are special cases of lists, with the list components consisting of the data frame's columns. Thus, if you call lapply() on a data frame with a specified function f(), then f() will be called on each of the frame's columns, with the return values placed in a list.

For instance, with our previous example, we can use lapply as follows:

```
> d
  kids ages
1 Jack   12
2 Jill   10
> dl <- lapply(d,sort)
> dl
$kids
[1] "Jack" "Jill"

$ages
[1] 10 12
```

So, dl is a list consisting of two vectors, the sorted versions of kids and ages.

Note that dl is just a list, not a data frame. We could coerce it to a data frame, like this:

```
as.data.frame(dl)
  kids ages
1 Jack   10
2 Jill   12
```

But this would make no sense, as the correspondence between names and ages has been lost. Jack, for instance, is now listed as 10 years old instead of 12. (But if we wished to sort the data frame with respect to one of the columns, preserving the correspondences, we could follow the approach presented on page 135.)

5.4.2   Extended Example: Applying Logistic Regression Models

Let's run a logistic regression model on the abalone data we used in Section 2.9.2, predicting gender from the other eight variables: height, weight, rings, and so on, one at a time.

The logistic model is used to predict a 0- or 1-valued random variable Y from one or more explanatory variables. The function value is the probability that $Y = 1$, given the explanatory variables. Let's say we have just one of the latter, X. Then the model is as follows:

$$Pr(Y = 1 | X = t) = \frac{1}{1 + \exp[-(\beta_0 + \beta_1 t)]}$$

As with linear regression models, the β_i values are estimated from the data, using the function glm() with the argument family=binomial.

We can use `sapply()` to fit eight single-predictor models—one for each of the eight variables other than gender in this data set—all in just one line of code.

```
1  aba <- read.csv("abalone.data",header=T)
2  abamf <- aba[aba$Gender != "I",]   # exclude infants from the analysis
3  lftn <- function(clmn) {
4     glm(abamf$Gender ~ clmn, family=binomial)$coef
5  }
6  loall <- sapply(abamf[,-1],lftn)
```

In lines 1 and 2, we read in the data frame and then exclude the observations for infants. In line 6, we call `sapply()` on the subdata frame in which column 1, named Gender, has been excluded. In other words, this is an eight-column subframe consisting of our eight explanatory variables. Thus, `lftn()` is called on each column of that subframe.

Taking as input a column from the subframe, accessed via the formal argument `clmn`, line 4 fits a logistic model that predicts gender from that column and hence from that explanatory variable. Recall from Section 1.5 that the ordinary regression function `lm()` returns a class `"lm"` object containing many components, one of which is `$coefficients`, the vector of estimated β_i. This component is also in the return value of `glm()`. Also recall that list component names can be abbreviated if there is no ambiguity. Here, we've shortened `coefficients` to `coef`.

In the end, line 6 returns eight pairs of estimated β_i. Let's check it out.

```
> loall
             Length    Diameter  Height     WholeWt    ShuckedWt  ViscWt
(Intercept)  1.275832  1.289130  1.027872   0.4300827  0.2855054  0.4829153
clmn        -1.962613 -2.533227 -5.643495  -0.2688070 -0.2941351 -1.4647507
             ShellWt    Rings
(Intercept)  0.5103942  0.64823569
col         -1.2135496 -0.04509376
```

Sure enough, we get a 2-by-8 matrix, with the jth column given the pair of estimated β_i values obtained when we do a logistic regression using the jth explanatory variable.

We could actually get the same result using the ordinary matrix/data frame `apply()` function, but when I tried it, I found that method somewhat slower. The discrepancy may be due to the matrix allocation time.

Note the class of the return value of `glm()`:

```
> class(loall)
[1] "glm" "lm"
```

This says that `loall` actually has *two* classes: `"glm"` and `"lm"`. This is because the `"glm"` class is a subclass of `"lm"`. We'll discuss classes in detail in Chapter 9.

5.4.3 Extended Example: Aids for Learning Chinese Dialects

Standard Chinese, often referred to as Mandarin outside China, is officially termed *putonghua* or *guoyu*. It is spoken today by the vast majority of people in China and among many ethnic Chinese outside China, but the dialects, such as Cantonese and Shanghainese, still enjoy wide usage too. Thus, a Chinese businessman in Beijing who intends to do business in Hong Kong may find it helpful to learn some Cantonese. Similarly, many in Hong Kong may wish to improve their Mandarin. Let's see how such a learning process might be shortened and how R can help.

The differences among the dialects are sometimes startling. The character for "down," 下, is pronounced *xia* in Mandarin, *ha* in Cantonese, and *wu* in Shanghainese. Indeed, because of these differences, and differences in grammar as well, many linguists consider these tongues separate languages rather than dialects. We will call them *fangyan* (meaning "regional speech") here, the Chinese term.

Let's see how R can help speakers of one fangyan learn another one. The key is that there are often patterns in the correspondences between the fangyans. For instance, the initial consonant transformation $x \rightarrow h$ seen in 下 in the previous paragraph (*xia* $\rightarrow$ *ha*) is common, arising also in characters such as 香 (meaning "fragrant"), pronounced *xiang* in Mandarin and *heung* in Cantonese. Note, too, the transformation *iang* $\rightarrow$ *eung* for the non–initial consonant portions of these pronunciations, which is also common. Knowing transformations such as these could speed up the learning curve considerably for the Mandarin-speaking learner of Cantonese, which is the setting we'll illustrate here.

We haven't mentioned the tones yet. All the fangyan are tonal, and sometimes there are patterns there as well, potentially providing further learning aids. However, this avenue will not be pursued here. You'll see that our code does need to make some use of the tones, but we will not attempt to analyze how tones transform from one fangyan to another. For simplicity, we also will not consider characters beginning with vowels, characters that have more than one reading, toneless characters, and other refinements.

Though the initial consonant *x* in Mandarin often maps to *h*, as seen previously, it also often maps to *s*, *y*, and other consonants. For example, the character *xie*, 謝, in the famous Mandarin term *xiexie* (for "thank you") is pronounced *je* in Cantonese. Here, there is an $x \rightarrow j$ transformation on the consonant.

It would be very helpful for the learner to have a list of transformations and their frequencies of occurrence. This a job made for R! The function `mapsound()`, shown a little later in the chapter, does exactly this. It relies on some support functions, also to be presented shortly.

To explain what `mapsound()` does, let's devise some terminology, illustrated by the $x \to h$ example earlier. We'll call x the *source value*, with h, s, and so on being the *mapped values.*

Here are the formal parameters:

- `df`: A data frame consisting of the pronunciation data of two fangyan

- `fromcol` and `tocol`: Names in `df` of the source and mapped columns

- `sourceval`: The source value to be mapped, such as x in the preceding example

Here is the head of a typical two-fangyan data frame, `canman8`, that would be used for `df`:

```
> head(canman8)
  Ch char    Can    Man Can cons Can sound Can tone Man cons Man sound Man tone
1        一  yat1   yi1        y        at        1        y         i 1
2        丁 ding1 ding1        d       ing        1        d       ing 1
3        七 chat1   qi1       ch        at        1        q         i 1
4        丈 jeung6 zhang4       j      eung        6       zh       ang 4
5        上 seung5 shang4       s      eung        5       sh       ang 3
6        下   ha5  xia4        h         a        5        x        ia 4
```

The function returns a list consisting of two components:

- counts: A vector of integers, indexed by the mapped values, showing the counts of those values. The elements of the vector are named according to the mapped values.

- images: A list of character vectors. Again, the indices of the list are the mapped values, and each vector consists of all the characters that correspond to the given mapped value.

To make this concrete, let's try it out:

```
> m2cx <- mapsound(canman8,"Man cons","Can cons","x")
> m2cx$counts
ch  f  g  h  j  k kw  n  s  y
15  2  1 87 12  4  2  1 81 21
```

We see that x maps to *ch* 15 times, to *f* 2 times, and so on. Note that we could have called `sort()` to `m2cx$counts` to view the mapped images in order, from most to least frequent.

The Mandarin-speaking learner of Cantonese can then see that if he wishes to know the Cantonese pronunciation of a word whose Mandarin romanized form begins with x, the Cantonese almost certainly begins with h or s. Little aids like this should help the learning process quite a bit.

To try to discern more patterns, the learner may wish to determine in which characters x maps to *ch*, for example. We know from the result of the preceding example that there are six such characters. Which ones are they?

That information is stored in images. The latter, as mentioned, is a list of vectors. We are interested in the vector corresponding to ch:

```
> head(m2cx$images[["ch"]])
     Ch char   Can  Man Can cons Can sound Can tone Man cons Man sound Man tone
613      嗅 chau3 xiu4       ch        au        3        x       iu 4
982      尋 cham4 xin2       ch        am        4        x       in 2
1050     巡 chun3 xun2       ch        un        3        x       un 2
1173     徐 chui4 xu2        ch        ui        4        x        u 2
1184     循 chun3 xun2       ch        un        3        x       un 2
1566     斜 che4 xie2        ch         e        4        x       ie 2
```

Now, let's look at the code. Before viewing the code for mapsound() itself, let's consider another routine we need for support. It is assumed here that the data frame df that is input to mapsound() is produced by merging two frames for individual fangyans. In this case, for instance, the head of the Cantonese input frame is as follows:

```
> head(can8)
  Ch char    Can
1       一   yat1
2       乙  yuet3
3       丁  ding1
4       七  chat1
5       乃  naai5
6       九   gau2
```

The one for Mandarin is similar. We need to merge these two frames into canman8, seen earlier. I've written the code so that this operation not only combines the frames but also separates the romanization of a character into initial consonant, the remainder of the romanization, and a tone number. For example, *ding1* is separated into *d*, *ing*, and *1*.

We could similarly explore transformations in the other direction, from Cantonese to Mandarin, and involving the nonconsonant remainders of characters. For example, this call determines which characters have *eung* as the nonconsonant portion of their Cantonese pronunciation:

```
> c2meung <- mapsound(canman8,c("Can cons","Man cons"),"eung")
```

We could then investigate the associated Mandarin sounds.

Here is the code to accomplish all this:

```
1  # merges data frames for 2 fangyans
2  merge2fy <- function(fy1,fy2) {
3     outdf <- merge(fy1,fy2)
4     # separate tone from sound, and create new columns
5     for (fy in list(fy1,fy2)) {
6        # saplout will be a matrix, init cons in row 1, remainders in row
```

```
 7      # 2, and tones in row 3
 8      saplout <- sapply((fy[[2]]),sepsoundtone)
 9      # convert it to a data frame
10      tmpdf <- data.frame(fy[,1],t(saplout),row.names=NULL,
11          stringsAsFactors=F)
12      # add names to the columns
13      consname <- paste(names(fy)[[2]]," cons",sep="")
14      restname <- paste(names(fy)[[2]]," sound",sep="")
15      tonename <- paste(names(fy)[[2]]," tone",sep="")
16      names(tmpdf) <- c("Ch char",consname,restname,tonename)
17      # need to use merge(), not cbind(), due to possibly different
18      # ordering of fy, outdf
19      outdf <- merge(outdf,tmpdf)
20      }
21      return(outdf)
22   }
23
24   # separates romanized pronunciation pronun into initial consonant, if any,
25   # the remainder of the sound, and the tone, if any
26   sepsoundtone <- function(pronun) {
27      nchr <- nchar(pronun)
28      vowels <- c("a","e","i","o","u")
29      # how many initial consonants?
30      numcons <- 0
31      for (i in 1:nchr) {
32          ltr <- substr(pronun,i,i)
33          if (!ltr %in% vowels) numcons <- numcons + 1 else break
34      }
35      cons <- if (numcons > 0) substr(pronun,1,numcons) else NA
36      tone <- substr(pronun,nchr,nchr)
37      numtones <- tone %in% letters  # T is 1, F is 0
38      if (numtones == 1) tone <- NA
39      therest <- substr(pronun,numcons+1,nchr-numtones)
40      return(c(cons,therest,tone))
41   }
```

So, even the merging code is not so simple. And this code makes some simplifying assumptions, excluding some important cases. Textual analysis is never for the faint of heart!

Not surprisingly, the merging process begins with a call to merge(), in line 3. This creates a new data frame, outdf, to which we will append new columns for the separated sound components.

The real work, then, involves the separation of a romanization into its sound components. For that, there is a loop in line 5 across the two input data frames. In each iteration, the current data frame is split into sound components, with the result appended to outdf in line 19. Note the comment preceding that line regarding the unsuitability of cbind() in this situation.

The actual separation into sound components is done in line 8. Here, we take a column of romanizations, such the following:

```
yat1
yuet3
ding1
chat1
naai5
gau2
```

We split it into three columns, consisting of initial consonant, remainder of the sound, and tone. For instance, *yat1* will be split into *y*, *at*, and *1*.

This is a very natural candidate for some kind of "apply" function, and indeed sapply() is used in line 8. Of course, this call requires that we write a suitable function to be applied. (If we had been lucky, there would have been an existing R function that worked, but no such good fortune here.) The function we use is sepsoundtone(), starting in line 26.

The sepsoundtone() function makes heavy use of R's substr() (for *substring*) function, described in detail in Chapter 11. In line 31, for example, we loop until we collect all the initial consonants, such *ch*. The return value, in line 40, consists of the three sound components extracted from the given romanized form, the formal parameter pronun.

Note the use of R's built-in constant, letters, in line 37. We use this to sense whether a given character is numeric, which means it's a tone. Some romanizations are toneless.

Line 8 will then return a 3-by-1 matrix, with one row for each of the three sound components. We wish to convert this to a data frame for merging with outdf in line 19, and we prepare for this in line 10.

Note that we call the matrix transpose function t() to put our information into columns rather than rows. This is needed because data-frame storage is by columns. Also, we include a column fy[,1], the Chinese characters themselves, to have a column in common in the call to merge() in line 19.

Now let's turn to the code for mapsound(), which actually is simpler than the preceding merging code.

```
1   mapsound <- function(df,fromcol,tocol,sourceval) {
2       base <- which(df[[fromcol]] == sourceval)
3       basedf <- df[base,]
4       # determine which rows of basedf correspond to the various mapped
5       # values
6       sp <- split(basedf,basedf[[tocol]])
7       retval <- list()
8       retval$counts <- sapply(sp,nrow)
9       retval$images <- sp
10      return(retval)
11  }
```

Recall that the argument df is the two-fangyan data frame, output from merge2fy(). The arguments fromcol and tocol are the names of the source and mapped columns. The string sourceval is the source value to be mapped. For concreteness, consider the earlier examples in which sourceval was *x*.

The first task is to determine which rows in df correspond to sourceval. This is accomplished via a straightforward application of which() in line 2. This information is then used in line 3 to extract the relevant subdata frame.

In that latter frame, consider the form that basedf[[tocol]] will take in line 6. These will be the values that *x* maps to—that is, *ch*, *h*, and so on. The purpose of line 6 is to determine which rows of basedf contain which of these mapped values. Here, we use R's split() function. We'll discuss split() in detail in Section 6.2.2, but the salient point is that sp will be a list of data frames: one for *ch*, one for *h*, and so on.

This sets up line 8. Since sp will be a list of data frames—one for each mapped value—applying the nrow() function via sapply() will give us the counts of the numbers of characters for each of the mapped values, such as the number of characters in which the map *x* → *ch* occurs (15 times, as seen in the example call).

The complexity of the code here makes this a good time to comment on programming style. Some readers may point out, correctly, that lines 2 and 3 could be replaced by a one-liner:

```
basedf <- df[df[[fromcol]] == sourceval,]
```

But to me, that line, with its numerous brackets, is harder to read. My personal preference is to break down operations if they become too complex.

Similarly, the last few lines of code could be compacted to another one-liner:

```
list(counts=sapply(sp,nrow),images=sp)
```

Among other things, this dispenses with the return(), conceivably speeding up the code. Recall that in R, the last value computed by a function is automatically returned anyway, without a return() call. However, the time savings here are really small and rarely matter, and again, my personal belief is that including the return() call is clearer.

6

FACTORS AND TABLES

Factors form the basis for many of R's powerful operations, including many of those performed on tabular data. The motivation for factors comes from the notion of *nominal*, or *categorical*, variables in statistics. These values are nonnumerical in nature, corresponding to categories such as Democrat, Republican, and Unaffiliated, although they may be coded using numbers.

In this chapter, we'll begin by looking at the extra information contained in factors and then focus on the functions used with factors. We'll also explore tables and common table operations.

6.1   Factors and Levels

An R *factor* might be viewed simply as a vector with a bit more information added (though, as seen below, it's different from this internally). That extra information consists of a record of the distinct values in that vector, called *levels*. Here's an example:

```
> x <- c(5,12,13,12)
> xf <- factor(x)
```

```
> xf
[1] 5  12 13 12
Levels: 5 12 13
```

The distinct values in xf—5, 12, and 13—are the levels here.

Let's take a look inside:

```
> str(xf)
 Factor w/ 3 levels "5","12","13": 1 2 3 2
> unclass(xf)
[1] 1 2 3 2
attr(,"levels")
[1] "5"  "12" "13"
```

This is revealing. The core of xf here is not (5,12,13,12) but rather (1,2,3,2). The latter means that our data consists first of a level-1 value, then level-2 and level-3 values, and finally another level-2 value. So the data has been recoded by level. The levels themselves are recorded too, of course, though as characters such as "5" rather than 5.

The length of a factor is still defined in terms of the length of the data rather than, say, being a count of the number of levels:

```
> length(xf)
[1] 4
```

We can anticipate future new levels, as seen here:

```
> x <- c(5,12,13,12)
> xff <- factor(x,levels=c(5,12,13,88))
> xff
[1] 5  12 13 12
Levels: 5 12 13 88
> xff[2] <- 88
> xff
[1] 5  88 13 12
Levels: 5 12 13 88
```

Originally, xff did not contain the value 88, but in defining it, we allowed for that future possibility. Later, we did indeed add the value.

By the same token, you cannot sneak in an "illegal" level. Here's what happens when you try:

```
> xff[2] <- 28
Warning message:
In `[<-.factor`(`*tmp*`, 2, value = 28) :
  invalid factor level, NAs generated
```

6.2 Common Functions Used with Factors

With factors, we have yet another member of the family of apply functions, tapply. We'll look at that function, as well as two other functions commonly used with factors: split() and by().

6.2.1 The tapply() Function

As motivation, suppose we have a vector x of ages of voters and a factor f showing some nonnumeric trait of those voters, such as party affiliation (Democrat, Republican, Unaffiliated). We might wish to find the mean ages in x within each of the party groups.

In typical usage, the call tapply(x,f,g) has x as a vector, f as a factor or list of factors, and g as a function. The function g() in our little example above would be R's built-in mean() function. If we wanted to group by both party and another factor, say gender, we would need f to consist of the two factors, party and gender.

Each factor in f must have the same length as x. This makes sense in light of the voter example above; we should have as many party affiliations as ages. If a component of f is a vector, it will be coerced into a factor by applying as.factor() to it.

The operation performed by tapply() is to (temporarily) split x into groups, each group corresponding to a level of the factor (or a combination of levels of the factors in the case of multiple factors), and then apply g() to the resulting subvectors of x. Here's a little example:

```
> ages <- c(25,26,55,37,21,42)
> affils <- c("R","D","D","R","U","D")
> tapply(ages,affils,mean)
 D  R  U
41 31 21
```

Let's look at what happened. The function tapply() treated the vector ("R","D","D","R","U","D") as a factor with levels "D", "R", and "U". It noted that "D" occurred in indices 2, 3 and 6; "R" occurred in indices 1 and 4; and "U" occurred in index 5. For convenience, let's refer to the three index vectors (2,3,6), (1,4), and (5) as x, y, and z, respectively. Then tapply() computed mean(u[x]), mean(u[y]), and mean(u[z]) and returned those means in a three-element vector. And that vector's element names are "D", "R", and "U", reflecting the factor levels that were used by tapply().

What if we have two or more factors? Then each factor yields a set of groups, as in the preceding example, and the groups are ANDed together. As an example, suppose that we have an economic data set that includes variables for gender, age, and income. Here, the call tapply(x,f,g) might have x as income and f as a pair of factors: one for gender and the other coding whether the person is older or younger than 25. We may be interested in finding mean income, broken down by gender and age. If we set g() to be mean(), tapply() will return the mean incomes in each of four subgroups:

- Male and under 25 years old

- Female and under 25 years old

- Male and over 25 years old

- Female and over 25 years old

Here's a toy example of that setting:

```
> d <- data.frame(list(gender=c("M","M","F","M","F","F"),
+   age=c(47,59,21,32,33,24),income=c(55000,88000,32450,76500,123000,45650)))
> d
  gender age income
1      M  47  55000
2      M  59  88000
3      F  21  32450
4      M  32  76500
5      F  33 123000
6      F  24  45650
> d$over25 <- ifelse(d$age > 25,1,0)
> d
  gender age income over25
1      M  47  55000      1
2      M  59  88000      1
3      F  21  32450      0
4      M  32  76500      1
5      F  33 123000      1
6      F  24  45650      0
> tapply(d$income,list(d$gender,d$over25),mean)
       0         1
F  39050 123000.00
M     NA  73166.67
```

We specified two factors, gender and indicator variable for age over or under 25. Since each of these factors has two levels, tapply() partitioned the income data into four groups, one for each combination of gender and age, and then applied to mean() function to each group.

6.2.2 The split() Function

In contrast to tapply(), which splits a vector into groups and then applies a specified function on each group, split() stops at that first stage, just forming the groups.

The basic form, without bells and whistles, is split(x,f), with x and f playing roles similar to those in the call tapply(x,f,g); that is, x being a vector or data frame and f being a factor or a list of factors. The action is to split x into groups, which are returned in a list. (Note that x is allowed to be a data frame with split() but not with tapply().)

Let's try it out with our earlier example.

```
> d
  gender age income over25
1      M  47  55000      1
2      M  59  88000      1
3      F  21  32450      0
4      M  32  76500      1
5      F  33 123000      1
6      F  24  45650      0
> split(d$income,list(d$gender,d$over25))
$F.0
[1] 32450 45650

$M.0
numeric(0)

$F.1
[1] 123000

$M.1
[1] 55000 88000 76500
```

The output of split() is a list, and recall that list components are denoted by dollar signs. So the last vector, for example, was named "M.1" to indicate that it was the result of combining "M" in the first factor and 1 in the second.

As another illustration, consider our abalone example from Section 2.9.2. We wanted to determine the indices of the vector elements corresponding to male, female, and infant. The data in that little example consisted of the seven-observation vector ("M","F","F","I","M","M","F"), assigned to g. We can do this in a flash with split().

```
> g <- c("M","F","F","I","M","M","F")
> split(1:7,g)
$F
[1] 2 3 7

$I
[1] 4

$M
[1] 1 5 6
```

The results show the female cases are in records 2, 3, and 7; the infant case is in record 4; and the male cases are in records 1, 5, and 6.

Let's dissect this step-by-step. The vector g, taken as a factor, has three levels: "M", "F", and "I". The indices corresponding to the first level are 1, 5, and 6, which means that g[1], g[5], and g[6] all have the value "M". So, R sets the M component of the output to elements 1, 5, and 6 of 1:7, which is the vector (1,5,6).

We can take a similar approach to simplify the code in our text concordance example from Section 4.2.4. There, we wished to input a text file, determine which words were in the text, and then output a list giving the words and their locations within the text. We can use split() to make short work of writing the code, as follows:

```
1  findwords <- function(tf) {
2      # read in the words from the file, into a vector of mode character
3      txt <- scan(tf,"")
4      words <- split(1:length(txt),txt)
5      return(words)
6  }
```

The call to scan() returns a list txt of the words read in from the file tf. So, txt[[1]] will contain the first word input from the file, txt[[2]] will contain the second word, and so on; length(txt) will thus be the total number of words read. Suppose for concreteness that that number is 220.

Meanwhile, txt itself, as the second argument in split() above, will be taken as a factor. The levels of that factor will be the various words in the file. If, for instance, the file contains the word *world* 6 times and *climate* was there 10 times, then "world" and "climate" will be two of the levels of txt. The call to split() will then determine where these and the other words appear in txt.

6.2.3   The by() Function

Suppose in the abalone example we wish to do regression analyses of diameter against length separately for each gender code: males, females, and infants. At first, this seems like something tailor-made for tapply(), but the first argument of that function must be a vector, not a matrix or a data frame. The function to be applied can be multivariate—for example, range()—but the input must be a vector. Yet the input for regression is a matrix (or data frame) with at least two columns: one for the predicted variable and one or more for predictor variables. In our abalone data application, the matrix would consist of a column for the diameter data and a column for length.

The by() function can be used here. It works like tapply() (which it calls internally, in fact), but it is applied to objects rather than vectors. Here's how to use it for the desired regression analyses:

```
> aba <- read.csv("abalone.data",header=TRUE)
> by(aba,aba$Gender,function(m) lm(m[,2]~m[,3]))
aba$Gender: F
```

```
Call:
lm(formula = m[, 2] ~ m[, 3])

Coefficients:
(Intercept)        m[, 3]
    0.04288       1.17918


-----------------------------------------------------------
aba$Gender: I

Call:
lm(formula = m[, 2] ~ m[, 3])

Coefficients:
(Intercept)        m[, 3]
    0.02997       1.21833


-----------------------------------------------------------
aba$Gender: M

Call:
lm(formula = m[, 2] ~ m[, 3])

Coefficients:
(Intercept)        m[, 3]
    0.03653       1.19480
```

Calls to by() look very similar to calls to tapply(), with the first argument specifying our data, the second the grouping factor, and the third the function to be applied to each group.

Just as tapply() forms groups of indices of a vector according to levels of a factor, this by() call finds groups of row numbers of the data frame aba. That creates three subdata frames: one for each gender level of M, F, and I.

The anonymous function we defined regresses the second column of its matrix argument m against the third column. This function will be called three times—once for each of the three subdata frames created earlier—thus producing the three regression analyses.

6.3   Working with Tables

To begin exploring R tables, consider this example:

```
> u <- c(22,8,33,6,8,29,-2)
> fl <- list(c(5,12,13,12,13,5,13),c("a","bc","a","a","bc","a","a"))
> tapply(u,fl,length)
   a bc
5  2 NA
```

```
12 1  1
13 2  1
```

Here, `tapply()` again temporarily breaks u into subvectors, as you saw earlier, and then applies the `length()` function to each subvector. (Note that this is independent of what's in u. Our focus now is purely on the factors.) Those subvector lengths are the counts of the occurrences of each of the $3 \times 2 = 6$ combinations of the two factors. For instance, 5 occurred twice with "a" and not at all with "bc"; hence the entries 2 and NA in the first row of the output. In statistics, this is called a *contingency table*.

There is one problem in this example: the NA value. It really should be 0, meaning that in no cases did the first factor have level 5 and the second have level "bc". The `table()` function creates contingency tables correctly.

```
> table(fl)
    fl.2
fl.1 a bc
  5  2  0
  12 1  1
  13 2  1
```

The first argument in a call to `table()` is either a factor or a list of factors. The two factors here were (5,12,13,12,13,5,13) and ("a","bc","a","a","bc", "a","a"). In this case, an object that is interpretable as a factor is counted as one.

Typically a data frame serves as the `table()` data argument. Suppose for instance the file *ct.dat* consists of election-polling data, in which candidate X is running for reelection. The *ct.dat* file looks like this:

```
"Vote for X" "Voted For X Last Time"
"Yes" "Yes"
"Yes" "No"
"No" "No"
"Not Sure" "Yes"
"No" "No"
```

In the usual statistical fashion, each row in this file represents one subject under study. In this case, we have asked five people the following two questions:

- Do you plan to vote for candidate X?
- Did you vote for X in the last election?

This gives us five rows in the data file.

Let's read in the file:

```
> ct <- read.table("ct.dat",header=T)
> ct
```

```
     Vote.for.X Voted.for.X.Last.Time
1          Yes                     Yes
2          Yes                     No
3           No                     No
4     Not Sure                     Yes
5           No                     No
```

We can use the `table()` function to compute the contingency table for this data:

```
> cttab <- table(ct)
> cttab
          Voted.for.X.Last.Time
Vote.for.X No Yes
  No        2   0
  Not Sure  0   1
  Yes       1   1
```

The 2 in the upper-left corner of the table shows that we had, for example, two people who said "no" to the first and second questions. The 1 in the middle-right indicates that one person answered "not sure" to the first question and "yes" to the second question.

We can also get one-dimensional counts, which are counts on a single factor, as follows:

```
> table(c(5,12,13,12,8,5))

 5  8 12 13
 2  1  2  1
```

Here's an example of a three-dimensional table, involving voters' genders, race (white, black, Asian, and other), and political views (liberal or conservative):

```
> v # the data frame
  gender race pol
1 M W L
2 M W L
3 F A C
4 M O L
5 F B L
6 F B C
> vt <- table(v)
> vt
, , pol = C
```

```
          race
gender A B O W
     F 1 1 0 0
     M 0 0 0 0


, , pol = L


          race
gender A B O W
     F 0 1 0 0
     M 0 0 1 2
```

R prints out a three-dimensional table as a series of two-dimensional tables. In this case, it generates a table of gender and race for conservatives and then a corresponding table for liberals. For example, the second two-dimensional table says that there were two white male liberals.

6.3.1   Matrix/Array-Like Operations on Tables

Just as most (nonmathematical) matrix/array operations can be used on data frames, they can be applied to tables, too. (This is not surprising, given that the cell counts portion of a table object is an array.)

For example, we can access the table cell counts using matrix notation. Let's apply this to our voting example from the previous section.

```
> class(cttab)
[1] "table"
> cttab[1,1]
[1] 2
> cttab[1,]
 No Yes
  2   0
```

In the second command, even though the first command had shown that cttab had class "cttab", we treated it as a matrix and printed out its "[1,1] element." Continuing this idea, the third command printed the first column of this "matrix."

We can multiply the matrix by a scalar. For instance, here's how to change cell counts to proportions:

```
> cttab/5
         Voted.for.X.Last.Time
Vote.for.X  No Yes
  No       0.4 0.0
  Not Sure 0.0 0.2
  Yes      0.2 0.2
```

In statistics, the *marginal* values of a variable are those obtained when this variable is held constant while others are summed. In the voting example, the marginal values of the Vote.for.X variable are 2 + 0 = 2, 0 + 1 = 1, and 1 + 1 = 2. We can of course obtain these via the matrix apply() function:

```
> apply(cttab,1,sum)
      No Not Sure      Yes
       2        1        2
```

Note that the labels here, such as No, came from the row names of the matrix, which table() produced.

But R supplies a function addmargins() for this purpose—that is, to find marginal totals. Here's an example:

```
> addmargins(cttab)
          Voted.for.X.Last.Time
Vote.for.X No Yes Sum
  No         2   0   2
  Not Sure   0   1   1
  Yes        1   1   2
  Sum        3   2   5
```

Here, we got the marginal data for both dimensions at once, conveniently superimposed onto the original table.

We can get the names of the dimensions and levels through dimnames(), as follows:

```
> dimnames(cttab)
$Vote.for.X
[1] "No"       "Not Sure" "Yes"

$Voted.for.X.Last.Time
[1] "No"  "Yes"
```

6.3.2 Extended Example: Extracting a Subtable

Let's continue working with our voting example:

```
> cttab
          Voted.for.X.Last.Time
Vote.for.X No Yes
  No         2   0
  Not Sure   0   1
  Yes        1   1
```

Suppose we wish to present this data at a meeting, concentrating on those respondents who know they will vote for X in the current election. In other words, we wish to eliminate the Not Sure entries and present a sub-table that looks like this:

```
                Voted.for.X.Last.Time
Vote.for.X No Yes
   No          2   0
   Yes         1   1
```

The function subtable() below performs subtable extraction. It has two arguments:

- tbl: The table of interest, of class "table".

- subnames: A list specifying the desired subtable extraction. Each component of this list is named after some dimension of tbl, and the value of that component is a vector of the names of the desired levels.

So, let's review what we have in this example before looking at the code. The argument cttab will be a two-dimensional table, with dimension names Voted.for.X and Voted.for.X.Last.Time. Within those two dimensions, the level names are No, Not Sure, and Yes in the first dimension, and No and Yes in the second. Of those, we wish to exclude the Not Sure cases, so our actual argument corresponding to the formal argument subnames is as follows:

```
list(Vote.for.X=c("No","Yes"),Voted.for.X.Last.Time=c("No","Yes"))
```

We can now call the function.

```
> subtable(cttab,list(Vote.for.X=c("No","Yes"),
+    Voted.for.X.Last.Time=c("No","Yes")))
          Voted.for.X.Last.Time
Vote.for.X No Yes
       No   2   0
       Yes  1   1
```

Now that we have a feel for what the function does, let's take a look at its innards.

```
1  subtable <- function(tbl,subnames) {
2     # get array of cell counts in tbl
3     tblarray <- unclass(tbl)
4     # we'll get the subarray of cell counts corresponding to subnames by
5     # calling do.call() on the "[" function; we need to build up a list
6     # of arguments first
7     dcargs <- list(tblarray)
8     ndims <- length(subnames) # number of dimensions
```

```
 9    for (i in 1:ndims) {
10        dcargs[[i+1]] <- subnames[[i]]
11    }
12    subarray <- do.call("[",dcargs)
13    # now we'll build the new table, consisting of the subarray, the
14    # numbers of levels in each dimension, and the dimnames() value, plus
15    # the "table" class attribute
16    dims <- lapply(subnames,length)
17    subtbl <- array(subarray,dims,dimnames=subnames)
18    class(subtbl) <- "table"
19    return(subtbl)
20  }
```

So, what's happening here? To prepare for writing this code, I first did a little detective work to determine the structure of objects of class "table". Looking through the code of the function table(), I found that at its core, an object of class "table" consists of an array whose elements are the cell counts. So the strategy is to extract the desired subarray, then add names to the dimensions of the subarray, and then bestow "table" class status to the result.

For the code here, then, the first task is to form the subarray corresponding to the user's desired subtable, and this constitutes most of the code. To this end, in line 3, we first extract the full cell counts array, storing it in tblarray. The question is how to use that to find the desired subarray. In principle, this is easy. In practice, that's not always the case.

To get the desired subarray, I needed to form a subsetting expression on the array tblarray—something like this:

```
tblarray[some index ranges here]
```

In our voting example, the expression is as follows:

```
tblarray[c("No","Yes"),c("No","Yes")]
```

This is simple in concept but difficult to do directly, since tblarray could be of different dimensions (two, three, or anything else). Recall that R's array subscripting is actually done via a function named "[" (). This function takes a variable number of arguments: two for two-dimensional arrays, three for three-dimensional arrays, and so on.

This problem is solved by using R's do.call(). This function has the following basic form:

```
do.call(f,argslist)
```

where f is a function and argslist is a list of arguments on which to call f(). In other words, the preceding code basically does this:

```
f(argslist[[1]],argslist[[2]],...)
```

This makes it easy to call a function with a variable number of arguments.

For our example, we need to form a list consisting first of tblarray and then the user's desired levels for each dimension. Our list looks like this:

```
list(tblarray,Vote.for.X=c("No","Yes"),Voted.for.X.Last.Time=c("No","Yes"))
```

Lines 7 through 11 build up this list for the general case. That's our sub-array. Then we need to attach the names and set the class to "table". The former operation can be done via R's array() function, which has the following arguments:

- data: The data to be placed into the new array. In our case, this is subarray.

- dim: The dimension lengths (number of rows, number of columns, number of layers, and so on). In our case, this is the value ndims, computed in line 16.

- dimnames: The dimension names and the names of their levels, already given to us by the user as the argument subnames.

This was a somewhat conceptually complex function to write, but it gets easier once you've mastered the inner structures of the "table" class.

6.3.3 Extended Example: Finding the Largest Cells in a Table

It can be difficult to view a table that is very big, with a large number of rows or dimensions. One approach might be to focus on the cells with the largest frequencies. That's the purpose of the tabdom() function developed below—it reports the dominant frequencies in a table. Here's a simple call:

```
tabdom(tbl,k)
```

This reports the cells in the table tbl that have the k largest frequencies.
Here's an example:

```
> d <- c(5,12,13,4,3,28,12,12,9,5,5,13,5,4,12)
> dtab <- table(d)
> tabdom(dtab,3)
   d Freq
3  5    4
5 12    4
2  4    2
```

The function tells us that the values 5 and 12 were the most frequent in d, with four instances each, and the next most frequent value was 4, with two instances. (The 3, 5, and 2 on the left are actually extraneous information; see the following discussion regarding converting a table to a data frame.)

As another example, consider our table cttab in the examples in the preceding sections:

```
> tabdom(cttab,2)
  Vote.for.X Voted.For.X.Last.Time Freq
1        No                     No    2
3       Yes                     No    1
```

So the combination No-No was most frequent, with two instances, with the second most frequent being Yes-No, with one instance.[1]

Well, how is this accomplished? It looks fairly complicated, but actually the work is made pretty easy by a trick, exploiting the fact that you can present tables in data frame format. Let's use our cttab table again.

```
> as.data.frame(cttab)
  Vote.for.X Voted.For.X.Last.Time Freq
1        No                     No    2
2  Not Sure                     No    0
3       Yes                     No    1
4        No                    Yes    0
5  Not Sure                    Yes    1
6       Yes                    Yes    1
```

Note that this is *not* the original data frame ct from which the table cttab was constructed. It is simply a different presentation of the table itself. There is one row for each combination of the factors, with a Freq column added to show the number of instances of each combination. This latter feature makes our task quite easy.

```
1  # finds the cells in table tbl with the k highest frequencies; handling
2  # of ties is unrefined
3  tabdom <- function(tbl,k) {
4     # create a data frame representation of tbl, adding a Freq column
5     tbldf <- as.data.frame(tbl)
6     # determine the proper positions of the frequencies in a sorted order
7     freqord <- order(tbldf$Freq,decreasing=TRUE)
8     # rearrange the data frame in that order, and take the first k rows
9     dom <- tbldf[freqord,][1:k,]
10    return(dom)
11 }
```

The comments should make the code self-explanatory.

---

[1] But didn't the Not Sure–Yes and Yes-Yes combinations also have one instance and thus should be tied with Yes-No for second place? Yes, definitely. My code is cavalier regarding ties, and the reader is encouraged to refine it in that direction.

The sorting approach in line 7, which makes use of order(), is the standard way to sort a data frame (worth remembering, since the situation arises rather frequently).

The approach taken here—converting a table to a data frame—could also be used in Section 6.3.2. However, you would need to be careful to remove levels from the factors to avoid zeros in cells.

6.4   Other Factor- and Table-Related Functions

R includes a number of other functions that are handy for working with tables and factors. We'll discuss two of them here: aggregate() and cut().

NOTE   *Hadley Wickham's reshape package "lets you flexibly restructure and aggregate data using just two functions: melt and cast." This package may take a while to learn, but it is extremely powerful. His plyr package is also quite versatile. You can download both packages from R's CRAN repository. See Appendix B for more details about downloading and installing packages.*

6.4.1   The aggregate() Function

The aggregate() function calls tapply() once for each variable in a group. For example, in the abalone data, we could find the median of each variable, broken down by gender, as follows:

```
> aggregate(aba[,-1],list(aba$Gender),median)
  Group.1 Length Diameter Height WholeWt ShuckedWt ViscWt ShellWt Rings
1       F  0.590    0.465  0.160 1.03850   0.44050 0.2240   0.295 10
2       I  0.435    0.335  0.110 0.38400   0.16975 0.0805   0.113 8
3       M  0.580    0.455  0.155 0.97575   0.42175 0.2100   0.276 10
```

The first argument, aba[,-1], is the entire data frame except for the first column, which is Gender itself. The second argument, which must be a list, is our Gender factor as before. Finally, the third argument tells R to compute the median on each column in each of the data frames generated by the subgrouping corresponding to our factors. There are three such subgroups in our example here and thus three rows in the output of aggregate().

6.4.2   The cut() Function

A common way to generate factors, especially for tables, is the cut() function. You give it a data vector x and a set of bins defined by a vector b. The function then determines which bin each of the elements of x falls into.

The following is the form of the call we'll use here:

```
y <- cut(x,b,labels=FALSE)
```

where the bins are defined to be the semi-open intervals (b[1],b[2]],
(b[2],b[3]],.... Here's an example:

```
> z
[1] 0.88114802 0.28532689 0.58647376 0.42851862 0.46881514 0.24226859 0.05289197
[8] 0.88035617
> seq(from=0.0,to=1.0,by=0.1)
 [1] 0.0 0.1 0.2 0.3 0.4 0.5 0.6 0.7 0.8 0.9 1.0
> binmarks <- seq(from=0.0,to=1.0,by=0.1)
> cut(z,binmarks,labels=F)
[1] 9 3 6 5 5 3 1 9
```

This says that z[1], 0.88114802, fell into bin 9, which was (0.8,0.9]; z[2],
0.28532689, fell into bin 3; and so on.

This returns a vector, as seen in the example's result. But we can convert
it into a factor and possibly then use it to build a table. For instance, you can
imagine using this to write your own specialized histogram function. (The R
function findInterval() would be useful for this, too.)

7

R PROGRAMMING STRUCTURES

 R is a block-structured language in the manner of the ALGOL-descendant family, such as C, C++, Python, Perl, and so on. As you've seen, blocks are delineated by braces, though braces are optional if the block consists of just a single statement. Statements are separated by newline characters or, optionally, by semicolons.

Here, we cover the basic structures of R as a programming language. We'll review some more details on loops and the like and then head straight into the topic of functions, which will occupy most of the chapter.

In particular, issues of variable scope will play a major role. As with many scripting languages, you do not "declare" variables in R. Programmers who have a background in, say, the C language, will find similarities in R at first but then will see that R has a richer scoping structure.

7.1 Control Statements

Control statements in R look very similar to those of the ALGOL-descendant family languages mentioned above. Here, we'll look at loops and if-else statements.

7.1.1 Loops

In Section 1.3, we defined the `oddcount()` function. In that function, the following line should have been instantly recognized by Python programmers:

```
for (n in x)  {
```

It means that there will be one iteration of the loop for each component of the vector x, with n taking on the values of those components—in the first iteration, n = x[1]; in the second iteration, n = x[2]; and so on. For example, the following code uses this structure to output the square of every element in a vector:

```
> x <- c(5,12,13)
> for (n in x) print(n^2)
[1] 25
[1] 144
[1] 169
```

C-style looping with `while` and `repeat` is also available, complete with `break`, a statement that causes control to leave the loop. Here is an example that uses all three:

```
> i <- 1
> while (i <= 10) i <- i+4
> i
[1] 13
>
> i <- 1
> while(TRUE) {  # similar loop to above
+     i <- i+4
+     if (i > 10) break
+ }
> i
[1] 13
>
> i <- 1
> repeat {  # again similar
+     i <- i+4
+     if (i > 10) break
+ }
> i
[1] 13
```

In the first code snippet, the variable i took on the values 1, 5, 9, and 13 as the loop went through its iterations. In that last case, the condition i <= 10 failed, so the break took hold and we left the loop.

This code shows three different ways of accomplishing the same thing, with break playing a key role in the second and third ways.

Note that repeat has no Boolean exit condition. You must use break (or something like return()). Of course, break can be used with for loops, too.

Another useful statement is next, which instructs the interpreter to skip the remainder of the current iteration of the loop and proceed directly to the next one. This provides a way to avoid using complexly nested if-then-else constructs, which can make the code confusing. Let's take a look at an example that uses next. The following code comes from an extended example in Chapter 8:

```
sim <- function(nreps) {
   commdata <- list()
   commdata$countabsamecomm <- 0
   for (rep in 1:nreps) {
      commdata$whosleft <- 1:20
      commdata$numabchosen <- 0
      commdata <- choosecomm(commdata,5)
      if (commdata$numabchosen > 0) next
      commdata <- choosecomm(commdata,4)
      if (commdata$numabchosen > 0) next
      commdata <- choosecomm(commdata,3)
   }
   print(commdata$countabsamecomm/nreps)
}
```

There are next statements in lines 8 and 10. Let's see how they work and how they improve on the alternatives. The two next statements occur within the loop that starts at line 4. Thus, when the if condition holds in line 8, lines 9 through 11 will be skipped, and control will transfer to line 4. The situation in line 10 is similar.

Without using next, we would need to resort to nested if statements, something like these:

```
sim <- function(nreps) {
   commdata <- list()
   commdata$countabsamecomm <- 0
   for (rep in 1:nreps) {
      commdata$whosleft <- 1:20
      commdata$numabchosen <- 0
      commdata <- choosecomm(commdata,5)
      if (commdata$numabchosen == 0) {
         commdata <- choosecomm(commdata,4)
         if (commdata$numabchosen == 0) {
            commdata <- choosecomm(commdata,3)
         }
      }
```

```
14    print(commdata$countabsamecomm/nreps)
15  }
```

Because this simple example has just two levels, it's not too bad. However, nested if statements can become confusing when you have more levels.

The for construct works on any vector, regardless of mode. You can loop over a vector of filenames, for instance. Say we have a file named *file1* with the following contents:

```
1
2
3
4
5
6
```

We also have a file named *file2* with these contents:

```
5
12
13
```

The following loop reads and prints each of these files. We use the scan() function here to read in a file of numbers and store those values in a vector. We'll talk more about scan() in Chapter 10.

```
> for (fn in c("file1","file2")) print(scan(fn))
Read 6 items
[1] 1 2 3 4 5 6
Read 3 items
[1]  5 12 13
```

So, fn is first set to *file1*, and the file of that name is read in and printed out. Then the same thing happens for *file2*.

7.1.2   Looping Over Nonvector Sets

R does not directly support iteration over nonvector sets, but there are a couple of indirect yet easy ways to accomplish it:

- Use lapply(), assuming that the iterations of the loop are independent of each other, thus allowing them to be performed in any order.

- Use get(). As its name implies, this function takes as an argument a character string representing the name of some object and returns the object of that name. It sounds simple, but get() is a very powerful function.

Let's look at an example of using get(). Say we have two matrices, u and v, containing statistical data, and we wish to apply R's linear regression function lm() to each of them.

```
> u
     [,1] [,2]
[1,]   1    1
[2,]   2    2
[3,]   3    4
> v
     [,1] [,2]
[1,]    8   15
[2,]   12   10
[3,]   20    2
> for (m in c("u","v")) {
+     z <- get(m)
+     print(lm(z[,2] ~ z[,1]))
+ }

Call:
lm(formula = z[, 2] ~ z[, 1])

Coefficients:
(Intercept)        z[, 1]
    -0.6667        1.5000

Call:
lm(formula = z[, 2] ~ z[, 1])

Coefficients:
(Intercept)        z[, 1]
     23.286        -1.071
```

Here, m was first set to u. Then these lines assign the matrix u to z, which allows the call to lm() on u:

```
z <- get(m)
print(lm(z[,2] ~ z[,1]))
```

The same then occurs with v.

7.1.3   if-else

The syntax for if-else looks like this:

```
if (r == 4) {
    x <- 1
```

```
} else {
   x <- 3
   y <- 4
}
```

It looks simple, but there is an important subtlety here. The if section consists of just a single statement:

```
x <- 1
```

So, you might guess that the braces around that statement are not necessary. However, they are indeed needed.

The right brace before the else is used by the R parser to deduce that this is an if-else rather than just an if. In interactive mode, without braces, the parser would mistakenly think the latter and act accordingly, which is not what we want.

An if-else statement works as a function call, and as such, it returns the last value assigned.

```
v <- if (cond) expression1 else expression2
```

This will set v to the result of expression1 or expression2, depending on whether cond is true. You can use this fact to compact your code. Here's a simple example:

```
> x <- 2
> y <- if(x == 2) x else x+1
> y
[1] 2
> x <- 3
> y <- if(x == 2) x else x+1
> y
[1] 4
```

Without taking this tack, the code

```
y <- if(x == 2) x else x+1
```

would instead consist of the somewhat more cluttered

```
if(x == 2) y <- x else y <- x+1
```

In more complex examples, expression1 and/or expression2 could be function calls. On the other hand, you probably should not let compactness take priority over clarity.

When working with vectors, use the ifelse() function, as discussed in Chapter 2, as it will likely produce faster code.

7.2 Arithmetic and Boolean Operators and Values

Table 7-1 lists the basic operators.

Table 7-1: Basic R Operators

Operation	Description
x + y	Addition
x - y	Subtraction
x * y	Multiplication
x / y	Division
x ^ y	Exponentiation
x %% y	Modular arithmetic
x %/% y	Integer division
x == y	Test for equality
x <= y	Test for less than or equal to
x >= y	Test for greater than or equal to
x && y	Boolean AND for scalars
x || y	Boolean OR for scalars
x & y	Boolean AND for vectors (vector x,y,result)
x | y	Boolean OR for vectors (vector x,y,result)
!x	Boolean negation

Though R ostensibly has no scalar types, with scalars being treated as one-element vectors, we see the exception in Table 7-1: There are different Boolean operators for the scalar and vector cases. This may seem odd, but a simple example will demonstrate the need for such a distinction.

```
> x
[1]  TRUE FALSE  TRUE
> y
[1]  TRUE  TRUE FALSE
> x & y
[1]  TRUE FALSE FALSE
> x[1] && y[1]
[1] TRUE
> x && y  # looks at just the first elements of each vector
[1] TRUE
> if (x[1] && y[1]) print("both TRUE")
[1] "both TRUE"
> if (x & y) print("both TRUE")
[1] "both TRUE"
Warning message:
In if (x & y) print("both TRUE") :
  the condition has length > 1 and only the first element will be used
```

The central point is that in evaluating an if, we need a single Boolean, not a vector of Booleans, hence the warning seen in the preceding example, as well as the need for having both the & and && operators.

The Boolean values TRUE and FALSE can be abbreviated as T and F (both must be capitalized). These values change to 1 and 0 in arithmetic expressions:

```
> 1 < 2
[1] TRUE
> (1 < 2) * (3 < 4)
[1] 1
> (1 < 2) * (3 < 4) * (5 < 1)
[1] 0
> (1 < 2) == TRUE
[1] TRUE
> (1 < 2) == 1
[1] TRUE
```

In the second computation, for instance, the comparison 1 < 2 returns TRUE, and 3 < 4 yields TRUE as well. Both values are treated as 1 values, so the product is 1.

On the surface, R functions look similar to those of C, Java, and so on. However, they have much more of a functional programming flavor, which has direct implications for the R programmer.

7.3   Default Values for Arguments

In Section 5.1.2, we read in a data set from a file named exams:

```
> testscores <- read.table("exams",header=TRUE)
```

The argument header=TRUE tells R that we have a header line, so R should not count that first line in the file as data.

This is an example of the use of *named arguments*. Here are the first few lines of the function:

```
> read.table
function (file, header = FALSE, sep = "", quote = "\"'", dec = ".",
    row.names, col.names, as.is = !stringsAsFactors, na.strings = "NA",
    colClasses = NA, nrows = -1, skip = 0, check.names = TRUE,
    fill = !blank.lines.skip, strip.white = FALSE, blank.lines.skip = TRUE,
    comment.char = "#", allowEscapes = FALSE, flush = FALSE,
    stringsAsFactors = default.stringsAsFactors(), encoding = "unknown")
{
    if (is.character(file)) {
        file <- file(file, "r")
        on.exit(close(file))
...
...
```

The second formal argument is named header. The = FALSE field means that this argument is optional, and if we don't specify it, the default value will be FALSE. If we don't want the default value, we must name the argument in our call:

```
> testscores <- read.table("exams",header=TRUE)
```

Hence the terminology *named argument*.

Note, though, that because R uses *lazy evaluation*—it does not evaluate an expression until/unless it needs to—the named argument may not actually be used.

7.4 Return Values

The return value of a function can be any R object. Although the return value is often a list, it could even be another function.

You can transmit a value back to the caller by explicitly calling return(). Without this call, the value of the last executed statement will be returned by default. For instance, consider the oddcount() example from Chapter 1:

```
> oddcount
function(x)  {
   k <- 0  # assign 0 to k
   for (n in x)  {
      if (n %% 2 == 1) k <- k+1   # %% is the modulo operator
   }
   return(k)
}
```

This function returns the count of odd numbers in the argument. We could slightly simplify the code by eliminating the call to return(). To do this, we evaluate the expression to be returned, k, as our last statement in the code:

```
oddcount <- function(x) {
   k <- 0
   pagebreak
   for (n in x) {
      if (n %% 2 == 1) k <- k+1
   }
   k
}
```

On the other hand, consider this code:

```
oddcount <- function(x) {
   k <- 0
```

```
    for (n in x) {
        if (n %% 2 == 1) k <- k+1
    }
}
```

It wouldn't work, for a rather subtle reason: The last executed statement here is the call to for(), which returns the value NULL (and does so, in R parlance, *invisibly*, meaning that it is discarded if not stored by assignment). Thus, there would be no return value at all.

7.4.1   Deciding Whether to Explicitly Call return()

The prevailing R idiom is to avoid explicit calls to return(). One of the reasons cited for this approach is that calling that function lengthens execution time. However, unless the function is very short, the time saved is negligible, so this might not be the most compelling reason to refrain from using return(). But it usually isn't needed nonetheless.

Consider our second example from the preceding section:

```
oddcount <- function(x) {
    k <- 0
    for (n in x) {
        if (n %% 2 == 1) k <- k+1
    }
    k
}
```

Here, we simply ended with a statement listing the expression to be returned—in this case, k. A call to return() wasn't necessary. Code in this book usually does include a call to return(), for clarity for beginners, but it is customary to omit it.

Good software design, however, should mean that you can glance through a function's code and immediately spot the various points at which control is returned to the caller. The easiest way to accomplish this is to use an explicit return() call in all lines in the middle of the code that cause a return. (You can still omit a return() call at the end of the function if you wish.)

7.4.2   Returning Complex Objects

Since the return value can be any R object, you can return complex objects. Here is an example of a function being returned:

```
> g
function() {
    t <- function(x) return(x^2)
    return(t)
}
```

```
> g()
function(x) return(x^2)
<environment: 0x8aafbc0>
```

If your function has multiple return values, place them in a list or other container.

7.5 Functions Are Objects

R functions are *first-class objects* (of the class "function", of course), meaning that they can be used for the most part just like other objects. This is seen in the syntax of function creation:

```
> g <- function(x) {
+    return(x+1)
+ }
```

Here, function() is a built-in R function whose job is to create functions! On the right-hand side, there are really two arguments to function(): The first is the formal argument list for the function we're creating—here, just x—and the second is the body of that function—here, just the single statement return(x+1). That second argument must be of class "expression". So, the point is that the right-hand side creates a function object, which is then assigned to g.

By the way, even the "{" is a function, as you can verify by typing this:

```
> ?"{"
```

Its job is the make a single unit of what could be several statements.

These two arguments to function() can later be accessed via the R functions formals() and body(), as follows:

```
> formals(g)
$x


> body(g)
{
    return(x + 1)
}
```

Recall that when using R in interactive mode, simply typing the name of an object results in printing that object to the screen. Functions are no exception, since they are objects just like anything else.

```
> g
function(x) {
    return(x+1)
}
```

This is handy if you're using a function that you wrote but which you've forgotten the details of. Printing out a function is also useful if you are not quite sure what an R library function does. By looking at the code, you may understand it better. For example, if you are not sure as to the exact behavior of the graphics function abline(), you could browse through its code to better understand how to use it.

```
> abline
function (a = NULL, b = NULL, h = NULL, v = NULL, reg = NULL,
    coef = NULL, untf = FALSE, ...)
{
    int_abline <- function(a, b, h, v, untf, col = par("col"),
        lty = par("lty"), lwd = par("lwd"), ...) .Internal(abline(a,
        b, h, v, untf, col, lty, lwd, ...))
    if (!is.null(reg)) {
        if (!is.null(a))
            warning("'a' is overridden by 'reg'")
        a <- reg
    }

    if (is.object(a) || is.list(a)) {
        p <- length(coefa <- as.vector(coef(a)))
...
...
```

If you wish to view a lengthy function in this way, run it through page():

```
> page(abline)
```

An alternative is to edit it using the edit() function, which we'll discuss in Section 7.11.2.

Note, though, that some of R's most fundamental built-in functions are written directly in C, and thus they are not viewable in this manner. Here's an example:

```
> sum
function (..., na.rm = FALSE)  .Primitive("sum")
```

Since functions are objects, you can also assign them, use them as arguments to other functions, and so on.

```
> f1 <- function(a,b) return(a+b)
> f2 <- function(a,b) return(a-b)
> f <- f1
> f(3,2)
[1] 5
> f <- f2
```

```
> f(3,2)
[1] 1
> g <- function(x) x^2
> body(g) <- quote(2*x+3)
> g
function (x)
2 * x + 3
> g(8)
[1] 19
```

And since functions are objects, you can loop through a list consisting of several functions. This would be useful, for instance, if you wished to write a loop to plot a number of functions on the same graph, as follows:

```
> g1 <- function(x) return(sin(x))
> g2 <- function(x) return(sqrt(x^2+1))
> g3 <- function(x) return(2*x-1)
> plot(c(0,1),c(-1,1.5))  # prepare the graph, specifying X and Y ranges
> for (f in c(g1,g2,g3)) plot(f,0,1,add=T)  # add plot to existing graph
```

The functions formals() and body() can even be used as replacement functions. We'll discuss replacement functions in Section 7.10, but for now, consider how you could change the body of a function by assignment:

```
> g <- function(h,a,b) h(a,b)
> body(g) <- quote(2*x + 3)
> g
function (x)
2 * x + 3
> x <- 3
> g(3)
[1] 9
```

The reason quote() was needed is that technically, the body of a function has the class "call", which is the class produced by quote(). Without the call to quote(), R would try to evaluate the quantity 2*x+3. So if x had been defined and equal to 3, for example, we would assign 9 to the body of g(), certainly not what we want. By the way, since * and + are functions (as discussed in Section 2.4.1), as a language object, 2*x+3 is indeed a call—in fact, it is one function call nested within another.

7.6   Environment and Scope Issues

A function—formally referred to as a *closure* in the R documentation— consists not only of its arguments and body but also of its *environment*. The latter is made up of the collection of objects present at the time the function is created. An understanding of how environments work in R is essential for writing effective R functions.

7.6.1 The Top-Level Environment

Consider this example:

```
> w <- 12
> f <- function(y) {
+     d <- 8
+     h <- function() {
+         return(d*(w+y))
+     }
+     return(h())
+ }
> environment(f)
<environment: R_GlobalEnv>
```

Here, the function f() is created at the *top level*—that is, at the interpreter command prompt—and thus has the top-level environment, which in R output is referred to as R_GlobalEnv but which confusingly you refer to in R code as .GlobalEnv. If you run an R program as a batch file, that is considered top level, too.

The function ls() lists the objects of an environment. If you call it at the top level, you get the top-level environment. Let's try it with our example code:

```
> ls()
[1] "f" "w"
```

As you can see, the top-level environment here includes the variable w, which is actually used within f(). Note that f() is here too, as functions are indeed objects and we did create it at the top level. At levels other than the top, ls() works a little differently, as you'll see in Section 7.6.3.

You get a bit more information from ls.str():

```
> ls.str()
f : function (y)
w :   num 12
```

Next, we'll look at how w and other variables come into play within f().

7.6.2 The Scope Hierarchy

Let's first get an intuitive overview of how scope works in R and then relate it to environments.

If we were working with the C language (as usual, background in C is not assumed), we would say that the variable w in the previous section is *global* to f(), while d is *local* to f(). Things are similar in R, but R is more hierarchical. In C, we would not have functions defined within functions, as we have with h() inside f() in our example. Yet, since functions are objects, it is possible—and sometimes desirable from the point of view of the encapsulation goal of object-oriented programming—to define a function within a function; we are simply creating an object, which we can do anywhere.

Here, we have h() being local to f(), just like d. In such a situation, it makes sense for scope to be hierarchical. Thus, R is set up so that d, which is local to f(), is in turn global to h(). The same is true for y, as arguments are considered locals in R.

Similarly, the hierarchical nature of scope implies that since w is global to f(), it is global to h() as well. Indeed, we do use w within h().

In terms of environments then, h()'s environment consists of whatever objects are defined at the time h() comes into existence; that is, at the time that this assignment is executed:

```
h <- function() {
   return(d*(w+y))
}
```

(If f() is called multiple times, h() will come into existence multiple times, going out of existence each time f() returns.)

What, then, will be in h()'s environment? Well, at the time h() is created, there are the objects d and y created within f(), *plus* f()'s environment (w). In other words, if one function is defined within another, then that inner function's environment consists of the environment of the outer one, plus whatever locals have been created so far within the outer one. With multiple nesting of functions, you have a nested sequence of larger and larger environments, with the "root" consisting of the top-level objects.

Let's try out the code:

```
> f(2)
[1] 112
```

What happened? The call f(2) resulted in setting the local variable d to 8, followed by the call h(). The latter evaluated d*(w+y)—that is, 8*(12+2)—giving us 112.

Note carefully the role of w. The R interpreter found that there was no local variable of that name, so it ascended to the next higher level—in this case, the top level—where it found a variable w with value 12.

Keep in mind that h() is local to f() and invisible at the top level.

```
> h
Error: object 'h' not found
```

It's possible (though not desirable) to deliberately allow name conflicts in this hierarchy. In our example, for instance, we could have a local variable d within h(), conflicting with the one in f(). In such a situation, the innermost environment is used first. In this case, a reference to d within h() would refer to h()'s d, not f()'s.

Environments created by inheritance in this manner are generally referred to by their memory locations. Here is what happened after adding a print statement to f() (using edit(), not shown here) and then running the code:

```
> f
function(y) {
   d <- 8
   h <- function() {
      return(d*(w+y))
   }
   print(environment(h))
   return(h())
}
> f(2)
<environment: 0x875753c>
[1] 112
```

Compare all this to the situation in which the functions are not nested:

```
> f
function(y) {
   d <- 8
   return(h())
}


> h
function() {
   return(d*(w+y))
}
```

The result is as follows:

```
> f(5)
Error in h() : object 'd' not found
```

This does not work, as d is no longer in the environment of h(), because h() is defined at the top level. Thus, an error is generated.

Worse, if by happenstance there had been some unrelated variable d in the top-level environment, we would not get an error message but instead would have incorrect results.

You might wonder why R didn't complain about the lack of y in the alternate definition of h() in the preceding example. As mentioned earlier, R doesn't evaluate a variable until it needs it under a policy called lazy evaluation. In this case, R had already encountered an error with d and thus never got to the point where it would try to evaluate y.

The fix is to pass d and y as arguments:

```
> f
function(y) {
   d <- 8
   return(h(d,y))
}
> h
function(dee,yyy) {
   return(dee*(w+yyy))
}
> f(2)
[1] 112
```

Okay, let's look at one last variation:

```
> f
function(y,ftn) {
   d <- 8
   print(environment(ftn))
   return(ftn(d,y))
}
> h
function(dee,yyy) {
   return(dee*(w+yyy))
}


> w <- 12
> f(3,h)
<environment: R_GlobalEnv>
[1] 120
```

When f() executed, the formal argument ftn was matched by the actual argument h. Since arguments are treated as locals, you might guess that ftn could have a different environment than top level. But as discussed, a closure includes environment, and thus ftn has h's environment.

Note carefully that all the examples so far involving nonlocal variables are for reads, not writes. The case of writes is crucial, and it will be covered in Section 7.8.1.

7.6.3   More on ls()

Without arguments, a call to ls() from within a function returns the names of the current local variables (including arguments). With the envir argument, it will print the names of the locals of any frame in the call chain.

Here's an example:

```
> f
function(y) {
    d <- 8
    return(h(d,y))
}
> h
function(dee,yyy) {
    print(ls())
    print(ls(envir=parent.frame(n=1)))
    return(dee*(w+yyy))
}



> f(2)
[1] "dee" "yyy"
[1] "d" "y"
[1] 112
```

With parent.frame(), the argument n specifies how many frames to go up in the call chain. Here, we were in the midst of executing h(), which had been called from f(), so specifying n = 1 gives us f()'s frame, and thus we get its locals.

7.6.4   Functions Have (Almost) No Side Effects

Yet another influence of the functional programming philosophy is that functions do not change nonlocal variables; that is, generally, there are no *side effects*. Roughly speaking, the code in a function has read access to its nonlocal variables, but it does not have write access to them. Our code can appear to reassign those variables, but the action will affect only copies, not the variables themselves. Let's demonstrate this by adding some more code to our previous example.

```
> w <- 12
> f
function(y) {
    d <- 8
    w <- w + 1
    y <- y - 2
    print(w)
    h <- function() {
        return(d*(w+y))
    }
    return(h())
}
```

```
> t <- 4
> f(t)
[1] 13
[1] 120
> w
[1] 12
> t
[1] 4
```

So, w at the top level did not change, even though it appeared to change
within f(). Only a local *copy* of w, within f(), changed. Similarly, the top-level
variable t didn't change, even though its associated formal argument y did
change.

NOTE   *More precisely, references to the local w actually go to the same memory location as the
global one, until the value of the local changes. In that case, a new memory location
is used.*

An important exception to this read-only nature of globals arises with
the superassignment operator, which we'll discuss later in Section 7.8.1.

7.6.5   Extended Example: A Function to Display the Contents of a Call Frame

In single-stepping through your code in a debugging setting, you often want
to know the values of the local variables in your current function. You may
also want to know the values of the locals in the parent function—that is,
the one from which the current function was called. Here, we will develop
code to display these values, thereby further demonstrating access to the
environment hierarchy. (The code is adapted from my edtdbg debugging
tool in R's CRAN code repository.)

For example, consider the following code:

```
f <- function() {
   a <- 1
   return(g(a)+a)
}

g <- function(aa) {
   b <- 2
   aab <- h(aa+b)
   return(aab)
}

h <- function(aaa) {
   c <- 3
   return(aaa+c)
}
```

When we call f(), it in turn calls g(), which then calls h(). In the debugging setting, say we are currently about to execute the return() within g(). We want to know the values of the local variables of the current function, say the variables aa, b, and aab. And while we're in g(), we also wish to know the values of the locals in f() at the time of the call to g(), as well as the values of the global variables. Our function showframe() will do all this.

The showframe() function has one argument, upn, which is the number of frames to go up the call stack. A negative value of the argument signals that we want to view the globals—the top-level variables.

Here's the code:

```
# shows the values of the local variables (including arguments) of the
# frame upn frames above the one from which showframe() is called; if
# upn < 0, the globals are shown; function objects are not shown
showframe <- function(upn) {
   # determine the proper environment
   if (upn < 0) {
      env <- .GlobalEnv
   } else {
      env <- parent.frame(n=upn+1)
   }
   # get the list of variable names
   vars <- ls(envir=env)
   # for each variable name, print its value
   for (vr in vars) {
      vrg <- get(vr,envir=env)
      if (!is.function(vrg)) {
         cat(vr,":\n",sep="")
         print(vrg)
      }
   }
}
```

Let's try it out. Insert some calls into g():

```
> g
function(aa) {
   b <- 2
   showframe(0)
   showframe(1)
   aab <- h(aa+b)
   return(aab)
}
```

Now run it:

```
> f()
aa:
```

```
[1] 1
b:
[1] 2
a:
[1] 1
```

To see how this works, we'll first look at the get() function, one of the most useful utilities in R. Its job is quite simple: Given the name of an object, it fetches the object itself. Here's an example:

```
> m <- rbind(1:3,20:22)
> m
     [,1] [,2] [,3]
[1,]    1    2    3
[2,]   20   21   22
> get("m")
     [,1] [,2] [,3]
[1,]    1    2    3
[2,]   20   21   22
```

This example with m involves the current call frame, but in our showframe() function, we deal with various levels in the environment hierarchy. So, we need to specify the level via the envir argument of get():

```
vrg <- get(vr,envir=env)
```

The level itself is determined largely by calling parent.frame():

```
if (upn < 0) {
   env <- .GlobalEnv
} else {
   env <- parent.frame(n=upn+1)
}
```

Note that ls() can also be called in the context of a particular level, thus enabling you to determine which variables exist at the level of interest and then inspect them. Here's an example:

```
vars <- ls(envir=env)
for (vr in vars) {
```

This code picks up the names of all the local variables in the given frame and then loops through them, setting things up for get() to do its work.

7.7   No Pointers in R

R does not have variables corresponding to *pointers* or *references* like those of, say, the C language. This can make programming more difficult in some cases. (As of this writing, the current version of R has an experimental feature called *reference classes*, which may reduce the difficulty.)

For example, you cannot write a function that directly changes its arguments. In Python, for instance, you can do this:

```
>>> x = [13,5,12]
>>> x.sort()
>>> x
[5, 12, 13]
```

Here, the value of x, the argument to sort(), changed. By contrast, here's how it works in R:

```
> x <- c(13,5,12)
> sort(x)
[1]  5 12 13
> x
[1] 13  5 12
```

The argument to sort() does not change. If we do want x to change in this R code, the solution is to reassign the arguments:

```
> x <- sort(x)
> x
[1]  5 12 13
```

What if our function has several variables of output? A solution is to gather them together into a list, call the function with this list as an argument, have the function return the list, and then reassign to the original list.

An example is the following function, which determines the indices of odd and even numbers in a vector of integers:

```
> oddsevens
function(v){
  odds <- which(v %% 2 == 1)
  evens <- which(v %% 2 == 0)
  list(o=odds,e=evens)
}
```

In general, our function f() changes variables x and y. We might store them in a list lxy, which would then be our argument to f(). The code, both called and calling, might have a pattern like this:

```
f <- function(lxxyy) {
  ...
  lxxyy$x <- ...
  lxxyy$y <- ...
  return(lxxyy)
}
```

```
# set x and y
lxy$x <- ...
lxy$y <- ...
lxy <- f(lxy)
# use new x and y
... <- lxy$x
... <- lxy$y
```

However, this may become unwieldy if your function will change many
variables. It can be especially awkward if your variables, say x and y in the
example, are themselves lists, resulting in a return value consisting of lists
within a list. This can still be handled, but it makes the code more syntactically complex and harder to read.

Alternatives include the use of global variables, which we will look at in
Section 7.8.4, and the new R reference classes mentioned earlier.

Another class of applications in which lack of pointers causes difficulties
is that of treelike data structures. C code normally makes heavy use of pointers for these kinds of structures. One solution for R is to revert to what was
done in the "good old days" before C, when programmers formed their own
"pointers" as vector indices. See Section 7.9.2 for an example.

7.8 Writing Upstairs

As mentioned earlier, code that exists at a certain level of the environment
hierarchy has at least read access to all the variables at the levels above it.
On the other hand, direct write access to variables at higher levels via the
standard <- operator is not possible.

If you wish to write to a global variable—or more generally, to any variable higher in the environment hierarchy than the level at which your write
statement exists—you can use the superassignment operator, <<-, or the
assign() function. Let's discuss the superassignment operator first.

7.8.1 Writing to Nonlocals with the Superassignment Operator

Consider the following code:

```
> two <- function(u) {
+     u <<- 2*u
+     z <- 2*z
+ }
> x <- 1
> z <- 3
> u
Error: object "u" not found
> two(x)
> x
```

```
[1] 1
> z
[1] 3
> u
[1] 2
```

Let's look at the impact (or not) on the three top-level variables x, z, and u:

- x: Even though x was the actual argument to two() in the example, it retained the value 1 after the call. This is because its value 1 was copied to the formal argument u, which is treated as a local variable within the function. Thus, when u changed, x did not change with it.

- z: The two z values are entirely unrelated to each other—one is top level, and the other is local to two(). The change in the local variable has no effect on the global variable. Of course, having two variables with the same name is probably not good programming practice.

- u: The u value did not even exist as a top-level variable prior to our calling two(), hence the "not found" error message. However, it was created as a top-level variable by the superassignment operator within two(), as confirmed after the call.

Though <<- is typically used to write to top-level variables, as in our example, technically, it does something a bit different. Use of this operator to write to a variable w will result in a search up the environment hierarchy, stopping at the first level at which a variable of that name is encountered. If none is found, then the level selected will be global. Look what happens in this little example:

```
> f
function() {
    inc <- function() {x <<- x + 1}
    x <- 3
    inc()
    return(x)
}
> f()
[1] 4
> x
Error: object 'x' not found
```

Here, inc() is defined within f(). When inc() is executing, and the R interpreter sees a superassignment to x, it starts going up the hierarchy. At the first level up—the environment within f()—it does find an x, and so that x is the one that is written to, not x at the top level.

7.8.2 Writing to Nonlocals with assign()

You can also use the `assign()` function to write to upper-level variables. Here's an altered version of the previous example:

```
> two
function(u) {
    assign("u",2*u,pos=.GlobalEnv)
    z <- 2*z
}
> two(x)
> x
[1] 1
> u
[1] 2
```

Here, we replaced the superassignment operator with a call to `assign()`. That call instructs R to assign the value `2*u` (this is the local u) to a variable u further up the call stack, specifically in the top-level environment. In this case, that environment is only one call level higher, but if we had a chain of calls, it could be much further up.

The fact that you reference variables using character strings in `assign()` can come in handy. Recall the example in Chapter 5 concerning analysis of hiring patterns of various large corporations. We wanted to form a subdata frame for each firm, extracted from the overall data frame, `all2006`. For instance, consider this call:

```
makecorpdfs(c("MICROSOFT CORPORATION","ms","INTEL CORPORATION","intel","
    SUN MICROSYSTEMS, INC.","sun","GOOGLE INC.","google"))
```

This would first extract all Microsoft records from the overall data frame, naming the resulting subdata frame `ms2006`. It would then create `intel2006` for Intel, and so on. Here is the code (changed to function form, for clarity):

```
makecorpdfs <- function(corplist) {
    for (i in 1:(length(corplist)/2)) {
        corp <- corplist[2*i-1]
        newdtf <- paste(corplist[2*i],"2006",sep="")
        assign(newdtf,makecorp(corp),pos=.GlobalEnv)
    }
}
```

In the iteration i = 1, the code uses `paste()` to splice together the strings `"ms"` and `"2006"`, resulting in `"ms2006"`, the desired name.

7.8.3 Extended Example: Discrete-Event Simulation in R

Discrete-event simulation (DES) is widely used in business, industry, and government. The term *discrete event* refers to the fact that the state of the system changes only in discrete quantities, rather than changing continuously.

A typical example would involve a queuing system, say people lining up to use an ATM. Let's define the state of our system at time t to be the number of people in the queue at that time. The state changes only by $+1$, when someone arrives, or by -1, when a person finishes an ATM transaction. This is in contrast to, for instance, a simulation of weather, in which temperature, barometric pressure, and so on change continuously.

This will be one of the longer, more involved examples in this book. But it exemplifies a number of important issues in R, especially concerning global variables, and will serve as an example when we discuss appropriate use of global variables in the next section. Your patience will turn out to be a good investment of time. (It is not assumed here that the reader has any prior background in DES.)

Central to DES operation is maintenance of the *event list*, which is simply a list of scheduled events. This is a general DES term, so the word *list* here does not refer to the R data type. In fact, we'll represent the event list by a data frame.

In the ATM example, for instance, the event list might at some point in the simulation look like this:

```
customer 1 arrives at time 23.12
customer 2 arrives at time 25.88
customer 3 arrives at time 25.97
customer 1 finishes service at time 26.02
```

Since the earliest event must always be handled next, the simplest form of coding the event list is to store it in time order, as in the example. (Readers with computer science background might notice that a more efficient approach might be to use some kind of binary tree for storage.) Here, we will implement it as a data frame, with the first row containing the earliest scheduled event, the second row containing the second earliest, and so on.

The main loop of the simulation repeatedly iterates. Each iteration pulls the earliest event off of the event list, updates the simulated time to reflect the occurrence of that event, and reacts to this event. The latter action will typically result in the creation of new events. For example, if a customer arrival occurs when the queue is empty, that customer's service will begin—one event triggers setting up another. Our code must determine the customer's service time, and then it will know the time at which service will be finished, which is another event that must be added to the event list.

One of the oldest approaches to writing DES code is the *event-oriented paradigm*. Here, the code to handle the occurrence of one event directly sets up another event, reflecting our preceding discussion.

As an example to guide your thinking, consider the ATM situation. At time 0, the queue is empty. The simulation code randomly generates the time of the first arrival, say 2.3. At this point, the event list is simply

(2.3,"arrival"). This event is pulled off the list, simulated time is updated to 2.3, and we react to the arrival event as follows:

- The queue for the ATM is empty, so we start the service by randomly generating the service time—say it is 1.2 time units. Then the completion of service will occur at simulated time $2.3 + 1.2 = 3.5$.

- We add the completion of service event to the event list, which will now consist of (3.5,"service done")).

- We also generate the time to the next arrival, say 0.6, which means the arrival will occur at time 2.9. Now the event list consists of (2.9,"arrival") and (3.5,"service done").

The code consists of a generally applicable library. We also have an example application, which simulates an M/M/1 queue, which is a single-server queue in which both interarrival time and service time are exponentially distributed.

NOTE   *The code in this example is hardly optimal, and the reader is invited to improve it, especially by rewriting some portions in C. (Chapter 15 shows how to interface C to R.) This example does, however, serve to illustrate a number of the issues we have discussed in this chapter.*

Here is a summary of the library functions:

- schedevnt(): Inserts a newly created event into the event list.
- getnextevnt(): Pulls the earliest event off the event list.
- dosim(): Includes the core loop of the simulation. Repeatedly calls getnextevnt() to get the earliest of the pending events; updates the current simulated time, sim$currtime, to reflect the occurrence of that event; and calls the application-specific function reactevnt() to process this newly occurred event.

The code uses the following application-specific functions:

- initglbls(): Initializes the application-specific global variables.
- reactevnt(): Takes the proper actions when an event occurs, typically generating new events as a result.
- prntrslts(): Prints the application-specific results of the simulation.

Note that initglbls(), reactevnt(), and prntrslts() are written by the application programmer and then passed to dosim() as arguments. In the M/M/1 queue example included here, these functions are named mm1initglbls(), mm1reactevnt(), and mm1prntrslts(), respectively. Thus, in correspondence with the definition of dosim(),

```
dosim <- function(initglbls,reactevnt,prntrslts,maxsimtime,apppars=NULL,dbg=FALSE){
```

our call is as follows:

```
dosim(mm1initglbls,mm1reactevnt,mm1prntrslts,10000.0,
    list(arrvrate=0.5,srvrate=1.0))
```

Here's the library code:

```
1   # DES.R:  R routines for discrete-event simulation (DES)
2
3   # each event will be represented by a data frame row consisting of the
4   # following components:  evnttime, the time the event is to occur;
5   # evnttype, a character string for the programmer-defined event type;
6   # optional application-specific components, e.g.
7   # the job's arrival time in a queuing app
8
9   # a global list named "sim" holds the events data frame, evnts, and
10  # current simulated time, currtime; there is also a component dbg, which
11  # indicates debugging mode
12
13  # forms a row for an event of type evntty that will occur at time
14  # evnttm; see comments in schedevnt() regarding appin
15  evntrow <- function(evnttm,evntty,appin=NULL) {
16     rw <- c(list(evnttime=evnttm,evnttype=evntty),appin)
17     return(as.data.frame(rw))
18  }
19
20  # insert event with time evnttm and type evntty into event list;
21  # appin is an optional set of application-specific traits of this event,
22  # specified in the form a list with named components
23  schedevnt <- function(evnttm,evntty,appin=NULL) {
24     newevnt <- evntrow(evnttm,evntty,appin)
25     # if the event list is empty, set it to consist of evnt and return
26     if (is.null(sim$evnts)) {
27        sim$evnts <<- newevnt
28        return()
29     }
30     # otherwise, find insertion point
31     inspt <- binsearch((sim$evnts)$evnttime,evnttm)
32     # now "insert," by reconstructing the data frame; we find what
33     # portion of the current matrix should come before the new event and
34     # what portion should come after it, then string everything together
35     before <-
36        if (inspt == 1) NULL else sim$evnts[1:(inspt-1),]
37     nr <- nrow(sim$evnts)
38     after <- if (inspt <= nr) sim$evnts[inspt:nr,] else NULL
39     sim$evnts <<- rbind(before,newevnt,after)
40  }
41
```

```
42  # binary search of insertion point of y in the sorted vector x; returns
43  # the position in x before which y should be inserted, with the value
44  # length(x)+1 if y is larger than x[length(x)]; could be changed to C
45  # code for efficiency
46  binsearch <- function(x,y) {
47     n <- length(x)
48     lo <- 1
49     hi <- n
50     while(lo+1 < hi) {
51        mid <- floor((lo+hi)/2)
52        if (y == x[mid]) return(mid)
53        if (y < x[mid]) hi <- mid else lo <- mid
54     }
55     if (y <= x[lo]) return(lo)
56     if (y < x[hi]) return(hi)
57     return(hi+1)
58  }
59
60  # start to process next event (second half done by application
61  # programmer via call to reactevnt())
62  getnextevnt <- function() {
63     head <- sim$evnts[1,]
64     # delete head
65     if (nrow(sim$evnts) == 1) {
66        sim$evnts <<- NULL
67     } else sim$evnts <<- sim$evnts[-1,]
68     return(head)
69  }
70
71  # simulation body
72  # arguments:
73  #    initglbls:  application-specific initialization function; inits
74  #      globals to statistical totals for the app, etc.; records apppars
75  #      in globals; schedules the first event
76  #    reactevnt: application-specific event handling function, coding the
77  #       proper action for each type of event
78  #    prntrslts:  prints application-specific results, e.g. mean queue
79  #       wait
80  #    apppars:  list of application-specific parameters, e.g.
81  #       number of servers in a queuing app
82  #    maxsimtime:  simulation will be run until this simulated time
83  #    dbg:  debug flag; if TRUE, sim will be printed after each event
84  dosim <- function(initglbls,reactevnt,prntrslts,maxsimtime,apppars=NULL,
85        dbg=FALSE) {
86     sim <<- list()
87     sim$currtime <<- 0.0  # current simulated time
88     sim$evnts <<- NULL  # events data frame
```

```
89    sim$dbg <<- dbg
90    initglbls(apppars)
91    while(sim$currtime < maxsimtime) {
92        head <- getnextevnt()
93        sim$currtime <<- head$evnttime  # update current simulated time
94        reactevnt(head)  # process this event
95        if (dbg) print(sim)
96    }
97    prntrslts()
98 }
```

The following is an example application of the code. Again, the simulation models an M/M/1 queue, which is a single-server queuing system in which service times and times between job arrivals are exponentially distributed.

```
1  # DES application:  M/M/1 queue, arrival rate 0.5, service rate 1.0
2
3  # the call
4  # dosim(mm1initglbls,mm1reactevnt,mm1prntrslts,10000.0,
5  #    list(arrvrate=0.5,srvrate=1.0))
6  # should return a value of about 2 (may take a while)
7
8  # initializes global variables specific to this app
9  mm1initglbls <- function(apppars) {
10     mm1glbls <<- list()
11     # simulation parameters
12     mm1glbls$arrvrate <<- apppars$arrvrate
13     mm1glbls$srvrate <<- apppars$srvrate
14     # server queue, consisting of arrival times of queued jobs
15     mm1glbls$srvq <<- vector(length=0)
16     # statistics
17     mm1glbls$njobsdone <<- 0  # jobs done so far
18     mm1glbls$totwait <<- 0.0  # total wait time so far
19     # set up first event, an arrival; the application-specific data for
20     # each event will consist of its arrival time, which we need to
21     # record in order to later calculate the job's residence time in the
22     # system
23     arrvtime <- rexp(1,mm1glbls$arrvrate)
24     schedevnt(arrvtime,"arrv",list(arrvtime=arrvtime))
25 }
26
27 # application-specific event processing function called by dosim()
28 # in the general DES library
29 mm1reactevnt <- function(head) {
30     if (head$evnttype == "arrv") {  # arrival
31         # if server free, start service, else add to queue (added to queue
32         # even if empty, for convenience)
```

```
33      if (length(mm1glbls$srvq) == 0) {
34          mm1glbls$srvq <<- head$arrvtime
35          srvdonetime <- sim$currtime + rexp(1,mm1glbls$srvrate)
36          schedevnt(srvdonetime,"srvdone",list(arrvtime=head$arrvtime))
37      } else mm1glbls$srvq <<- c(mm1glbls$srvq,head$arrvtime)
38      # generate next arrival
39      arrvtime <- sim$currtime + rexp(1,mm1glbls$arrvrate)
40      schedevnt(arrvtime,"arrv",list(arrvtime=arrvtime))
41   } else {  # service done
42      # process job that just finished
43      # do accounting
44      mm1glbls$njobsdone <<- mm1glbls$njobsdone + 1
45      mm1glbls$totwait <<-
46          mm1glbls$totwait + sim$currtime - head$arrvtime
47      # remove from queue
48      mm1glbls$srvq <<- mm1glbls$srvq[-1]
49      # more still in the queue?
50      if (length(mm1glbls$srvq) > 0) {
51          # schedule new service
52          srvdonetime <- sim$currtime + rexp(1,mm1glbls$srvrate)
53          schedevnt(srvdonetime,"srvdone",list(arrvtime=mm1glbls$srvq[1]))
54      }
55   }
56 }
57
58 mm1prntrslts <- function() {
59   print("mean wait:")
60   print(mm1glbls$totwait/mm1glbls$njobsdone)
61 }
```

To see how all this works, take a look at the M/M/1 application code. There, we have set up a global variable, mm1glbls, which contains variables relevant to the M/M/1 code, such as mm1glbls$totwait, the running total of the wait time of all jobs simulated so far. As you can see, the superassignment operator is used to write to such variables, as in this statement:

```
mm1glbls$srvq <<- mm1glbls$srvq[-1]
```

Let's look at mm1reactevnt() to see how the simulation works, focusing on the code portion in which a "service done" event is handled.

```
} else {  # service done
   # process job that just finished
   # do accounting
   mm1glbls$njobsdone <<- mm1glbls$njobsdone + 1
   mm1glbls$totwait <<-
      mm1glbls$totwait + sim$currtime - head$arrvtime
   # remove this job from queue
```

```
mm1glbls$srvq <<- mm1glbls$srvq[-1]
# more still in the queue?
if (length(mm1glbls$srvq) > 0) {
    # schedule new service
    srvdonetime <- sim$currtime + rexp(1,mm1glbls$srvrate)
    schedevnt(srvdonetime,"srvdone",list(arrvtime=mm1glbls$srvq[1]))
}
}
```

First, this code does some bookkeeping, updating the totals of number of jobs completed and wait time. It then removes this newly completed job from the server queue. Finally, it checks if there are still jobs in the queue and, if so, calls schedevnt() to arrange for the service of the one at the head.

What about the DES library code itself? First note that the simulation state, consisting of the current simulated time and the event list, has been placed in an R list structure, sim. This was done in order to encapsulate all the main information into one package, which in R, typically means using a list. The sim list has been made a global variable.

As mentioned, a key issue in writing a DES library is the event list. This code implements it as a data frame, sim$evnts. Each row of the data frame corresponds to one scheduled event, with information about the event time, a character string representing the event type (say arrival or service completion), and any application-specific data the programmer wishes to add. Since each row consists of both numeric and character data, it was natural to choose a data frame for representing this event list. The rows of the data frame are in ascending order of event time, which is contained in the first column.

The main loop of the simulation is in dosim() of the DES library code, beginning at line 91:

```
while(sim$currtime < maxsimtime) {
    head <- getnextevnt()
    sim$currtime <<- head$evnttime  # update current simulated time
    reactevnt(head)  # process this event
    if (dbg) print(sim)
}
```

First, getnextevnt() is called to remove the head (the earliest event) from the event list. (Note the side effect: The event list changes.) Then the current simulated time is updated according to the scheduled time in the head event. Finally, the programmer-supplied function reactevnt() is called to process the event (as seen in the M/M/1 code discussed earlier).

The main potential advantage of using a data frame as our structure here is that it enables us to maintain the event list in ascending order by time via a binary search operation by event time. This is done in line 31 within schedevnt(), the function that inserts a newly created event into the event list:

```
inspt <- binsearch((sim$evnts)$evnttime,evnttm)
```

Here, we wish to insert a newly created event into the event list, and the fact that we are working with a vector enables the use of a fast binary search. (As noted in the comments in the code, though, this really should be implemented in C for good performance.)

A later line in schedevnt()is a good example of the use of rbind():

```
sim$evnts <<- rbind(before,newevnt,after)
```

Now, we have extracted the events in the event list whose times are earlier than that of evnt and stored them in before. We also constructed a similar set in after for the events whose times are later than that of newevnt. We then use rbind() to put all these together in the proper order.

7.8.4   When Should You Use Global Variables?

Use of global variables is a subject of controversy in the programming community. Obviously, the question raised by the title of this section cannot be answered in any formulaic way, as it is a matter of personal taste and style. Nevertheless, most programmers would probably consider the outright banning of global variables, which is encouraged by many teachers of programming, to be overly rigid. In this section, we will explore the possible value of globals in the context of the structures of R. Here, the term *global variable*, or just *global*, will be used to include any variable located higher in the environment hierarchy than the level of the given code of interest.

The use of global variables in R is more common than you may have guessed. You might be surprised to learn that R itself makes very substantial use of globals internally, both in its C code and in its R routines. The superassignment operator <<-, for instance, is used in many of the R library functions (albeit typically in writing to a variable just one level up in the environment hierarchy). *Threaded* code and *GPU* code, which are used for writing fast programs (as described in Chapter 16), tend to make heavy use of global variables, which provide the main avenue of communication between parallel actors.

Now, to make our discussion concrete, let's return to the earlier example from Section 7.7:

```
f <- function(lxxyy) {  # lxxyy is a list containing x and y
  ...
  lxxyy$x <- ...
  lxxyy$y <- ...
  return(lxxyy)
}
```

```
# set x and y
lxy$x <- ...
lxy$y <- ...
lxy <- f(lxy)
# use new x and y
... <- lxy$x
... <- lxy$y
```

As noted earlier, this code might be a bit unwieldy, especially if x and y are themselves lists.

By contrast, here is an alternate pattern that uses globals:

```
f <- function() {
   ...
   x <<- ...
   y <<- ...
}

# set x and y
x <- ...
y <- ...
f()  # x and y are changed in here
# use new x and y
... <- x
... <- y
```

Arguably, this second version is much cleaner, being less cluttered and not requiring manipulation of lists. Cleaner code is usually easier to write, debug, and maintain.

It is for these reasons—avoiding clutter and simplifying the code—that we chose to use globals, rather than to return lists, in the DES code earlier in this chapter. Let's explore that example further.

We had two global variables (both lists, encapsulating various information): sim, associated with the library code, and mm1glbls, associated with our M/M/1 application code. Let's consider sim first.

Even many programmers who have reservations about using globals agree that such variables may be justified if they are truly global, in the sense that they are used broadly in the program. This is the case for sim in our DES example. It is used both in the library code (in schedevnt(), getnextevnt(), and dosim()) and in in our M/M/1 application code (in mm1reactevnt()). The latter access to sim is on a read-only basis in this particular instance, but it could involve writes in some applications. A common example of such writes is when an event needs to be canceled. This might arise in modeling a "whichever comes first" situation; two events are scheduled, and when one of them occurs, the other must be canceled.

So, using sim as a global seems justified. Nevertheless, if we were bound and determined to avoid using globals, we could have placed sim as a local within dosim(). This function would then pass sim as an argument to all of the functions mentioned in the previous paragraph (schedevnt(), getnextevnt(), and so on), and each of these functions would return the modified sim. Line 94 for example, would change from this:

```
reactevnt(head)
```

to this:

```
sim <- reactevnt(head)
```

We would then need to add a line like the following to our application-specific function mm1reactevnt():

```
return(sim)
```

We could do something similar with mm1glbls, placing a variable called, say, appvars as a local within dosim(). However, if we did this with sim as well, we would need to place them together in a list so that both would be returned, as in our earlier example function f(). We would then have the lists-within-lists clutter described earlier—well, lists within lists within lists in this case.

On the other hand, critics of the use of global variables counter that the simplicity of the code comes at a price. They worry that it may be difficult during debugging to track down locations at which a global variable changes value, since such a change could occur anywhere in the program. This seems to be less of a concern in view of our modern text editors and integrated development tools (the original article calling for avoiding use of globals was published in 1970!), which can be used to find all instances of a variable. However, it should be taken into consideration.

Another concern raised by critics involves situations in which a function is called in several unrelated parts of the overall program using different values. For example, consider using our example f() function in different parts of our program, each call with its own values of x and y, rather than just a single value of each, as assumed earlier. This could be solved by setting up vectors of x and y values, with one element for each instance of f() in your program. You would lose some of the simplicity of using globals, though.

The above issues apply generally, not just to R. However, for R there is an additional concern for globals at the top level, as the user will typically have lots of variables there. The danger is that code that uses globals may accidentally overwrite an unrelated variable with the same name.

This can be avoided easily, of course, by simply choosing long, very application-specific names for globals in your code. But a compromise is also available in the form of environments, such as the following for the DES example above.

Within dosim(), the line

```
sim <<- list()
```

would be replaced by

```
assign("simenv",new.env(),envir=.GlobalEnv)
```

This would create a new environment, pointed to by simenv at the top level. It would serve as a package in which to encapsulate our globals. We would access them via get() and assign(). For instance, the lines

```
if (is.null(sim$evnts)) {
    sim$evnts <<- newevnt
```

in schedevnt() would become

```
if (is.null(get("evnts",envir=simenv))) {
    assign("evnts",newevnt,envir=simenv)
```

Yes, this is cluttered too, but at least it is not complex like lists of lists of lists. And it does protect against unwittingly writing to an unrelated variable the user has at the top level. Using the superassignment operator still yields the least cluttered code, but this compromise is worth considering.

As usual, there is no single style of programming that produces the best solution in all applications. The globals approach is another option to consider for your programming tool kit.

7.8.5 Closures

Recall that an R *closure* consists of a function's arguments and body together with its *environment* at the time of the call. The fact that the environment is included is exploited in a type of programming that uses a feature also known (in a slight overloading of terminology) as a *closure*.

A closure consists of a function that sets up a local variable and then creates another function that accesses that variable. This is a very abstract description, so let's go right to an example.[1]

```
1  > counter
2  function () {
3      ctr <- 0
4      f <- function() {
5          ctr <<- ctr + 1
6          cat("this count currently has value",ctr,"\n")
7      }
```

[1] Adapted from an example in "Top-level Task Callbacks in R," by Duncan Temple Lang (2001), *http://developer.r-project.org/TaskHandlers.pdf*.

```
8      return(f)
9  }
```

Let's try this out before going into the internal details:

```
> c1 <- counter()
> c2 <- counter()
> c1
function() {
     ctr <<- ctr + 1
     cat("this count currently has value",ctr,"\n")
  }
<environment: 0x8d445c0>
> c2
function() {
     ctr <<- ctr + 1
     cat("this count currently has value",ctr,"\n")
  }
<environment: 0x8d447d4>
> c1()
this count currently has value 1
> c1()
this count currently has value 2
> c2()
this count currently has value 1
> c2()
this count currently has value 2
> c2()
this count currently has value 3
> c1()
this count currently has value 3
```

Here, we called counter() twice, assigning the results to c1 and c2. As expected, those two variables will consist of functions, specifically copies of f().

However, f() accesses a variable ctr through the superassignment operator, and that variable will be the one of that name that is local to counter(), as it is the first one up the environment hierarchy. It is part of the environment of f() and, as such, is packaged in what is returned to the caller of counter().

The key point is that each time counter() is called, the variable ctr will be in a different environment (in the example, the environments were at memory addresses 0x8d445c0 and 0x8d447d4). In other words, different calls to counter() will produce physically different ctrs.

The result, then, is that our functions c1() and c2() serve as completely independent counters, as seen in the example, where we invoke each of them a few times.

7.9 Recursion

Once a mathematics PhD student whom I knew to be quite bright, but who had little programming background, sought my advice on how to write a certain function. I quickly said, "You don't even need to tell me what the function is supposed to do. The answer is to use recursion." Startled, he asked what recursion is. I advised him to read about the famous Towers of Hanoi problem. Sure enough, he returned the next day, reporting that he was able to solve his problem in just a few lines of code, using recursion. Obviously, recursion can be a powerful tool. Well then, what is it?

A *recursive* function calls itself. If you have not encountered this concept before, it may sound odd, but the idea is actually simple. In rough terms, the idea is this:

To solve a problem of type X by writing a recursive function f():

1. Break the original problem of type X into one or more smaller problems of type X.
2. Within f(), call f() on each of the smaller problems.
3. Within f(), piece together the results of (2) to solve the original problem.

7.9.1 A Quicksort Implementation

A classic example is Quicksort, an algorithm used to sort a vector of numbers from smallest to largest. For instance, suppose we wish to sort the vector (5,4,12,13,3,8,88). We first compare everything to the first element, 5, to form two subvectors: one consisting of the elements less than 5 and the other consisting of the elements greater than or equal to 5. That gives us subvectors (4,3) and (12,13,8,88). We then call the function on the subvectors, returning (3,4) and (8,12,13,88). We string those together with the 5, yielding (3,4,5,8,12,13,88), as desired.

R's vector-filtering capability and its c() function make implementation of Quicksort quite easy.

NOTE   *This example is for the purpose of demonstrating recursion. R's own sort function, sort(), is much faster, as it is written in C.*

```
qs <- function(x) {
   if (length(x) <= 1) return(x)
   pivot <- x[1]
   therest <- x[-1]
   sv1 <- therest[therest < pivot]
   sv2 <- therest[therest >= pivot]
   sv1 <- qs(sv1)
   sv2 <- qs(sv2)
   return(c(sv1,pivot,sv2))
}
```

Note carefully the *termination condition*:

```
if (length(x) <= 1) return(x)
```

Without this, the function would keep calling itself repeatedly on empty vectors, executing forever. (Actually, the R interpreter would eventually refuse to go any further, but you get the idea.)

Sounds like magic? Recursion certainly is an elegant way to solve many problems. But recursion has two potential drawbacks:

- It's fairly abstract. I knew that the graduate student, as a fine mathematician, would take to recursion like a fish to water, because recursion is really just the inverse of proof by mathematical induction. But many programmers find it tough.

- Recursion is very lavish in its use of memory, which may be an issue in R if applied to large problems.

7.9.2 Extended Example: A Binary Search Tree

Treelike data structures are common in both computer science and statistics. In R, for example, the rpart library for a recursive partioning approach to regression and classification is very popular. Trees obviously have applications in genealogy, and more generally, graphs form the basis of analysis of social networks.

However, there are real issues with tree structures in R, many of them related to the fact that R does not have pointer-style references, as discussed in Section 7.7. Indeed, for this reason and for performance purposes, a better option is often to write the core code in C with an R wrapper, as we'll discuss in Chapter 15. Yet trees can be implemented in R itself, and if performance is not an issue, using this approach may be more convenient.

For the sake of simplicity, our example here will be a binary search tree, a classic computer science data structure that has the following property:

> In each node of the tree, the value at the left link, if any, is less than or equal to that of the parent, while the value at the right link, if any, is greater than that of the parent.

Here is an example:

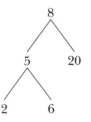

We've stored 8 in the *root*—that is, the head—of the tree. Its two child nodes contain 5 and 20, and the former itself has two child nodes, which store 2 and 6.

Note that the nature of binary search trees implies that at any node, all of the elements in the node's left subtree are less than or equal to the value stored in this node, while the right subtree stores the elements that are larger than the value in this node. In our example tree, where the root node contains 8, all of the values in the left subtree—5, 2 and 6—are less than 8, while 20 is greater than 8.

If implemented in C, a tree node would be represented by a C struct, similar to an R list, whose contents are the stored value, a pointer to the left child, and a pointer to the right child. But since R lacks pointer variables, what can we do?

Our solution is to go back to the basics. In the old prepointer days in FORTRAN, linked data structures were implemented in long arrays. A pointer, which in C is a memory address, was an array index instead.

Specifically, we'll represent each node by a row in a three-column matrix. The node's stored value will be in the third element of that row, while the first and second elements will be the left and right links. For instance, if the first element in a row is 29, it means that this node's left link points to the node stored in row 29 of the matrix.

Remember that allocating space for a matrix in R is a time-consuming activity. In an effort to amortize the memory-allocation time, we allocate new space for a tree's matrix several rows at a time, instead of row by row. The number of rows allocated each time will be given in the variable inc. As is common with tree traversal, we implement our algorithm with recursion.

NOTE   *If you anticipate that the matrix will become quite large, you may wish to double its size at each allocation, rather than grow it linearly as we have here. This would further reduce the number of time-consuming disruptions.*

Before discussing the code, let's run through a quick session of tree building using its routines.

```
> x <- newtree(8,3)
> x
$mat
     [,1] [,2] [,3]
[1,]   NA   NA    8
[2,]   NA   NA   NA
[3,]   NA   NA   NA

$nxt
[1] 2

$inc
[1] 3

> x <- ins(1,x,5)
> x
$mat
```

```
       [,1] [,2] [,3]
[1,]     2   NA    8
[2,]    NA   NA    5
[3,]    NA   NA   NA


$nxt
[1] 3

$inc
[1] 3

> x <- ins(1,x,6)
> x
$mat
       [,1] [,2] [,3]
[1,]     2   NA    8
[2,]    NA    3    5
[3,]    NA   NA    6

$nxt
[1] 4

$inc
[1] 3

> x <- ins(1,x,2)
> x
$mat
       [,1] [,2] [,3]
[1,]     2   NA    8
[2,]     4    3    5
[3,]    NA   NA    6
[4,]    NA   NA    2
[5,]    NA   NA   NA
[6,]    NA   NA   NA

$nxt
[1] 5

$inc
[1] 3

> x <- ins(1,x,20)
> x
$mat
       [,1] [,2] [,3]
```

```
[1,]     2    5    8
[2,]     4    3    5
[3,]    NA   NA    6
[4,]    NA   NA    2
[5,]    NA   NA   20
[6,]    NA   NA   NA

$nxt
[1] 6

$inc
[1] 3
```

What happened here? First, the command containing our call newtree(8,3) creates a new tree, assigned to x, storing the number 8. The argument 3 specifies that we allocate storage room three rows at a time. The result is that the matrix component of the list x is now as follows:

```
      [,1] [,2] [,3]
[1,]    NA   NA    8
[2,]    NA   NA   NA
[3,]    NA   NA   NA
```

Three rows of storage are indeed allocated, and our data now consists just of the number 8. The two NA values in that first row indicate that this node of the tree currently has no children.

We then make the call ins(1,x,5) to insert a second value, 5, into the tree x. The argument 1 specifies the root. In other words, the call says, "Insert 5 in the subtree of x whose root is in row 1." Note that we need to reassign the return value of this call back to x. Again, this is due to the lack of pointer variables in R. The matrix now looks like this:

```
      [,1] [,2] [,3]
[1,]     2   NA    8
[2,]    NA   NA    5
[3,]    NA   NA   NA
```

The element 2 means that the left link out of the node containing 8 is meant to point to row 2, where our new element 5 is stored.

The session continues in this manner. Note that when our initial allotment of three rows is full, ins() allocates three new rows, for a total of six. In the end, the matrix is as follows:

```
      [,1] [,2] [,3]
[1,]     2    5    8
[2,]     4    3    5
[3,]    NA   NA    6
```

```
[4,]   NA   NA    2
[5,]   NA   NA   20
[6,]   NA   NA   NA
```

This represents the tree we graphed for this example.

The code follows. Note that it includes only routines to insert new items and to traverse the tree. The code for deleting a node is somewhat more complex, but it follows a similar pattern.

```
1   # routines to create trees and insert items into them are included
2   # below; a deletion routine is left to the reader as an exercise
3
4   # storage is in a matrix, say m, one row per node of the tree; if row
5   # i contains (u,v,w), then node i stores the value w, and has left and
6   # right links to rows u and v; null links have the value NA
7
8   # the tree is represented as a list (mat,nxt,inc), where mat is the
9   # matrix, nxt is the next empty row to be used, and inc is the number of
10  # rows of expansion to be allocated whenever the matrix becomes full
11
12  # print sorted tree via in-order traversal
13  printtree <- function(hdidx,tr) {
14     left <- tr$mat[hdidx,1]
15     if (!is.na(left)) printtree(left,tr)
16     print(tr$mat[hdidx,3])  # print root
17     right <- tr$mat[hdidx,2]
18     if (!is.na(right)) printtree(right,tr)
19  }
20
21  # initializes a storage matrix, with initial stored value firstval
22  newtree <- function(firstval,inc) {
23     m <- matrix(rep(NA,inc*3),nrow=inc,ncol=3)
24     m[1,3] <- firstval
25     return(list(mat=m,nxt=2,inc=inc))
26  }
27
28  # inserts newval into the subtree of tr, with the subtree's root being
29  # at index hdidx; note that return value must be reassigned to tr by the
30  # caller (including ins() itself, due to recursion)
31  ins <- function(hdidx,tr,newval) {
32     # which direction will this new node go, left or right?
33     dir <- if (newval <= tr$mat[hdidx,3]) 1 else 2
34     # if null link in that direction, place the new node here, otherwise
35     # recurse
36     if (is.na(tr$mat[hdidx,dir])) {
37        newidx <- tr$nxt  # where new node goes
38        # check for room to add a new element
39        if (tr$nxt == nrow(tr$mat) + 1) {
```

```
40        tr$mat <-
41            rbind(tr$mat, matrix(rep(NA,tr$inc*3),nrow=tr$inc,ncol=3))
42        }
43        # insert new tree node
44        tr$mat[newidx,3] <- newval
45        # link to the new node
46        tr$mat[hdidx,dir] <- newidx
47        tr$nxt <- tr$nxt + 1  # ready for next insert
48        return(tr)
49   } else tr <- ins(tr$mat[hdidx,dir],tr,newval)
50  }
```

There is recursion in both printtree() and ins(). The former is definitely the easier of the two, so let's look at that first. It prints out the tree, in sorted order.

Recall our description of a recursive function f() that solves a problem of category X: We have f() split the original X problem into one or more smaller X problems, call f() on them, and combine the results. In this case, our problem's category X is to print a tree, which could be a subtree of a larger one. The role of the function on line 13 is to print the given tree, which it does by calling itself in lines 15 and 18. There, it prints first the left subtree and then the right subtree, pausing in between to print the root.

This thinking—print the left subtree, then the root, then the right subtree—forms the intuition in writing the code, but again we must make sure to have a proper termination mechanism. This mechanism is seen in the if() statements in lines 15 and 18. When we come to a null link, we do not continue to recurse.

The recursion in ins() follows the same principles but is considerably more delicate. Here, our "category X" is an insertion of a value into a subtree. We start at the root of a tree, determine whether our new value must go into the left or right subtree (line 33), and then call the function again on that subtree. Again, this is not hard in principle, but a number of details must be attended to, including the expansion of the matrix if we run out of room (lines 40–41).

One difference between the recursive code in printtree() and ins() is that the former includes two calls to itself, while the latter has only one. This implies that it may not be difficult to write the latter in a nonrecursive form.

7.10   Replacement Functions

Recall the following example from Chapter 2:

```
> x <- c(1,2,4)
> names(x)
NULL
> names(x) <- c("a","b","ab")
> names(x)
```

```
[1] "a"  "b"  "ab"
> x
 a  b  ab
 1  2  4
```

Consider one line in particular:

```
> names(x) <- c("a","b","ab")
```

Looks totally innocuous, eh? Well, no. In fact, it's outrageous! How on Earth can we possibly assign a value to the result of a function call? The resolution to this odd state of affairs lies in the R notion of *replacement functions*.

The preceding line of R code actually is the result of executing the following:

```
x <- "names<-"(x,value=c("a","b","ab"))
```

No, this isn't a typo. The call here is indeed to a function named names<-(). (We need to insert the quotation marks due to the special characters involved.)

7.10.1 What's Considered a Replacement Function?

Any assignment statement in which the left side is not just an identifier (meaning a variable name) is considered a replacement function. When encountering this:

```
g(u) <- v
```

R will try to execute this:

```
u <- "g<-"(u,value=v)
```

Note the "try" in the preceding sentence. The statement will fail if you have not previously defined g<-(). Note that the replacement function has one more argument than the original function g(), a named argument value, for reasons explained in this section.

In earlier chapters, you've seen this innocent-looking statement:

```
x[3] <- 8
```

The left side is not a variable name, so it must be a replacement function, and indeed it is, as follows.

Subscripting operations are functions. The function "["() is for reading vector elements, and "[<-"() is used to write. Here's an example:

```
> x <- c(8,88,5,12,13)
> x
```

```
[1]  8 88  5 12 13
> x[3]
[1] 5
```

```
> "["(x,3)
[1] 5
> x <- "[<-"(x,2:3,value=99:100)
> x
[1]   8  99 100  12  13
```

Again, that complicated call in this line:

```
> x <- "[<-"(x,2:3,value=99:100)
```

is simply performing what happens behind the scenes when we execute this:

```
x[2:3] <- 99:100
```

We can easily verify what's occurring like so:

```
> x <- c(8,88,5,12,13)
> x[2:3] <- 99:100
> x
[1]   8  99 100  12  13
```

7.10.2   Extended Example: A Self-Bookkeeping Vector Class

Suppose we have vectors on which we need to keep track of writes. In other words, when we execute the following:

```
x[2] <- 8
```

we would like not only to change the value in x[2] to 8 but also increment a count of the number of times x[2] has been written to. We can do this by writing class-specific versions of the generic replacement functions for vector subscripting.

NOTE   *This code uses classes, which we'll discuss in detail in Chapter 9. For now, all you need to know is that S3 classes are constructed by creating a list and then anointing it as a class by calling the class() function.*

```
1   # class "bookvec" of vectors that count writes of their elements
2
3   # each instance of the class consists of a list whose components are the
4   # vector values and a vector of counts
5
```

```
6   # construct a new object of class bookvec
7   newbookvec <- function(x) {
8       tmp <- list()
9       tmp$vec <- x # the vector itself
10      tmp$wrts <- rep(0,length(x)) # counts of the writes, one for each element
11      class(tmp) <- "bookvec"
12      return(tmp)
13  }
14
15  # function to read
16  "[.bookvec" <- function(bv,subs) {
17      return(bv$vec[subs])
18  }
19
20  # function to write
21  "[<-.bookvec" <- function(bv,subs,value) {
22      bv$wrts[subs] <- bv$wrts[subs] + 1 # note the recycling
23      bv$vec[subs] <- value
24      return(bv)
25  }
```

Let's test it.

```
> b <- newbookvec(c(3,4,5,5,12,13))
> b
$vec
[1]  3  4  5  5 12 13

$wrts
[1] 0 0 0 0 0 0

attr(,"class")
[1] "bookvec"
> b[2]
[1] 4
> b[2] <- 88  # try writing
> b[2]  # worked?
[1] 88
> b$wrts  # write count incremented?
[1] 0 1 0 0 0 0
```

We have named our class "bookvec", because these vectors will do their own bookkeeping—that is, keep track of write counts. So, the subscripting functions will be [.bookvec() and [<-.bookvec().

Our function newbookvec() (line 7) does the construction for this class. In it, you can see the structure of the class: An object will consist of the vector itself, vec (line 9), and a vector of write counts, wrts (line 10).

By the way, note in line 11 that the function class() itself is a replacement function!

The functions [.bookvec() and [<-.bookvec() are fairly straightforward. Just remember to return the entire object in the latter.

7.11   Tools for Composing Function Code

If you are writing a short function that's needed only temporarily, a quick-and-dirty way to do this is to write it on the spot, right there in your interactive terminal session. Here's an example:

```
> g <- function(x) {
+    return(x+1)
+ }
```

This approach obviously is infeasible for longer, more complex functions. Now, let's look at some better ways to compose R code.

7.11.1   Text Editors and Integrated Development Environments

You can use a text editor such as Vim, Emacs, or even Notepad, or an editor within an integrated development environment (IDE) to write your code in a file and then read it into R from the file. To do the latter, you can use R's source() function.

For instance, suppose we have functions f() and g() in a file *xyz.R*. In R, we give this command:

```
> source("xyz.R")
```

This reads f() and g() into R as if we had typed them using the quick-and-dirty way shown at the beginning of this section.

If you don't have much code, you can cut and paste from your editor window to your R window.

Some general-purpose editors have special plug-ins available for R, such as ESS for Emacs and Vim-R for Vim. There are also IDEs for R, such as the commercial one by Revolution Analytics, and open source products such as StatET, JGR, Rcmdr, and RStudio.

7.11.2   The edit() Function

A nice implication of the fact that functions are objects is that you can edit functions from within R's interactive mode. Most R programmers do their code editing with a text editor in a separate window, but for a small, quick change, the edit() function can be handy.

For instance, we could edit the function f1() by typing this:

```
> f1 <- edit(f1)
```

This opens the default editor on the code for f1, which we could then edit and assign back to f1.

Or, we might be interested in having a function f2() very similar to f1() and thus could execute the following:

```
> f2 <- edit(f1)
```

This gives us a copy of f1() to start from. We would do a little editing and then save to f2(), as seen in the preceding command.

The editor involved will depend on R's internal options variable editor. In UNIX-class systems, R will set this from your shell's EDITOR or VISUAL environment variable, or you can set it yourself, as follows:

```
> options(editor="/usr/bin/vim")
```

For more details on using options, see the online documentation by typing the following:

```
> ?options
```

You can use edit() to edit data structures, too.

7.12   Writing Your Own Binary Operations

You can invent your own operations! Just write a function whose name begins and ends with %, with two arguments of a certain type, and a return value of that type.

For example, here's a binary operation that adds double the second operand to the first:

```
> "%a2b%" <- function(a,b) return(a+2*b)
> 3 %a2b% 5
[1] 13
```

A less trivial example is given in the section about set operations in Section 8.5.

7.13   Anonymous Functions

As remarked at several points in this book, the purpose of the R function function() is to create functions. For instance, consider this code:

```
inc <- function(x) return(x+1)
```

It instructs R to create a function that adds 1 to its argument and then assigns that function to inc. However, that last step—the assignment—is not always taken. We can simply use the function object created by our call to function() without naming that object. The functions in that context are called *anonymous*, since they have no name. (That is somewhat misleading, since even nonanonymous functions only have a name in the sense that a variable is pointing to them.)

Anonymous functions can be convenient if they are short one-liners and are called by another function. Let's go back to our example of using apply in Section 3.3:

```
> z
     [,1] [,2]
[1,]   1    4
[2,]   2    5
[3,]   3    6
> f <- function(x) x/c(2,8)
> y <- apply(z,1,f)
> y
  [,1] [,2] [,3]
[1,] 0.5 1.000 1.50
[2,] 0.5 0.625 0.75
```

Let's bypass the middleman—that is, skip the assignment to f—by using an anonymous function within our call to apply(), as follows:

```
> y <- apply(z,1,function(x) x/c(2,8))
> y
     [,1]  [,2] [,3]
[1,]  0.5 1.000 1.50
[2,]  0.5 0.625 0.75
```

What really happened here? The third formal argument to apply() must be a function, which is exactly what we supplied here, since the return value of function() is a function!

Doing things this way is often clearer than defining the function externally. Of course, if the function is more complicated, that clarity is not attained.

8

DOING MATH AND SIMULATIONS IN R

 R contains built-in functions for your favorite math operations and, of course, for statistical distributions. This chapter provides an overview of using these functions. Given the mathematical nature of this chapter, the examples assume a slightly higher-level knowledge than those in other chapters. You should be familiar with calculus and linear algebra to get the most out of these examples.

8.1 Math Functions

R includes an extensive set of built-in math functions. Here is a partial list:

- `exp()`: Exponential function, base e
- `log()`: Natural logarithm
- `log10()`: Logarithm base 10
- `sqrt()`: Square root
- `abs()`: Absolute value

- `sin()`, `cos()`, and so on: Trig functions
- `min()` and `max()`: Minimum value and maximum value within a vector
- `which.min()` and `which.max()`: Index of the minimal element and maximal element of a vector
- `pmin()` and `pmax()`: Element-wise minima and maxima of several vectors
- `sum()` and `prod()`: Sum and product of the elements of a vector
- `cumsum()` and `cumprod()`: Cumulative sum and product of the elements of a vector
- `round()`, `floor()`, and `ceiling()`: Round to the closest integer, to the closest integer below, and to the closest integer above
- `factorial()`: Factorial function

8.1.1   Extended Example: Calculating a Probability

As our first example, we'll work through calculating a probability using the `prod()` function. Suppose we have n independent events, and the ith event has the probability p_i of occurring. What is the probability of exactly one of these events occurring?

Suppose first that $n = 3$ and our events are named A, B, and C. Then we break down the computation as follows:

$$
\begin{aligned}
\text{P(exactly one event occurs)} &= \\
\text{P(A and not B and not C)} &+ \\
\text{P(not A and B and not C)} &+ \\
\text{P(not A and not B and C)} &
\end{aligned}
$$

P(A and not B and not C) would be $p_A(1 - p_B)(1 - p_C)$, and so on.

For general n, that is calculated as follows:

$$
\sum_{i=1}^{n} p_i(1 - p_1)...(1 - p_{i-1})(1 - p_{i+1})...(1 - p_n)
$$

(The ith term inside the sum is the probability that event i occurs and all the others do *not* occur.)

Here's code to compute this, with our probabilities p_i contained in the vector p:

```
exactlyone <- function(p) {
   notp <- 1 - p
   tot <- 0.0
   for (i in 1:length(p))
      tot <- tot + p[i] * prod(notp[-i])
   return(tot)
}
```

How does it work? Well, the assignment

```
notp <- 1 - p
```

creates a vector of all the "not occur" probabilities $1 - p_j$, using recycling. The expression prod(notp[-i]) computes the product of all the elements of notp, except the ith—exactly what we need.

8.1.2 Cumulative Sums and Products

As mentioned, the functions cumsum() and cumprod() return cumulative sums and products.

```
> x <- c(12,5,13)
> cumsum(x)
[1] 12 17 30
> cumprod(x)
[1]   12   60 780
```

In x, the sum of the first element is 12, the sum of the first two elements is 17, and the sum of the first three elements is 30.

The function cumprod() works the same way as cumsum(), but with the product instead of the sum.

8.1.3 Minima and Maxima

There is quite a difference between min() and pmin(). The former simply combines all its arguments into one long vector and returns the minimum value in that vector. In contrast, if pmin() is applied to two or more vectors, it returns a vector of the pair-wise minima, hence the name pmin.

Here's an example:

```
> z
     [,1] [,2]
[1,]   1    2
[2,]   5    3
[3,]   6    2
> min(z[,1],z[,2])
[1] 1
> pmin(z[,1],z[,2])
[1] 1 3 2
```

In the first case, min() computed the smallest value in (1,5,6,2,3,2). But the call to pmin() computed the smaller of 1 and 2, yielding 1; then the smaller of 5 and 3, which is 3; then finally the minimum of 6 and 2, giving 2. Thus, the call returned the vector (1,3,2).

You can use more than two arguments in pmin(), like this:

```
> pmin(z[1,],z[2,],z[3,])
[1] 1 2
```

The 1 in the output is the minimum of 1, 5, and 6, with a similar computation leading to the 2.

The max() and pmax() functions act analogously to min() and pmin().

Function minimization/maximization can be done via nlm() and optim(). For example, let's find the smallest value of $f(x) = x^2 - \sin(x)$.

```
> nlm(function(x) return(x^2-sin(x)),8)
$minimum
[1] -0.2324656

$estimate
[1] 0.4501831

$gradient
[1] 4.024558e-09

$code
[1] 1

$iterations
[1] 5
```

Here, the minimum value was found to be approximately -0.23, occurring at $x = 0.45$. A Newton-Raphson method (a technique from numerical analysis for approximating roots) is used, running five iterations in this case. The second argument specifies the initial guess, which we set to be 8. (This second argument was picked pretty arbitrarily here, but in some problems, you may need to experiment to find a value that will lead to convergence.)

8.1.4   Calculus

R also has some calculus capabilities, including symbolic differentiation and numerical integration, as you can see in the following example.

```
> D(expression(exp(x^2)),"x")   # derivative
exp(x^2) * (2 * x)
> integrate(function(x) x^2,0,1)
0.3333333 with absolute error < 3.7e-15
```

Here, R reported

$$\frac{d}{dx}e^{x^2} = 2xe^{x^2}$$

and

$$\int_0^1 x^2 \, dx \approx 0.3333333$$

You can find R packages for differential equations (odesolve), for interfacing R with the Yacas symbolic math system (ryacas), and for other calculus operations. These packages, and thousands of others, are available from the Comprehensive R Archive Network (CRAN); see Appendix B.

8.2 Functions for Statistical Distributions

R has functions available for most of the famous statistical distributions. Prefix the name as follows:

- With d for the density or probability mass function (pmf)
- With p for the cumulative distribution function (cdf)
- With q for quantiles
- With r for random number generation

The rest of the name indicates the distribution. Table 8-1 lists some common statistical distribution functions.

Table 8-1: Common R Statistical Distribution Functions

Distribution	Density/pmf	cdf	Quantiles	Random Numbers
Normal	dnorm()	pnorm()	qnorm()	rnorm()
Chi square	dchisq()	pchisq()	qchisq()	rchisq()
Binomial	dbinom()	pbinom()	qbinom()	rbinom()

As an example, let's simulate 1,000 chi-square variates with 2 degrees of freedom and find their mean.

```
> mean(rchisq(1000,df=2))
[1] 1.938179
```

The r in rchisq specifies that we wish to generate random numbers—in this case, from the chi-square distribution. As seen in this example, the first argument in the r-series functions is the number of random variates to generate.

These functions also have arguments specific to the given distribution families. In our example, we use the df argument for the chi-square family, indicating the number of degrees of freedom.

NOTE   *Consult R's online help for details on the arguments for the statistical distribution functions. For instance, to find out more about the chi-square function for quantiles, type ?qchisq at the command prompt.*

Let's also compute the 95th percentile of the chi-square distribution with two degrees of freedom:

```
> qchisq(0.95,2)
[1] 5.991465
```

Here, we used q to indicate quantile—in this case, the 0.95 quantile, or the 95th percentile.

The first argument in the d, p, and q series is actually a vector so that we can evaluate the density/pmf, cdf, or quantile function at multiple points. Let's find both the 50th and 95th percentiles of the chi-square distribution with 2 degrees of freedom.

```
qchisq(c(0.5,0.95),df=2)
[1] 1.386294 5.991465
```

8.3   Sorting

Ordinary numerical sorting of a vector can be done with the sort() function, as in this example:

```
> x <- c(13,5,12,5)
> sort(x)
[1]  5  5 12 13
> x
[1] 13  5 12  5
```

Note that x itself did not change, in keeping with R's functional language philosophy.

If you want the indices of the sorted values in the original vector, use the order() function. Here's an example:

```
> order(x)
[1] 2 4 3 1
```

This means that x[2] is the smallest value in x, x[4] is the second smallest, x[3] is the third smallest, and so on.

You can use order(), together with indexing, to sort data frames, like this:

```
> y
    V1 V2
1  def  2
2   ab  5
3 zzzz  1
> r <- order(y$V2)
> r
[1] 3 1 2
> z <- y[r,]
> z
    V1 V2
3 zzzz  1
1  def  2
2   ab  5
```

What happened here? We called order() on the second column of y, yielding a vector r, telling us where numbers should go if we want to sort them. The 3 in this vector tells us that x[3,2] is the smallest number in x[,2]; the 1 tells us that x[1,2] is the second smallest; and the 2 tells us that x[2,2] is the third smallest. We then use indexing to produce the frame sorted by column 2, storing it in z.

You can use order() to sort according to character variables as well as numeric ones, as follows:

```
> d
   kids ages
1  Jack   12
2  Jill   10
3 Billy   13
> d[order(d$kids),]
   kids ages
3 Billy   13
1  Jack   12
2  Jill   10
> d[order(d$ages),]
   kids ages
2  Jill   10
1  Jack   12
3 Billy   13
```

A related function is rank(), which reports the rank of each element of a vector.

```
> x <- c(13,5,12,5)
> rank(x)
[1] 4.0 1.5 3.0 1.5
```

This says that 13 had rank 4 in x; that is, it is the fourth smallest. The value 5 appears twice in x, with those two being the first and second smallest, so the rank 1.5 is assigned to both. Optionally, other methods of handling ties can be specified.

8.4   Linear Algebra Operations on Vectors and Matrices

Multiplying a vector by a scalar works directly, as you saw earlier. Here's another example:

```
> y
[1]  1  3  4 10
> 2*y
[1]  2  6  8 20
```

If you wish to compute the inner product (or dot product) of two vectors, use crossprod(), like this:

```
> crossprod(1:3,c(5,12,13))
     [,1]
[1,]   68
```

The function computed $1 \cdot 5 + 2 \cdot 12 + 3 \cdot 13 = 68$.

Note that the name crossprod() is a misnomer, as the function does not compute the vector cross product. We'll develop a function to compute real cross products in Section 8.4.1.

For matrix multiplication in the mathematical sense, the operator to use is %*%, not *. For instance, here we compute the matrix product:

$$\begin{pmatrix} 1 & 2 \\ 3 & 4 \end{pmatrix} \begin{pmatrix} 1 & -1 \\ 0 & 1 \end{pmatrix} = \begin{pmatrix} 1 & 1 \\ 3 & 1 \end{pmatrix}$$

Here's the code:

```
> a
     [,1] [,2]
[1,]    1    2
[2,]    3    4
> b
     [,1] [,2]
[1,]    1   -1
[2,]    0    1
```

```
> a %*% b
     [,1] [,2]
[1,]   1    1
[2,]   3    1
```

The function solve() will solve systems of linear equations and even find matrix inverses. For example, let's solve this system:

$$x_1 + x_2 = 2$$

$$-x_1 + x_2 = 4$$

Its matrix form is as follows:

$$\begin{pmatrix} 1 & 1 \\ -1 & 1 \end{pmatrix} \begin{pmatrix} x_1 \\ x_2 \end{pmatrix} = \begin{pmatrix} 2 \\ 4 \end{pmatrix}$$

Here's the code:

```
> a <- matrix(c(1,-1,1,1),nrow=2)
> b <- c(2,4)
> solve(a,b)
[1] -1  3
> solve(a)
     [,1] [,2]
[1,]  0.5 -0.5
[2,]  0.5  0.5
```

In that second call to solve(), the lack of a second argument signifies that we simply wish to compute the inverse of the matrix.

Here are a few other linear algebra functions:

- t(): Matrix transpose
- qr(): QR decomposition
- chol(): Cholesky decomposition
- det(): Determinant
- eigen(): Eigenvalues/eigenvectors
- diag(): Extracts the diagonal of a square matrix (useful for obtaining variances from a covariance matrix and for constructing a diagonal matrix).
- sweep(): Numerical analysis sweep operations

Note the versatile nature of diag(): If its argument is a matrix, it returns a vector, and vice versa. Also, if the argument is a scalar, the function returns the identity matrix of the specified size.

```
> m
     [,1] [,2]
[1,]    1    2
[2,]    7    8
> dm <- diag(m)
> dm
[1] 1 8
> diag(dm)
     [,1] [,2]
[1,]    1    0
[2,]    0    8
> diag(3)
     [,1] [,2] [,3]
[1,]    1    0    0
[2,]    0    1    0
[3,]    0    0    1
```

The sweep() function is capable of fairly complex operations. As a simple example, let's take a 3-by-3 matrix and add 1 to row 1, 4 to row 2, and 7 to row 3.

```
> m
     [,1] [,2] [,3]
[1,]    1    2    3
[2,]    4    5    6
[3,]    7    8    9
> sweep(m,1,c(1,4,7),"+")
     [,1] [,2] [,3]
[1,]    2    3    4
[2,]    8    9   10
[3,]   14   15   16
```

The first two arguments to sweep() are like those of apply(): the array and the margin, which is 1 for rows in this case. The fourth argument is a function to be applied, and the third is an argument to that function (to the "+" function).

8.4.1   Extended Example: Vector Cross Product

Let's consider the issue of vector cross products. The definition is very simple: The cross product of vectors (x_1, x_2, x_3) and (y_1, y_2, y_3) in three-dimensional space is a new three-dimensional vector, as shown in Equation 8.1.

$$(x_2 y_3 - x_3 y_2, -x_1 y_3 + x_3 y_1, x_1 y_2 - x_2 y_1) \qquad (8.1)$$

This can be expressed compactly as the expansion along the top row of the determinant, as shown in Equation 8.2.

$$\begin{pmatrix} - & - & - \\ x_1 & x_2 & x_3 \\ y_1 & y_2 & y_3 \end{pmatrix} \tag{8.2}$$

Here, the elements in the top row are merely placeholders.

Don't worry about this bit of pseudomath. The point is that the cross product vector can be computed as a sum of subdeterminants. For instance, the first component in Equation 8.1, $x_2y_3 - x_3y_2$, is easily seen to be the determinant of the submatrix obtained by deleting the first row and first column in Equation 8.2, as shown in Equation 8.3.

$$\begin{pmatrix} x_2 & x_3 \\ y_2 & y_3 \end{pmatrix} \tag{8.3}$$

Our need to calculate subdeterminants—that is determinants of submatrices—fits perfectly with R, which excels at specifying submatrices. This suggests calling det() on the proper submatrices, as follows:

```
xprod <- function(x,y) {
   m <- rbind(rep(NA,3),x,y)
   xp <- vector(length=3)
   for (i in 1:3)
      xp[i] <- -(-1)^i * det(m[2:3,-i])
   return(xp)
}
```

Note that even R's ability to specify values as NA came into play here to deal with the "placeholders" mentioned above.

All this may seem like overkill. After all, it wouldn't have been hard to code Equation 8.1 directly, without resorting to use of submatrices and determinants. But while that may be true in the three-dimensional case, the approach shown here is quite fruitful in the n-ary case, in n-dimensional space. The cross product there is defined as an n-by-n determinant of the form shown in Equation 8.1, and thus the preceding code generalizes perfectly.

8.4.2   Extended Example: Finding Stationary Distributions of Markov Chains

A Markov chain is a random process in which we move among various *states*, in a "memoryless" fashion, whose definition need not concern us here. The state could be the number of jobs in a queue, the number of items stored in inventory, and so on. We will assume the number of states to be finite.

As a simple example, consider a game in which we toss a coin repeatedly and win a dollar whenever we accumulate three consecutive heads. Our state at any time i will the number of consecutive heads we have so far, so our state can be 0, 1, or 2. (When we get three heads in a row, our state reverts to 0.)

The central interest in Markov modeling is usually the long-run state distribution, meaning the long-run proportions of the time we are in each state. In our coin-toss game, we can use the code we'll develop here to calculate that distribution, which turns out to have us at states 0, 1, and 2 in proportions 57.1%, 28.6%, and 14.3% of the time. Note that we win our dollar if we are in state 2 and toss a head, so $0.143 \times 0.5 = 0.071$ of our tosses will result in wins.

Since R vector and matrix indices start at 1 rather than 0, it will be convenient to relabel our states here as 1, 2, and 3 rather than 0, 1, and 2. For example, state 3 now means that we currently have two consecutive heads.

Let p_{ij} denote the *transition probability* of moving from state i to state j during a time step. In the game example, for instance, $p_{23} = 0.5$, reflecting the fact that with probability $1/2$, we will toss a head and thus move from having one consecutive head to two. On the other hand, if we toss a tail while we are in state 2, we go to state 1, meaning 0 consecutive heads; thus $p_{21} = 0.5$.

We are interested in calculating the vector $\pi = (\pi_1, ..., \pi_s)$, where π_i is the long-run proportion of time spent at state i, over all states i. Let P denote the transition probability matrix whose i^{th} row, j^{th} column element is p_{ij}. Then it can be shown that π must satisfy Equation 8.4,

$$\pi = \pi P \qquad (8.4)$$

which is equivalent to Equation 8.5:

$$(I - P^T)\pi = 0 \qquad (8.5)$$

Here I is the identity matrix and P^T denotes the transpose of P.

Any single one of the equations in the system of Equation 8.5 is redundant. We thus eliminate one of them, by removing the last row of $I-P$ in Equation 8.5. That also means removing the last 0 in the 0 vector on the right-hand side of Equation 8.5.

But note that there is also the constraint shown in Equation 8.6.

$$\sum_i \pi_i = 1 \qquad (8.6)$$

In matrix terms, this is as follows:

$$1_n^T \pi = 1$$

where 1_n is a vector of n 1s.

So, in the modified version of Equation 8.5, we replace the removed row with a row of all 1s and, on the right-hand side, replace the removed 0 with a 1. We can then solve the system.

All this can be computed with R's solve() function, as follows:

```
findpi1 <- function(p) {
    n <- nrow(p)
    imp <- diag(n) - t(p)
```

```
 4      imp[n,] <- rep(1,n)
 5      rhs <- c(rep(0,n-1),1)
 6      pivec <- solve(imp,rhs)
 7      return(pivec)
 8   }
```

Here are the main steps:

1. Calculate $I - P^T$ in line 3. Note again that diag(), when called with a scalar argument, returns the identity matrix of the size given by that argument.

2. Replace the last row of P with 1 values in line 4.

3. Set up the right-hand side vector in line 5.

4. Solve for π in line 6.

Another approach, using more advanced knowledge, is based on eigenvalues. Note from Equation 8.4 that π is a left eigenvector of P with eigenvalue 1. This suggests using R's eigen() function, selecting the eigenvector corresponding to that eigenvalue. (A result from mathematics, the Perron-Frobenius theorem, can be used to carefully justify this.)

Since π is a left eigenvector, the argument in the call to eigen() must be P transpose rather than P. In addition, since an eigenvector is unique only up to scalar multiplication, we must deal with two issues regarding the eigenvector returned to us by eigen():

- It may have negative components. If so, we multiply by -1.

- It may not satisfy Equation 8.6. We remedy this by dividing by the length of the returned vector.

Here is the code:

```
 1   findpi2 <- function(p) {
 2      n <- nrow(p)
 3      # find first eigenvector of P transpose
 4      pivec <- eigen(t(p))$vectors[,1]
 5      # guaranteed to be real, but could be negative
 6      if (pivec[1] < 0) pivec <- -pivec
 7      # normalize to sum to 1
 8      pivec <- pivec / sum(pivec)
 9      return(pivec)
10   }
```

The return value of eigen() is a list. One of the list's components is a matrix named vectors. These are the eigenvectors, with the ith column being the eigenvector corresponding to the ith eigenvalue. Thus, we take column 1 here.

8.5 Set Operations

R includes some handy set operations, including these:

- union(x,y): Union of the sets x and y
- intersect(x,y): Intersection of the sets x and y
- setdiff(x,y): Set difference between x and y, consisting of all elements of x that are not in y
- setequal(x,y): Test for equality between x and y
- c %in% y: Membership, testing whether c is an element of the set y
- choose(n,k): Number of possible subsets of size k chosen from a set of size n

Here are some simple examples of using these functions:

```
> x <- c(1,2,5)
> y <- c(5,1,8,9)
> union(x,y)
[1] 1 2 5 8 9
> intersect(x,y)
[1] 1 5
> setdiff(x,y)
[1] 2
> setdiff(y,x)
[1] 8 9
> setequal(x,y)
[1] FALSE
> setequal(x,c(1,2,5))
[1] TRUE
> 2 %in% x
[1] TRUE
> 2 %in% y
[1] FALSE
> choose(5,2)
[1] 10
```

Recall from Section 7.12 that you can write your own binary operations. For instance, consider coding the symmetric difference between two sets—that is, all the elements belonging to exactly one of the two operand sets. Because the symmetric difference between sets x and y consists exactly of those elements in x but not y and vice versa, the code consists of easy calls to setdiff() and union(), as follows:

```
> symdiff
function(a,b) {
    sdfxy <- setdiff(x,y)
    sdfyx <- setdiff(y,x)
```

```
    return(union(sdfxy,sdfyx))
}
```

Let's try it.

```
> x
[1] 1 2 5
> y
[1] 5 1 8 9
> symdiff(x,y)
[1] 2 8 9
```

Here's another example: a binary operand for determining whether one set u is a subset of another set v. A bit of thought shows that this property is equivalent to the intersection of u and v being equal to u. Hence we have another easily coded function:

```
> "%subsetof%" <- function(u,v) {
+     return(setequal(intersect(u,v),u))
+ }
> c(3,8) %subsetof% 1:10
[1] TRUE
> c(3,8) %subsetof% 5:10
[1] FALSE
```

The function combn() generates combinations. Let's find the subsets of {1,2,3} of size 2.

```
> c32 <- combn(1:3,2)
> c32
     [,1] [,2] [,3]
[1,]   1    1    2
[2,]   2    3    3
> class(c32)
[1] "matrix"
```

The results are in the columns of the output. We see that the subsets of {1,2,3} of size 2 are (1,2), (1,3), and (2,3).

The function also allows you to specify a function to be called by combn() on each combination. For example, we can find the sum of the numbers in each subset, like this:

```
> combn(1:3,2,sum)
[1] 3 4 5
```

The first subset, {1,2}, has a sum of 2, and so on.

8.6 Simulation Programming in R

One of the most common uses of R is simulation. Let's see what kinds of tools R has available for this application.

8.6.1 Built-In Random Variate Generators

As mentioned, R has functions to generate variates from a number of different distributions. For example, rbinom() generates binomial or Bernoulli random variates.[1]

Let's say we want to find the probability of getting at least four heads out of five tosses of a coin (easy to find analytically, but a handy example). Here's how we can do this:

```
> x <- rbinom(100000,5,0.5)
> mean(x >= 4)
[1] 0.18829
```

First, we generate 100,000 variates from a binomial distribution with five trials and a success probability of 0.5. We then determine which of them has a value 4 or 5, resulting in a Boolean vector of the same length as x. The TRUE and FALSE values in that vector are treated as 1s and 0s by mean(), giving us our estimated probability (since the average of a bunch of 1s and 0s is the proportion of 1s).

Other functions include rnorm() for the normal distribution, rexp() for the exponential, runif() for the uniform, rgamma() for the gamma, rpois() for the Poisson, and so on.

Here is another simple example, which finds $E[\max(X, Y)]$, the expected value of the maximum of independent N(0,1) random variables X and Y:

```
sum <- 0
nreps <- 100000
for (i in 1:nreps) {
   xy <- rnorm(2)  # generate 2 N(0,1)s
   sum <- sum + max(xy)
}
print(sum/nreps)
```

We generated 100,000 pairs, found the maximum for each, and averaged those maxima to obtain our estimated expected value.

The preceding code, with an explicit loop, may be clearer, but as before, if we are willing to use some more memory, we can do this more compactly.

---

[1] A sequence of independent 0- and 1- valued random variables with the same probability of 1 for each is called *Bernoulli*.

```
> emax
function(nreps) {
   x <- rnorm(2*nreps)
   maxxy <- pmax(x[1:nreps],x[(nreps+1):(2*nreps)])
   return(mean(maxxy))
}
```

Here, we generated double nreps values. The first nreps value simulates X, and the remaining nreps value represents Y. The pmax() call then computes the pair-wise maxima that we need. Again, note the contrast here between max() and pmax(), the latter producing pair-wise maxima.

8.6.2   Obtaining the Same Random Stream in Repeated Runs

According to the R documentation, all random-number generators use 32-bit integers for seed values. Thus, other than round-off error, the same initial seed should generate the same stream of numbers.

By default, R will generate a different random number stream from run to run of a program. If you want the same stream each time—important in debugging, for instance—call set.seed(), like this:

```
> set.seed(8888)   # or your favorite number as an argument
```

8.6.3   Extended Example: A Combinatorial Simulation

Consider the following probability problem:

> Three committees, of sizes 3, 4 and 5, are chosen from 20 people. What is the probability that persons A and B are chosen for the same committee?

This problem is not hard to solve analytically, but we may wish to check our solution using simulation, and in any case, writing the code will demonstrate how R's set operations can come in handy in combinatorial settings. Here is the code:

```
1  sim <- function(nreps) {
2     commdata <- list() # will store all our info about the 3 committees
3     commdata$countabsamecomm <- 0
4     for (rep in 1:nreps) {
5        commdata$whosleft <- 1:20 # who's left to choose from
6        commdata$numabchosen <- 0 # number among A, B chosen so far
7        # choose committee 1, and check for A,B serving together
8        commdata <- choosecomm(commdata,5)
```

```
9       # if A or B already chosen, no need to look at the other comms.
10      if (commdata$numabchosen > 0) next
11      # choose committee 2 and check
12      commdata <- choosecomm(commdata,4)
13      if (commdata$numabchosen > 0) next
14      # choose committee 3 and check
15      commdata <- choosecomm(commdata,3)
16    }
17    print(commdata$countabsamecomm/nreps)
18  }
19
20  choosecomm <- function(comdat,comsize) {
21    # choose committee
22    committee <- sample(comdat$whosleft,comsize)
23    # count how many of A and B were chosen
24    comdat$numabchosen <- length(intersect(1:2,committee))
25    if (comdat$numabchosen == 2)
26      comdat$countabsamecomm <- comdat$countabsamecomm + 1
27    # delete chosen committee from the set of people we now have to choose from
28    comdat$whosleft <- setdiff(comdat$whosleft,committee)
29    return(comdat)
30  }
```

We number the potential committee members from 1 to 20, with persons A and B having ID 1 and 2. Recalling that R lists are often used to store several related variables in one basket, we set up a list comdat. Its components include the following:

- comdat$whosleft: We simulate the random selection of the committees by randomly choosing from this vector. Each time we choose a committee, we remove the committee members' IDs. It is initialized to 1:20, indicating that no one has been selected yet.

- comdat$numabchosen: This is a count of how many among the people A and B have been chosen so far. If we choose a committee and find this to be positive, we can skip choosing the remaining committees for the following reason: If this number is 2, we know definitely that A and B are on the same committee; if it is 1, we know definitely that A and B are *not* on the same committee.

- comdat$countabsamecomm: Here, we store a count of the number of times A and B are on the same committee.

Since committee selection involves subsets, it's not surprising that a couple of R's set operations—intersect() and setdiff()—come in handy here. Note, too, the use of R's next statement, which tells R to skip the rest of this iteration of the loop.

9

OBJECT-ORIENTED PROGRAMMING

Many programmers believe that object-oriented programming (OOP) makes for clearer, more reusable code. Though very different from the familiar OOP languages like C++, Java, and Python, R is very much OOP in outlook.

The following themes are key to R:

- Everything you touch in R—ranging from numbers to character strings to matrices—is an object.

- R promotes *encapsulation*, which is packaging separate but related data items into one class instance. Encapsulation helps you keep track of related variables, enhancing clarity.

- R classes are *polymorphic*, which means that the same function call leads to different operations for objects of different classes. For instance, a call to print() on an object of a certain class triggers a call to a print function tailored to that class. Polymorphism promotes reusability.

- R allows *inheritance*, which allows extending a given class to a more specialized class.

This chapter covers OOP in R. We'll discuss programming in the two types of classes, S3 and S4, and then present a few useful OOP-related R utilities.

9.1 S3 Classes

The original R structure for classes, known as S3, is still the dominant class paradigm in R use today. Indeed, most of R's own built-in classes are of the S3 type.

An S3 class consists of a list, with a class name attribute and *dispatch* capability added. The latter enables the use of generic functions, as we saw in Chapter 1. S4 classes were developed later, with goal of adding *safety*, meaning that you cannot accidentally access a class component that is not already in existence.

9.1.1 S3 Generic Functions

As mentioned, R is polymorphic, in the sense that the same function can lead to different operations for different classes. You can apply plot(), for example, to many different types of objects, getting a different type of plot for each. The same is true for print(), summary(), and many other functions.

In this manner, we get a uniform interface to different classes. For example, if you are writing code that includes plot operations, polymorphism may allow you to write your program without worrying about the various types of objects that might be plotted.

In addition, polymorphism certainly makes things easier to remember for the user and makes it fun and convenient to explore new library functions and associated classes. If a function is new to you, just try running plot() on the function's output; it will likely work. From a programmer's viewpoint, polymorphism allows writing fairly general code, without worrying about what type of object is being manipulated, because the underlying class mechanisms take care of that.

The functions that work with polymorphism, such as plot() and print(), are known as *generic functions*. When a generic function is called, R will then dispatch the call to the proper class method, meaning that it will reroute the call to a function defined for the object's class.

9.1.2 Example: OOP in the lm() Linear Model Function

As an example, let's look at a simple regression analysis run via R's lm() function. First, let's see what lm() does:

```
> ?lm
```

The output of this help query will tell you, among other things, that this function returns an object of class "lm".

Let's try creating an instance of this object and then printing it:

```
> x <- c(1,2,3)
> y <- c(1,3,8)
> lmout <- lm(y ~ x)
> class(lmout)
[1] "lm"
> lmout

Call:
lm(formula = y ~ x)

Coefficients:
(Intercept)            x
       -3.0          3.5
```

Here, we printed out the object lmout. (Remember that by simply typing the name of an object in interactive mode, the object is printed.) The R interpreter then saw that lmout was an object of class "lm" and thus called print.lm(), a special print method for the "lm" class. In R terminology, the call to the generic function print() was dispatched to the method print.lm() associated with the class "lm".

Let's take a look at the generic function and the class method in this case:

```
> print
function(x, ...) UseMethod("print")
<environment: namespace:base>
> print.lm
function (x, digits = max(3, getOption("digits") - 3), ...)
{
    cat("\nCall:\n", deparse(x$call), "\n\n", sep = "")
    if (length(coef(x))) {
        cat("Coefficients:\n")
        print.default(format(coef(x), digits = digits), print.gap = 2,
            quote = FALSE)
    }
    else cat("No coefficients\n")
    cat("\n")
    invisible(x)
}
<environment: namespace:stats>
```

You may be surprised to see that print() consists solely of a call to UseMethod(). But this is actually the dispatcher function, so in view of print()'s role as a generic function, you should not be surprised after all.

Don't worry about the details of print.lm(). The main point is that the printing depends on context, with a special print function called for the "lm" class. Now let's see what happens when we print this object with its class attribute removed:

```
> unclass(lmout)
$coefficients
(Intercept)           x
       -3.0         3.5

$residuals
    1     2     3
  0.5  -1.0   0.5

$effects
(Intercept)            x
 -6.928203   -4.949747    1.224745

$rank
[1] 2
...
```

I've shown only the first few lines here—there's a lot more. (Try running this on your own!) But you can see that the author of lm() decided to make print.lm() much more concise, limiting it to printing a few key quantities.

9.1.3   Finding the Implementations of Generic Methods

You can find all the implementations of a given generic method by calling methods(), like this:

```
> methods(print)
 [1] print.acf*
 [2] print.anova
 [3] print.aov*
 [4] print.aovlist*
 [5] print.ar*
 [6] print.Arima*
 [7] print.arima0*
 [8] print.AsIs
 [9] print.aspell*
[10] print.Bibtex*
[11] print.browseVignettes*
[12] print.by
[13] print.check_code_usage_in_package*
[14] print.check_demo_index*
[15] print.checkDocFiles*
```

```
[16] print.checkDocStyle*
[17] print.check_dotInternal*
[18] print.checkFF*
[19] print.check_make_vars*
[20] print.check_package_code_syntax*
...
```

Asterisks denote *nonvisible* functions, meaning ones that are not in the default namespaces. You can find these functions via getAnywhere() and then access them by using a namespace qualifier. An example is print.aspell(). The aspell() function itself does a spellcheck on the file specified in its argument. For example, suppose the file *wrds* consists of this line:

```
Which word is mispelled?
```

In this case, this function will catch the misspelled word, as follows:

```
aspell("wrds")
mispelled
  wrds:1:15
```

The output says that there is the indicated spelling error in line 1, character 15 of the input file. But what concerns us here is the mechanism by which that output was printed.

The aspell() function returns an object of class "aspell", which does have its own generic print function, print.aspell(). In fact, that function was invoked in our example, after the call to aspell(), and the return value was printed out. At that time, R called UseMethod() on the object of class "aspell". But if we call that print method directly, R won't recognize it:

```
> aspout <- aspell("wrds")
> print.aspell(aspout)
Error: could not find function "print.aspell"
```

However, we can find it by calling getAnywhere():

```
> getAnywhere(print.aspell)
A single object matching 'print.aspell' was found
It was found in the following places
  registered S3 method for print from namespace utils
  namespace:utils
with value

function (x, sort = TRUE, verbose = FALSE, indent = 2L, ...)
{
    if (!(nr <- nrow(x)))
...
```

So, the function is in the `utils` namespace, and we can execute it by adding such a qualifier:

```
> utils:::print.aspell(aspout)
mispelled
  wrds:1:15
```

You can see all the generic methods this way:

```
> methods(class="default")
...
```

9.1.4 Writing S3 Classes

S3 classes have a rather cobbled-together structure. A class instance is created by forming a list, with the components of the list being the member variables of the class. (Readers who know Perl may recognize this ad hoc nature in Perl's own OOP system.) The "class" attribute is set by hand by using the attr() or class() function, and then various implementations of generic functions are defined. We can see this in the case of lm() by inspecting the function:

```
> lm
...
z <- list(coefficients = if (is.matrix(y))
                matrix(,0,3) else numeric(0L), residuals = y,
              fitted.values = 0 * y, weights = w, rank = 0L,
              df.residual = if (is.matrix(y)) nrow(y) else length(y))
}
...
class(z) <- c(if(is.matrix(y)) "mlm", "lm")
...
```

Again, don't mind the details; the basic process is there. A list was created and assigned to z, which will serve as the framework for the "lm" class instance (and which will eventually be the value returned by the function). Some components of that list, such as residuals, were already assigned when the list was created. In addition, the class attribute was set to "lm" (and possibly to "mlm", as will be explained in the next section).

As an example of how to write an S3 class, let's switch to something simpler. Continuing our employee example from Section 4.1, we could write this:

```
> j <- list(name="Joe", salary=55000, union=T)
> class(j) <- "employee"
> attributes(j) # let's check
```

```
$names
[1] "name" "salary" "union"

$class
[1] "employee"
```

Before we write a print method for this class, let's see what happens when we call the default print():

```
> j
$name
[1] "Joe"

$salary
[1] 55000

$union
[1] TRUE

attr(,"class")
[1] "employee"
```

Essentially, j was treated as a list for printing purposes.

Now let's write our own print method:

```
print.employee <- function(wrkr) {
    cat(wrkr$name,"\n")
    cat("salary",wrkr$salary,"\n")
    cat("union member",wrkr$union,"\n")
}
```

So, any call to print() on an object of class "employee" should now be referred to print.employee(). We can check that formally:

```
> methods(,"employee")
[1] print.employee
```

Or, of course, we can simply try it out:

```
> j
Joe
salary 55000
union member TRUE
```

9.1.5 Using Inheritance

The idea of inheritance is to form new classes as specialized versions of old ones. In our previous employee example, for instance, we could form a new class devoted to hourly employees, "hrlyemployee", as a subclass of "employee", as follows:

```
k <- list(name="Kate", salary= 68000, union=F, hrsthismonth= 2)
class(k) <- c("hrlyemployee","employee")
```

Our new class has one extra variable: hrsthismonth. The name of the new class consists of two character strings, representing the new class and the old class. Our new class inherits the methods of the old one. For instance, print.employee() still works on the new class:

```
> k
Kate
salary 68000
union member FALSE
```

Given the goals of inheritance, that is not surprising. However, it's important to understand exactly what transpired here.

Once again, simply typing k resulted in the call print(k). In turn, that caused UseMethod() to search for a print method on the first of k's two class names, "hrlyemployee". That search failed, so UseMethod() tried the other class name, "employee", and found print.employee(). It executed the latter.

Recall that in inspecting the code for "lm", you saw this line:

```
class(z) <- c(if(is.matrix(y)) "mlm", "lm")
```

You can now see that "mlm" is a subclass of "lm" for vector-valued response variables.

9.1.6 Extended Example: A Class for Storing Upper-Triangular Matrices

Now it's time for a more involved example, in which we will write an R class "ut" for upper-triangular matrices. These are square matrices whose elements below the diagonal are zeros, such as shown in Equation 9.1.

$$\begin{pmatrix} 1 & 5 & 12 \\ 0 & 6 & 9 \\ 0 & 0 & 2 \end{pmatrix} \tag{9.1}$$

Our motivation here is to save storage space (though at the expense of a little extra access time) by storing only the nonzero portion of the matrix.

NOTE *The R class "dist" also uses such storage, though in a more focused context and without the class functions we have here.*

The component mat of this class will store the matrix. As mentioned, to save on storage space, only the diagonal and above-diagonal elements will be stored, in column-major order. Storage for the matrix (9.1), for instance, consists of the vector (1,5,6,12,9,2), and the component mat has that value.

We will include a component ix in this class, to show where in mat the various columns begin. For the preceding case, ix is c(1,2,4), meaning that column 1 begins at mat[1], column 2 begins at mat[2], and column 3 begins at mat[4]. This allows for handy access to individual elements or columns of the matrix.

The following is the code for our class.

```
1   # class "ut", compact storage of upper-triangular matrices
2
3   # utility function, returns 1+...+i
4   sum1toi <- function(i) return(i*(i+1)/2)
5
6   # create an object of class "ut" from the full matrix inmat (0s included)
7   ut <- function(inmat) {
8      n <- nrow(inmat)
9      rtrn <- list()  # start to build the object
10     class(rtrn) <- "ut"
11     rtrn$mat <- vector(length=sum1toi(n))
12     rtrn$ix <- sum1toi(0:(n-1)) + 1
13     for (i in 1:n) {
14        # store column i
15        ixi <- rtrn$ix[i]
16        rtrn$mat[ixi:(ixi+i-1)] <- inmat[1:i,i]
17     }
18     return(rtrn)
19  }
20
21  # uncompress utmat to a full matrix
22  expandut <- function(utmat) {
23     n <- length(utmat$ix)  # numbers of rows and cols of matrix
24     fullmat <- matrix(nrow=n,ncol=n)
25     for (j in 1:n) {
26        # fill jth column
27        start <- utmat$ix[j]
28        fin <- start + j - 1
29        abovediagj <- utmat$mat[start:fin] # above-diag part of col j
30        fullmat[,j] <- c(abovediagj,rep(0,n-j))
31     }
32     return(fullmat)
33  }
34
35  # print matrix
36  print.ut <- function(utmat)
37     print(expandut(utmat))
```

```
38
39    # multiply one ut matrix by another, returning another ut instance;
40    # implement as a binary operation
41    "%mut%" <- function(utmat1,utmat2) {
42        n <- length(utmat1$ix)   # numbers of rows and cols of matrix
43        utprod <- ut(matrix(0,nrow=n,ncol=n))
44        for (i in 1:n) {  # compute col i of product
45            # let a[j] and bj denote columns j of utmat1 and utmat2, respectively,
46            # so that, e.g. b2[1] means element 1 of column 2 of utmat2
47            # then column i of product is equal to
48            #    bi[1]*a[1] + ... + bi[i]*a[i]
49            # find index of start of column i in utmat2
50            startbi <- utmat2$ix[i]
51            # initialize vector that will become bi[1]*a[1] + ... + bi[i]*a[i]
52            prodcoli <- rep(0,i)
53            for (j in 1:i) {  # find bi[j]*a[j], add to prodcoli
54                startaj <- utmat1$ix[j]
55                bielement <- utmat2$mat[startbi+j-1]
56                prodcoli[1:j] <- prodcoli[1:j] +
57                    bielement * utmat1$mat[startaj:(startaj+j-1)]
58            }
59            # now need to tack on the lower 0s
60            startprodcoli <- sum1toi(i-1)+1
61            utprod$mat[startbi:(startbi+i-1)] <- prodcoli
62        }
63        return(utprod)
64    }
```

Let's test it.

```
> test
function() {
   utm1 <- ut(rbind(1:2,c(0,2)))
   utm2 <- ut(rbind(3:2,c(0,1)))
   utp <- utm1 %mut% utm2
   print(utm1)
   print(utm2)
   print(utp)
   utm1 <- ut(rbind(1:3,0:2,c(0,0,5)))
   utm2 <- ut(rbind(4:2,0:2,c(0,0,1)))
   utp <- utm1 %mut% utm2
   print(utm1)
   print(utm2)
   print(utp)
}
```

```
> test()
     [,1] [,2]
[1,] 1 2
[2,] 0 2
     [,1] [,2]
[1,] 3 2
[2,] 0 1
     [,1] [,2]
[1,] 3 4
[2,] 0 2
     [,1] [,2] [,3]
[1,] 1 2 3
[2,] 0 1 2
[3,] 0 0 5
     [,1] [,2] [,3]
[1,] 4 3 2
[2,] 0 1 2
[3,] 0 0 1
     [,1] [,2] [,3]
[1,] 4 5 9
[2,] 0 1 4
[3,] 0 0 5
```

Throughout the code, we take into account the fact that the matrices involved have a lot of zeros. For example, we avoid multiplying by zeros simply by not adding terms to sums when the terms include a 0 factor.

The ut() function is fairly straightforward. This function is a *constructor*, which is a function whose job it is to create an instance of the given class, eventually returning that instance. So in line 9, we create a list that will serve as the body of the class object, naming it rtrn as a reminder that this will be the class instance to be constructed and returned.

As noted earlier, the main member variables of our class will be mat and idx, implemented as components of the list. Memory for these two components is allocated in lines 11 and 12.

The loop that follows then fills in rtrn$mat column by column and assigns rtrn$idx element by element. A slicker way to do this for loop would be to use the rather obscure row() and col() functions. The row() function takes a matrix input and returns a new matrix of the same size, but with each element replaced by its row number. Here's an example:

```
> m
     [,1] [,2]
[1,] 1 4
[2,] 2 5
[3,] 3 6
```

```
> row(m)
     [,1] [,2]
[1,]  1    1
[2,]  2    2
[3,]  3    3
```

The col() function works similarly.

Using this idea, we could replace the for loop in ut() with a one-liner:

```
rtrn$mat <- inmat[row(inmat) <= col(inmat)]
```

Whenever possible, we should exploit vectorization. Take a look at line 12, for example:

```
rtrn$ix <- sum1toi(0:(n-1)) + 1
```

Since sum1toi() (which we defined on line 4) is based only on the vectorized functions "*"() and "+"(), sum1toi() itself is also vectorized. This allows us to apply sum1toi() to a vector above. Note that we used recycling as well.

We want our "ut" class to include some methods, not just variables. To this end, we have included three methods:

- The expandut() function converts from a compressed matrix to an ordinary one. In expandut(), the key lines are 27 and 28, where we use rtrn$ix to determine where in utmat$mat the jth column of our matrix is stored. That data is then copied to the jth column of fullmat in line 30. Note the use of rep() to generate the zeros in the lower portion of this column.

- The print.ut() function is for printing. This function is quick and easy, using expandut(). Recall that any call to print() on an object of type "ut" will be dispatched to print.ut(), as in our test cases earlier.

- The "%mut%"() function is for multiplying two compressed matrices (without uncompressing them). This function starts in line 39. Since this is a binary operation, we take advantage of the fact that R accommodates user-defined binary operations, as described in Section 7.12, and implement our matrix-multiply function as %mut%.

Let's look at the details of the "%mut%"() function. First, in line 43, we allocate space for the product matrix. Note the use of recycling in an unusual context. The first argument of matrix() is required to be a vector of a length compatible with the number of specified rows and columns, so the 0 we provide is recycled to a vector of length n^2. Of course, rep() could be used instead, but exploiting recycling makes for a bit shorter, more elegant code.

For both clarity and fast execution, the code here has been written around the fact that R stores matrices in column-major order. As mentioned in the comments, our code then makes use of the fact that column i of the product can be expressed as a linear combination of the columns of the first factor. It will help to see a specific example of this property, shown in Equation 9.2.

$$\begin{pmatrix} 1 & 2 & 3 \\ 0 & 1 & 2 \\ 0 & 0 & 5 \end{pmatrix} \begin{pmatrix} 4 & 3 & 2 \\ 0 & 1 & 2 \\ 0 & 0 & 1 \end{pmatrix} = \begin{pmatrix} 4 & 5 & 9 \\ 0 & 1 & 4 \\ 0 & 0 & 5 \end{pmatrix} \tag{9.2}$$

The comments say that, for instance, column 3 of the product is equal to the following:

$$2 \begin{pmatrix} 1 \\ 0 \\ 0 \end{pmatrix} + 2 \begin{pmatrix} 2 \\ 1 \\ 0 \end{pmatrix} + 1 \begin{pmatrix} 3 \\ 2 \\ 5 \end{pmatrix}$$

Inspection of Equation 9.2 confirms the relation.

Couching the multiplication problem in terms of columns of the two input matrices enables us to compact the code and to likely increase the speed. The latter again stems from vectorization, a benefit discussed in detail in Chapter 14. This approach is used in the loop beginning at line 53. (Arguably, in this case, the increase in speed comes at the expense of readability of the code.)

9.1.7 Extended Example: A Procedure for Polynomial Regression

As another example, consider a statistical regression setting with one predictor variable. Since any statistical model is merely an approximation, in principle, you can get better and better models by fitting polynomials of higher and higher degrees. However, at some point, this becomes overfitting, so that the prediction of new, future data actually deteriorates for degrees higher than some value.

The class "polyreg" aims to deal with this issue. It fits polynomials of various degrees but assesses fits via cross-validation to reduce the risk of overfitting. In this form of cross-validation, known as the *leaving-one-out method*, for each point we fit the regression to all the data *except* this observation, and then we predict that observation from the fit. An object of this class consists of outputs from the various regression models, plus the original data.

The following is the code for the "polyreg" class.

```
1   # "polyreg," S3 class for polynomial regression in one predictor variable
2
3   # polyfit(y,x,maxdeg) fits all polynomials up to degree maxdeg; y is
4   # vector for response variable, x for predictor; creates an object of
5   # class "polyreg"
6   polyfit <- function(y,x,maxdeg) {
7      # form powers of predictor variable, ith power in ith column
8      pwrs <- powers(x,maxdeg) # could use orthog polys for greater accuracy
9      lmout <- list() # start to build class
10     class(lmout) <- "polyreg" # create a new class
```

```
11     for (i in 1:maxdeg) {
12        lmo <- lm(y ~ pwrs[,1:i])
13        # extend the lm class here, with the cross-validated predictions
14        lmo$fitted.cvvalues <- lvoneout(y,pwrs[,1:i,drop=F])
15        lmout[[i]] <- lmo
16     }
17     lmout$x <- x
18     lmout$y <- y
19     return(lmout)
20  }
21
22  # print() for an object fits of class "polyreg": print
23  # cross-validated mean-squared prediction errors
24  print.polyreg <- function(fits) {
25     maxdeg <- length(fits) - 2
26     n <- length(fits$y)
27     tbl <- matrix(nrow=maxdeg,ncol=1)
28     colnames(tbl) <- "MSPE"
29     for (i in 1:maxdeg) {
30        fi <- fits[[i]]
31        errs <- fits$y - fi$fitted.cvvalues
32        spe <- crossprod(errs,errs) # sum of squared prediction errors
33        tbl[i,1] <- spe/n
34     }
35     cat("mean squared prediction errors, by degree\n")
36     print(tbl)
37  }
38
39  # forms matrix of powers of the vector x, through degree dg
40  powers <- function(x,dg) {
41     pw <- matrix(x,nrow=length(x))
42     prod <- x
43     for (i in 2:dg) {
44        prod <- prod * x
45        pw <- cbind(pw,prod)
46     }
47     return(pw)
48  }
49
50  # finds cross-validated predicted values; could be made much faster via
51  # matrix-update methods
52  lvoneout <- function(y,xmat) {
53     n <- length(y)
54     predy <- vector(length=n)
55     for (i in 1:n) {
56        # regress, leaving out ith observation
57        lmo <- lm(y[-i] ~ xmat[-i,])
58        betahat <- as.vector(lmo$coef)
```

```
59    # the 1 accommodates the constant term
60    predy[i] <- betahat %*% c(1,xmat[i,])
61  }
62  return(predy)
63 }
64
65 # polynomial function of x, coefficients cfs
66 poly <- function(x,cfs) {
67   val <- cfs[1]
68   prod <- 1
69   dg <- length(cfs) - 1
70   for (i in 1:dg) {
71     prod <- prod * x
72     val <- val + cfs[i+1] * prod
73   }
74 }
```

As you can see, "polyreg" consists of polyfit(), the constructor function, and print.polyreg(), a print function tailored to this class. It also contains several utility functions to evaluate powers and polynomials and to perform cross-validation. (Note that in some cases here, efficiency has been sacrificed for clarity.)

As an example of using the class, we'll generate some artificial data and create an object of class "polyreg" from it, printing out the results.

```
> n <- 60
> x <- (1:n)/n
> y <- vector(length=n)
> for (i in 1:n) y[i] <- sin((3*pi/2)*x[i]) + x[i]^2 + rnorm(1,mean=0,sd=0.5)
> dg <- 15
> (lmo <- polyfit(y,x,dg))
mean squared prediction errors, by degree
            MSPE
 [1,] 0.4200127
 [2,] 0.3212241
 [3,] 0.2977433
 [4,] 0.2998716
 [5,] 0.3102032
 [6,] 0.3247325
 [7,] 0.3120066
 [8,] 0.3246087
 [9,] 0.3463628
[10,] 0.4502341
[11,] 0.6089814
[12,] 0.4499055
[13,]        NA
[14,]        NA
[15,]        NA
```

Note first that we used a common R trick in this command:

```
> (lmo <- polyfit(y,x,dg))
```

By surrounding the entire assignment statement in parentheses, we get the printout and form `lmo` at the same time, in case we need the latter for other things.

The function `polyfit()` fits polynomial models up through a specified degree, in this case 15, calculating the cross-validated mean squared prediction error for each model. The last few values in the output were NA, because roundoff error considerations led R to refuse to fit polynomials of degrees that high.

So, how is it all done? The main work is handled by the function `polyfit()`, which creates an object of class "polyreg". That object consists mainly of the objects returned by the R regression fitter `lm()` for each degree.

In forming those objects, note line 14:

```
lmo$fitted.cvvalues <- lvoneout(y,pwrs[,1:i,drop=F])
```

Here, `lmo` is an object returned by `lm()`, but we are adding an extra component to it: `fitted.cvvalues`. Since we can add a new component to a list at any time, and since S3 classes are lists, this is possible.

We also have a method for the generic function `print()`, `print.polyreg()` in line 24. In Section 12.1.5, we will add a method for the `plot()` generic function, `plot.polyreg()`.

In computing prediction errors, we used cross-validation, or the leaving-one-out method, in a form that predicts each observation from all the others. To implement this, we take advantage of R's use of negative subscripts in line 57:

```
lmo <- lm(y[-i] ~ xmat[-i,])
```

So, we are fitting the model with the ith observation deleted from our data set.

NOTE *As mentioned in the comment in the code, we could make a much faster implementation by using a matrix-inverse update method, known as the Sherman-Morrison-Woodbury formula. For more information, see J. H. Venter and J. L. J. Snyman, "A Note on the Generalised Cross-Validation Criterion in Linear Model Selection," Biometrika, Vol. 82, no. 1, pp. 215–219.*

9.2 S4 Classes

Some programmers feel that S3 does not provide the safety normally associated with OOP. For example, consider our earlier employee database example, where our class "employee" had three fields: name, salary, and union. Here are some possible mishaps:

- We forget to enter the union status.

- We misspell *union* as *onion*.

- We create an object of some class other than "employee" but accidentally set its class attribute to "employee".

In each of these cases, R will not complain. The goal of S4 is to elicit a complaint and prevent such accidents.

S4 structures are considerably richer than S3 structures, but here we present just the basics. Table 9-1 shows an overview of the differences between the two classes.

Table 9-1: Basic R Operators

Operation	S3	S4
Define class	Implicit in constructor code	setClass()
Create object	Build list, set class attr	new()
Reference member variable	$	@
Implement generic f()	Define f.classname()	setMethod()
Declare generic	UseMethod()	setGeneric()

9.2.1   Writing S4 Classes

You define an S4 class by calling setClass(). Continuing our employee example, we could write the following:

```
> setClass("employee",
+    representation(
+        name="character",
+        salary="numeric",
+        union="logical")
+ )
[1] "employee"
```

This defines a new class, "employee", with three member variables of the specified types.

Now let's create an instance of this class, for Joe, using new(), a built-in constructor function for S4 classes:

```
> joe <- new("employee",name="Joe",salary=55000,union=T)
> joe
An object of class "employee"
Slot "name":
[1] "Joe"
```

```
Slot "salary":
[1] 55000

Slot "union":
[1] TRUE
```

Note that the member variables are called *slots*, referenced via the @ symbol. Here's an example:

```
> joe@salary
[1] 55000
```

We can also use the slot() function, say, as another way to query Joe's salary:

```
> slot(joe,"salary")
[1] 55000
```

We can assign components similarly. Let's give Joe a raise:

```
> joe@salary <- 65000
> joe
An object of class "employee"
Slot "name":
[1] "Joe"

Slot "salary":
[1] 65000

Slot "union":
[1] TRUE
```

Nah, he deserves a bigger raise that that:

```
> slot(joe,"salary") <- 88000
> joe
An object of class "employee"
Slot "name":
[1] "Joe"

Slot "salary":
[1] 88000

Slot "union":
[1] TRUE
```

As noted, an advantage of using S4 is safety. To illustrate this, suppose we were to accidentally spell *salary* as *salry*, like this:

```
> joe@salry <- 48000
Error in checkSlotAssignment(object, name, value) :
  "salry" is not a slot in class "employee"
```

By contrast, in S3 there would be no error message. S3 classes are just lists, and you are allowed to add a new component (deliberately or not) at any time.

9.2.2 Implementing a Generic Function on an S4 Class

To define an implementation of a generic function on an S4 class, use setMethod(). Let's do that for our class "employee" here. We'll implement the show() function, which is the S4 analog of S3's generic "print".

As you know, in R, when you type the name of a variable while in interactive mode, the value of the variable is printed out:

```
> joe
An object of class "employee"
Slot "name":
[1] "Joe"

Slot "salary":
[1] 88000

Slot "union":
[1] TRUE
```

Since joe is an S4 object, the action here is that show() is called. In fact, we would get the same output by typing this:

```
> show(joe)
```

Let's override that, with the following code:

```
setMethod("show", "employee",
   function(object) {
      inorout <- ifelse(object@union,"is","is not")
      cat(object@name,"has a salary of",object@salary,
         "and",inorout, "in the union", "\n")
   }
)
```

The first argument gives the name of the generic function for which we will define a class-specific method, and the second argument gives the class name. We then define the new function.

Let's try it out:

```
> joe
Joe has a salary of 55000 and is in the union
```

9.3 S3 Versus S4

The type of class to use is the subject of some controversy among R programmers. In essence, your view here will likely depend on your personal choice of which you value more—the convenience of S3 or the safety of S4.

John Chambers, the creator of the S language and one of the central developers of R, recommends S4 over S3 in his book *Software for Data Analysis* (Springer, 2008). He argues that S4 is needed in order to write "clear and reliable software." On the other hand, he notes that S3 remains quite popular.

Google's R Style Guide, which you can find at *http://google-styleguide .googlecode.com/svn/trunk/google-r-style.html*, is interesting in this regard. Google comes down squarely on the S3 side, stating "avoid S4 objects and methods when possible." (Of course, it's also interesting that Google even has an R style guide in the first place!)

NOTE *A nice, concrete comparison of the two methods is given in Thomas Lumley's "Programmer's Niche: A Simple Class, in S3 and S4," R News, April 1, 2004, pp. 33–36.*

9.4 Managing Your Objects

As a typical R session progresses, you tend to accumulate a large number of objects. Various tools are available to manage them. Here, we'll look at the following:

- The ls() function
- The rm() function
- The save() function
- Several functions that tell you more about the structure of an object, such as class() and mode()
- The exists() function

9.4.1 Listing Your Objects with the ls() Function

The ls() command will list all of your current objects. A useful named argument for this function is pattern, which enables *wildcards*. Here, you tell ls() to list only the objects whose names include a specified pattern. The following is an example.

```
> ls()
 [1] "acc"        "acc05"      "binomci"   "cmeans"    "divorg"    "dv"
 [7] "fit"        "g"          "genxc"     "genxnt"    "j"         "lo"
[13] "out1"       "out1.100"   "out1.25"   "out1.50"   "out1.75"   "out2"
[19] "out2.100"   "out2.25"    "out2.50"   "out2.75"   "par.set"   "prpdf"
[25] "ratbootci"  "simonn"     "vecprod"   "x"         "zout"      "zout.100"
[31] "zout.125"   "zout3"      "zout5"     "zout.50"   "zout.75"
> ls(pattern="ut")
 [1] "out1"       "out1.100"  "out1.25"   "out1.50"   "out1.75"   "out2"
 [7] "out2.100"   "out2.25"   "out2.50"   "out2.75"   "zout"      "zout.100"
[13] "zout.125"   "zout3"     "zout5"     "zout.50"   "zout.75"
```

In the second case, we asked for a list of all objects whose names include the string "ut".

9.4.2   Removing Specific Objects with the rm() Function

To remove objects you no longer need, use rm(). Here's an example:

```
> rm(a,b,x,y,z,uuu)
```

This code removes the six specified objects (a, b, and so on).

One of the named arguments of rm() is list, which makes it easier to remove multiple objects. This code assigns all of our objects to list, thus removing everything:

```
> rm(list = ls())
```

Using ls()'s pattern argument, this tool becomes even more powerful. Here's an example:

```
> ls()
 [1] "doexpt"            "notebookline"      "nreps"          "numcorrectcis"
 [5] "numnotebooklines"  "numrules"          "observationpt"  "prop"
 [9] "r"                 "rad"               "radius"         "rep"
[13] "s"                 "s2"                "sim"            "waits"
[17] "wbar"              "x"                 "y"              "z"
> ls(pattern="notebook")
[1] "notebookline"      "numnotebooklines"
> rm(list=ls(pattern="notebook"))
> ls()
 [1] "doexpt"            "nreps"             "numcorrectcis"  "numrules"
 [5] "observationpt"     "prop"              "r"              "rad"
 [9] "radius"            "rep"               "s"              "s2"
[13] "sim"               "waits"             "wbar"           "x"
[17] "y"                 "z"
```

Here, we found two objects whose names include the string "notebook" and then asked to remove them, which was confirmed by the second call to ls().

NOTE *You may find the function browseEnv() helpful. It will show in your web browser your globals (or objects in a different specified environment), with some details on each.*

9.4.3 Saving a Collection of Objects with the save() Function

Calling save() on a collection of objects will write them to disk for later retrieval by load(). Here's a quick example:

```
> z <- rnorm(100000)
> hz <- hist(z)
> save(hz,file="hzfile")
> ls()
[1] "hz" "z"
> rm(hz)
> ls()
[1] "z"
> load("hzfile")
> ls()
[1] "hz" "z"
> plot(hz)  # graph window pops up
```

Here, we generate some data and then draw a histogram of it. But we also save the output of hist() in a variable, hz. That variable is an object (of class "histogram", of course). Anticipating that we will want to reuse this object in a later R session, we use the save() function to save the object to the file *hzfile*. It can be reloaded in that future session via load(). To demonstrate this, we deliberately removed the hz object, then called load() to reload it, and then called ls() to show that it had indeed been reloaded.

I once needed to read in a very large data file, each record of which required processing. I then used save() to keep the R object version of the processed file for future R sessions.

9.4.4 "What Is This?"

Developers often need to know the exact structure of the object returned by a library function. If the documentation does not give sufficient details, what can we do?

The following R functions may be helpful:

- class(), mode()
- names(), attributes()
- unclass(), str()
- edit()

Let's go through an example. R includes facilities for constructing *contingency tables*, which we discussed in Section 6.4. An example in that section involved an election survey in which five respondents are asked whether they intend to vote for candidate X and whether they voted for X in the last election. Here is the resulting table:

```
> cttab <- table(ct)
> cttab
          Voted.for.X.Last.Time
Vote.for.X No Yes
  No        2   0
  Not Sure  0   1
  Yes       1   1
```

For instance, two respondents answered no to both questions.

The object cttab was returned by the function table and thus is likely of class "table". A check of the documentation (?table) confirms this. But what is in the class?

Let's explore the structure of that object cttab of class "table".

```
> ctu <- unclass(cttab)
> ctu
          Votes.for.X.Last.Time
Vote.for.X No Yes
  No        2   0
  Not Sure  0   1
  Yes       1   1
> class(ctu)
[1] "matrix"
```

So, the counts portion of the object is a matrix. (If the data had involved three or more questions, rather than just two, this would have been a higher-dimensional array.) Note that the names of the dimensions and of the individual rows and columns are there, too; they are associated with the matrix.

The unclass() function is quite useful as a first step. If you simply print an object, you are at the mercy of the version of print() associated with that class, which may in the name of succinctness hide or distort some valuable information. Printing the result of calling unclass() allows you to work around this problem, though there was no difference in this example. (You saw an instance in which it did make a difference in the section about S3 generic functions in Section 9.1.1 earlier.) The function str() serves the same purpose, in a more compact manner.

Note, though, applying unclass() to an object still results in an object with some basic class. Here, cttab had the class "table", but unclass(cttab) still had the class "matrix".

Let's try looking at the code for table(), the library function that produced cttab. We could simply type table, but since this is a somewhat longish function, a lot of the function would zoom by on the screen too fast for us to absorb it. We could use page() to solve this problem, but I prefer edit():

```
> edit(table)
```

This allows you to browse through the code with your text editor. In doing so, you'll find this code at the end:

```
y <- array(tabulate(bin, pd), dims, dimnames = dn)
class(y) <- "table"
y
```

Ah, interesting. This shows that table() is, to some extent, a wrapper for another function, tabulate(). But what might be more important here is that the structure of a "table" object is really pretty simple: It consists of an array created from the counts, with the class attribute tacked on. So, it's essentially just an array.

The function names() shows the components in an object, and attributes() gives you this and a bit more, notably the class name.

9.4.5   The exists() Function

The function exists() returns TRUE or FALSE, depending on whether the argument exists. Be sure to put the argument in quotation marks.

For example, the following code shows that the acc object exists:

```
> exists("acc")
[1] TRUE
```

Why would this function be useful? Don't we always know whether or not we've created an object and whether it's still there? Not necessarily. If you are writing general-purpose code, say to be made available to the world in R's CRAN code repository, your code may need to check whether a certain object exists, and if it doesn't, then your code must create it. For example, as you learned in Section 9.4.3, you can save objects to disk files using save() and then later restore them to R's memory space by calling load(). You might write general-purpose code that makes the latter call if the object is not already present, a condition you could check by calling exists().

10

INPUT/OUTPUT

One of the most underemphasized topics in many university programming courses is input/output (I/O). I/O plays a central role in most real-world applications of computers. Just consider an ATM cash machine, which uses multiple I/O operations for both input—reading your card and reading your typed-in cash request—and output—printing instructions on the screen, printing your receipt, and most important, controlling the machine to output your money!

R is not the tool you would choose for running an ATM, but it features a highly versatile array of I/O capabilities, as you will learn in this chapter. We'll start with the basics of access to the keyboard and monitor, and then go into considerable detail on reading and writing files, including the navigation of file directories. Finally, we discuss R's facilities for accessing the Internet.

10.1   Accessing the Keyboard and Monitor

R provides several functions for accesssing the keyboard and monitor. Here, we'll look at the scan(), readline(), print(), and cat() functions.

10.1.1   Using the scan() Function

You can use scan() to read in a vector, whether numeric or character, from a file or the keyboard. With a little extra work, you can even read in data to form a list.

Suppose we have files named *z1.txt*, *z2.txt*, *z3.txt*, and *z4.txt*. The *z1.txt* file contains the following:

```
123
4 5
6
```

The *z2.txt* file contents are as follows:

```
123
4.2 5
6
```

The *z3.txt* file contains this:

```
abc
de f
g
```

And finally, the *z4.txt* file has these contents:

```
abc
123 6
y
```

Let's see what we can do with these files using the scan() function.

```
> scan("z1.txt")
Read 4 items
[1] 123 4 5 6
> scan("z2.txt")
Read 4 items
[1] 123.0 4.2 5.0 6.0
> scan("z3.txt")
Error in scan(file, what, nmax, sep, dec, quote, skip, nlines, na.strings, :
  scan() expected 'a real', got 'abc'
> scan("z3.txt",what="")
```

```
Read 4 items
[1] "abc" "de" "f" "g"
> scan("z4.txt",what="")
Read 4 items
[1] "abc" "123" "6" "y"
```

In the first call, we got a vector of four integers (though the mode is numeric). The second time, since one number was nonintegral, the others were shown as floating-point numbers, too.

In the third case, we got an error. The scan() function has an optional argument named what, which specifies mode, defaulting to double mode. So, the nonnumeric contents of the file *z3* produced an error. But we then tried again, with what="". This assigns a character string to what, indicating that we want character mode. (We could have set what to any character string.)

The last call worked the same way. The first item was a character string, so it treated all the items that followed as strings too.

Of course, in typical usage, we would assign the return value of scan() to a variable. Here's an example:

```
> v <- scan("z1.txt")
```

By default, scan() assumes that the items of the vector are separated by *whitespace*, which includes blanks, carriage return/line feeds, and horizontal tabs. You can use the optional sep argument for other situations. As example, we can set sep to the newline character to read in each line as a string, as follows:

```
> x1 <- scan("z3.txt",what="")
Read 4 items
> x2 <- scan("z3.txt",what="",sep="\n")
Read 3 items
> x1
[1] "abc" "de"  "f"   "g"
> x2
[1] "abc"   "de f" "g"
> x1[2]
[1] "de"
> x2[2]
[1] "de f"
```

In the first case, the strings "de" and "f" were assigned to separate elements of x1. But in the second case, we specified that elements of x2 were to be delineated by end-of-line characters, not spaces. Since "de" and "f" are on the same line, they are assigned together to x[2].

More sophisticated methods for reading files will be presented later in this chapter, such as methods to read in a file one line at a time. But if you want to read the entire file at once, scan() provides a quick solution.

You can use scan() to read from the keyboard by specifying an empty string for the filename:

```
> v <- scan("")
1: 12 5 13
4: 3 4 5
7: 8
8:
Read 7 items
> v
[1] 12  5 13  3  4  5  8
```

Note that we are prompted with the index of the next item to be input, and we signal the end of input with an empty line.

If you do not wish scan() to announce the number of items it has read, include the argument quiet=TRUE.

10.1.2   Using the readline() Function

If you want to read in a single line from the keyboard, readline() is very handy.

```
> w <- readline()
abc de f
> w
[1] "abc de f"
```

Typically, readline() is called with its optional prompt, as follows:

```
> inits <- readline("type your initials:  ")
type your initials:  NM
> inits
[1] "NM"
```

10.1.3   Printing to the Screen

At the top level of interactive mode, you can print the value of a variable or expression by simply typing the variable name or expression. This won't work if you need to print from within the body of a function. In that case, you can use the print() function, like this:

```
> x <- 1:3
> print(x^2)
[1] 1 4 9
```

Recall that print() is a *generic* function, so the actual function called will depend on the class of the object that is printed. If, for example, the argument is of class "table", then the print.table() function will be called.

It's a little better to use cat() instead of print(), as the latter can print only one expression and its output is numbered, which may be a nuisance. Compare the results of the functions:

```
> print("abc")
[1] "abc"
> cat("abc\n")
abc
```

Note that we needed to supply our own end-of-line character, "\n", in the call to cat(). Without it, our next call would continue to write to the same line.

The arguments to cat() will be printed out with intervening spaces:

```
> x
[1] 1 2 3
> cat(x,"abc","de\n")
1 2 3 abc de
```

If you don't want the spaces, set sep to the empty string "", as follows:

```
> cat(x,"abc","de\n",sep="")
123abcde
```

Any string can be used for sep. Here, we use the newline character:

```
> cat(x,"abc","de\n",sep="\n")
1
2
3
abc
de
```

You can even set sep to be a vector of strings, like this:

```
> x <- c(5,12,13,8,88)
> cat(x,sep=c(".",".",".","\n","\n"))
5.12.13.8
88
```

10.2   Reading and Writing Files

Now that we've covered the basics of I/O, let's get to some more practical applications of reading and writing files. The following sections discuss reading data frames or matrices from files, working with text files, accessing files on remote machines, and getting file and directory information.

10.2.1 Reading a Data Frame or Matrix from a File

In Section 5.1.2, we discussed the use of the function read.table() to read in a data frame. As a quick review, suppose the file z looks like this:

```
name age
John 25
Mary 28
Jim 19
```

The first line contains an optional header, specifying column names. We could read the file this way:

```
> z <- read.table("z",header=TRUE)
> z
  name age
1 John  25
2 Mary  28
3  Jim  19
```

Note that scan() would not work here, because our file has a mixture of numeric and character data (and a header).

There appears to be no direct way of reading in a matrix from a file, but it can be done easily with other tools. A simple, quick way is to use scan() to read in the matrix row by row. You use the byrow option in the function matrix() to indicate that you are defining the elements of the matrix in a row-wise, rather than column-wise, manner.

For instance, say the file x contains a 5-by-3 matrix, stored row-wise:

```
1 0 1
1 1 1
1 1 0
1 1 0
0 0 1
```

We can read it into a matrix this way:

```
> x <- matrix(scan("x"),nrow=5,byrow=TRUE)
```

This is fine for quick, one-time operations, but for generality, you can use read.table(), which returns a data frame, and then convert via as.matrix(). Here is a general method:

```
read.matrix <- function(filename) {
   as.matrix(read.table(filename))
}
```

10.2.2 Reading Text Files

In computer literature, there is often a distinction made between *text files* and *binary files*. That distinction is somewhat misleading—every file is binary in the sense that it consists of 0s and 1s. Let's take the term *text file* to mean a file that consists mainly of ASCII characters or coding for some other human language (such as GB for Chinese) and that uses newline characters to give humans the perception of lines. The latter aspect will turn out to be central here. Nontext files, such as JPEG images or executable program files, are generally called *binary files*.

You can use readLines() to read in a text file, either one line at a time or in a single operation. For example, suppose we have a file *z1* with the following contents:

```
John 25
Mary 28
Jim 19
```

We can read the file all at once, like this:

```
> z1 <- readLines("z1")
> z1
[1] "John 25" "Mary 28" "Jim 19"
```

Since each line is treated as a string, the return value here is a vector of strings—that is, a vector of character mode. There is one vector element for each line read, thus three elements here.

Alternatively, we can read it in one line at a time. For this, we first need to create a connection, as described next.

10.2.3 Introduction to Connections

Connection is R's term for a fundamental mechanism used in various kinds of I/O operations. Here, it will be used for file access.

The connection is created by calling file(), url(), or one of several other R functions. To see a list of those functions, type this:

```
> ?connection
```

So, we can now read in the *z1* file (introduced in the previous section) line by line, as follows:

```
> c <- file("z1","r")
> readLines(c,n=1)
[1] "John 25"
> readLines(c,n=1)
[1] "Mary 28"
> readLines(c,n=1)
[1] "Jim 19"
```

```
> readLines(c,n=1)
character(0)
```

We opened the connection, assigned the result to c, and then read the file one line at a time, as specified by the argument n=1. When R encountered the end of file (EOF), it returned an empty result. We needed to set up a connection so that R could keep track of our position in the file as we read through it.

We can detect EOF in our code:

```
> c <- file("z","r")
> while(TRUE) {
+     rl <- readLines(c,n=1)
+     if (length(rl) == 0) {
+         print("reached the end")
+         break
+     } else print(rl)
+ }
[1] "John 25"
[1] "Mary 28"
[1] "Jim 19"
[1] "reached the end"
```

If we wish to "rewind"—to start again at the beginning of the file—we can use seek():

```
> c <- file("z1","r")
> readLines(c,n=2)
[1] "John 25" "Mary 28"
> seek(con=c,where=0)
[1] 16
> readLines(c,n=1)
[1] "John 25"
```

The argument where=0 in our call to seek() means that we wish to position the file pointer zero characters from the start of the file—in other words, directly at the beginning.

The call returns 16, meaning that the file pointer was at position 16 before we made the call. That makes sense. The first line consists of "John 25" *plus* the end-of-line character, for a total of eight characters, and the same is true for the second line. So, after reading the first two lines, we were at position 16.

You can close a connection by calling—what else?—close(). You would use this to let the system know that the file you have been writing is complete and should now be officially written to disk. As another example, in a client/server relationship over the Internet (see Section 10.3.1), a client would use close() to indicate to the server that the client is signing off.

10.2.4 Extended Example: Reading PUMS Census Files

The U.S. Census Bureau makes census data available in the form of Public Use Microdata Samples (PUMS). The term *microdata* here means that we are dealing with raw data and each record is for a real person, as opposed to statistical summaries. Data on many, many variables are included.

The data is organized by household. For each unit, there is first a Household record, describing the various characteristics of that household, followed by one Person record for each person in the household. Character positions 106 and 107 (with numbering starting at 1) in the Household record state the number of Person records for that household. (The number can be very large, since some institutions count as households.)

To enhance the integrity of the data, character position 1 contains H or P to confirm that this is a Household or Person record. So, if you read an H record, and it tells you there are three people in the household, then the following three records should be P records, followed by another H record; if not, you've encountered an error.

As our test file, we'll take the first 1,000 records of the year 2000 1 percent sample. The first few records look like this:

```
H000019510649     06010       99979997  70                                    631973
15758   5996765843665000001200000 0 0 0 0 0 0 0 0 0 0 0     0    0    0
0    0 0 0      0 0    0 0000 0    0    0  0 0    00000000000000000000000000000
000000000000000000000000000
P00001950100010923000420190010110000010147050600206011099999904200000 0040010000
00300280    28600  70   9997    99972020202020202220000040000000000000006000000
     00000  00   0000   00000000000000000132241057904MS    476041-20311010310
07000049010000000000900100000100000100001000001000001000139010000490000
H000040710649     06010       99979997  70                                    631973
15758   5996765843653008002000003001060605030101010102010 01200006000000100001
00600020 0     0 0    0 0000 0    0    0  0 0    02000102010102200000000010750
02321125100004000000040000
P00004070100005301000010380010110000010147030400100009005199901200000 0006010000
00100000    00000  00   0000   0000202020202020222000004000000000000000001000060
     06010  70   9997    99970101004900100000001018703221    770051-10111010500
40004000000000000000000000000000000000000000000000004000000040000349
P00004070200005303011010140010110000010147050000204004005199901200000 0006010000
00100000    00000  00   0000   000020202020 0 02000000000000000000000000050000
     00000  00   0000   000000000000000000000000000000000000000000000-00000000000
000    0    0    0    0    0    0    0    0    00000000349
H000061010649     06010       99979997  70                                    631973
15758   5996765843608011901000002002040305020101010102010 00770004800064000001
1    0 030    0 0    0 0340 00660000000170 0    06010000000004410039601000000
00021100000004940000000000
```

The records are very wide and thus wrap around. Each one occupies four lines on the page here.

We'll create a function called extractpums() to read in a PUMS file and create a data frame from its Person records. The user specifies the filename and lists fields to extract and names to assign to those fields.

We also want to retain the household serial number. This is good to have because data for persons in the same household may be correlated and we may want to add that aspect to our statistical model. Also, the household data may provide important covariates. (In the latter case, we would want to retain the covariate data as well.)

Before looking at the function code, let's see what the function does. In this data set, gender is in column 23 and age in columns 25 and 26. In the example, our filename is *pumsa*. The following call creates a data frame consisting of those two variables.

```
pumsdf <- extractpums("pumsa",list(Gender=c(23,23),Age=c(25,26)))
```

Note that we are stating here the names we want the columns to have in the resulting data frame. We can use any names we want—say Sex and Ancientness.

Here is the first part of that data frame:

```
> head(pumsdf)
  serno Gender Age
2   195      2  19
3   407      1  38
4   407      1  14
5   610      2  65
6  1609      1  50
7  1609      2  49
```

The following is the code for the extractpums() function.

```
1  # reads in PUMS file pf, extracting the Person records, returning a data
2  # frame; each row of the output will consist of the Household serial
3  # number and the fields specified in the list flds; the columns of
4  # the data frame will have the names of the indices in flds
5
6  extractpums <- function(pf,flds) {
7     dtf <- data.frame() # data frame to be built
8     con <- file(pf,"r") # connection
9     # process the input file
10    repeat {
11       hrec <- readLines(con,1) # read Household record
12       if (length(hrec) == 0) break # end of file, leave loop
13       # get household serial number
14       serno <- intextract(hrec,c(2,8))
```

```
15      # how many Person records?
16      npr <- intextract(hrec,c(106,107))
17      if (npr > 0)
18         for (i in 1:npr) {
19            prec <- readLines(con,1) # get Person record
20            # make this person's row for the data frame
21            person <- makerow(serno,prec,flds)
22            # add it to the data frame
23            dtf <- rbind(dtf,person)
24         }
25      }
26    return(dtf)
27 }
28
29 # set up this person's row for the data frame
30 makerow <- function(srn,pr,fl) {
31    l <- list()
32    l[["serno"]] <- srn
33    for (nm in names(fl)) {
34       l[[nm]] <- intextract(pr,fl[[nm]])
35    }
36    return(l)
37 }
38
39 # extracts an integer field in the string s, in character positions
40 # rng[1] through rng[2]
41 intextract <- function(s,rng) {
42    fld <- substr(s,rng[1],rng[2])
43    return(as.integer(fld))
44 }
```

Let's see how this works. At the beginning of extractpums(), we create an empty data frame and set up the connection for the PUMS file read.

```
dtf <- data.frame()  # data frame to be built
con <- file(pf,"r")  # connection
```

The main body of the code then consists of a repeat loop.

```
repeat {
    hrec <- readLines(con,1) # read Household record
    if (length(hrec) == 0) break # end of file, leave loop
    # get household serial number
    serno <- intextract(hrec,c(2,8))
    # how many Person records?
    npr <- intextract(hrec,c(106,107))
```

```
if (npr > 0)
   for (i in 1:npr) {
      ...
   }
}
```

This loop iterates until the end of the input file is reached. The latter condition will be sensed by encountering a zero-length Household record, as seen in the preceding code.

Within the repeat loop, we alternate reading a Household record and reading the associated Person records. The number of Person records for the current Household record is extracted from columns 106 and 107 of that record, storing this number in npr. That extraction is done by a call to our function intextract().

The for loop then reads in the Person records one by one, in each case forming the desired row for the output data frame and then attaching it to the latter via rbind():

```
for (i in 1:npr) {
   prec <- readLines(con,1)  # get Person record
   # make this person's row for the data frame
   person <- makerow(serno,prec,flds)
   # add it to the data frame
   dtf <- rbind(dtf,person)
}
```

Note how makerow() creates the row to be added for a given person. Here the formal arguments are srn for the household serial number, pr for the given Person record, and fl for the list of variable names and column fields.

```
makerow <- function(srn,pr,fl) {
   l <- list()
   l[["serno"]] <- srn
   for (nm in names(fl)) {
      l[[nm]] <- intextract(pr,fl[[nm]])
   }
   return(l)
}
```

For instance, consider our sample call:

```
pumsdf <- extractpums("pumsa",list(Gender=c(23,23),Age=c(25,26)))
```

When makerow() executes, fl will be a list with two elements, named Gender and Age. The string pr, the current Person record, will have Gender in column 23 and Age in columns 25 and 26. We call intextract() to pull out the desired numbers.

The intextract() function itself is a straightforward conversion of characters to numbers, such as converting the string "12" to the number 12.

Note that, if not for the presence of Household records, we could do all of this much more easily with a handy built-in R function: read.fwf(). The name of this function is an abbreviation for "read fixed-width formatted," alluding to the fact that each variable is stored in given character positions of a record. In essence, this function alleviates the need to write a function like intextract().

10.2.5   Accessing Files on Remote Machines via URLs

Certain I/O functions, such as read.table() and scan(), accept web URLs as arguments. (Check R's online help facility to see if your favorite function allows this.)

As an example, we'll read some data from the University of California, Irvine archive at *http://archive.ics.uci.edu/ml/datasets.html*, using the Echocardiogram data set. After navigating the links, we find the location of that file and then read it from R, as follows:

```
> uci <- "http://archive.ics.uci.edu/ml/machine-learning-databases/"
> uci <- paste(uci,"echocardiogram/echocardiogram.data",sep="")
> ecc <- read.csv(uci)
```

(We've built up the URL in stages here to fit the page.)

Let's take a look at what we downloaded:

```
> head(ecc)
  X11 X0 X71 X0.1 X0.260     X9 X4.600 X14    X1 X1.1 name X1.2 X0.2
1  19  0  72    0 0.380       6  4.100  14 1.700 0.588 name    1    0
2  16  0  55    0 0.260       4  3.420  14     1     1 name    1    0
3  57  0  60    0 0.253 12.062  4.603  16 1.450 0.788 name    1    0
4  19  1  57    0 0.160      22  5.750  18 2.250 0.571 name    1    0
5  26  0  68    0 0.260       5  4.310  12     1 0.857 name    1    0
6  13  0  62    0 0.230      31  5.430 22.5 1.875 0.857 name    1    0
```

We could then do our analyses. For example, the third column is age, so we could find its mean or perform other calculations on that data. See the echocardiogram.names page at *http://archive.ics.uci.edu/ml/machine-learning-databases/echocardiogram/echocardiogram.names* for descriptions of all of the variables.

10.2.6   Writing to a File

Given the statistical basis of R, file reads are probably much more common than writes. But writes are sometimes necessary, and this section will present methods for writing to files.

The function write.table() works very much like read.table(), except that it writes a data frame instead of reading one. For instance, let's take the little Jack and Jill example from the beginning of Chapter 5:

```
> kids <- c("Jack","Jill")
> ages <- c(12,10)
> d <- data.frame(kids,ages,stringsAsFactors=FALSE)
> d
  kids ages
1 Jack   12
2 Jill   10
> write.table(d,"kds")
```

The file *kds* will now have these contents:

```
"kids" "ages"
"1" "Jack" 12
"2" "Jill" 10
```

In the case of writing a matrix to a file, just state that you do not want row or column names, as follows:

```
> write.table(xc,"xcnew",row.names=FALSE,col.names=FALSE)
```

The function cat() can also be used to write to a file, one part at a time. Here's an example:

```
> cat("abc\n",file="u")
> cat("de\n",file="u",append=TRUE)
```

The first call to cat() creates the file *u*, consisting of one line with contents "abc". The second call appends a second line. Unlike the case of using the writeLines() function (which we'll discuss next), the file is automatically saved after each operation. For instance, after the previous calls, the file will look like this:

```
abc
de
```

You can write multiple fields as well. So:

```
> cat(file="v",1,2,"xyz\n")
```

would produce a file *v* consisting of a single line:

```
1 2 xyz
```

You can also use writeLines(), the counterpart of readLines(). If you use a connection, you must specify "w" to indicate you are writing to the file, not reading from it:

```
> c <- file("www","w")
> writeLines(c("abc","de","f"),c)
> close(c)
```

The file *www* will be created with these contents:

```
abc
de
f
```

Note the need to proactively close the file.

10.2.7   Getting File and Directory Information

R has a variety of functions for getting information about directories and files, setting file access permissions, and the like. The following are a few examples:

- file.info(): Gives file size, creation time, directory-versus-ordinary file status, and so on for each file whose name is in the argument, a character vector.

- dir(): Returns a character vector listing the names of all the files in the directory specified in its first argument. If the optional argument recursive=TRUE is specified, the result will show the entire directory tree rooted at the first argument.

- file.exists(): Returns a Boolean vector indicating whether the given file exists for each name in the first argument, a character vector.

- getwd() and setwd(): Used to determine or change the current working directory.

To see all the file- and directory-related functions, type the following:

```
> ?files
```

Some of these options will be demonstrated in the next example.

10.2.8   Extended Example: Sum the Contents of Many Files

Here, we'll develop a function to find the sum of the contents (assumed numeric) in all files in a directory tree. In our example, a directory *dir1* contains the files *filea* and *fileb*, as well as a subdirectory *dir2*, which holds the file *filec*. The contents of the files are as follows:

* *filea*: 5, 12, 13

* *fileb*: 3, 4, 5

* *filec*: 24, 25, 7

If *dir1* is in our current directory, the call sumtree("dir1") will yield the sum of those nine numbers, 98. Otherwise, we need to specify the full pathname of *dir1*, such as sumtree("/home/nm/dir1"). Here is the code:

```
1   sumtree <- function(drtr) {
2       tot <- 0
3       # get names of all files in the tree
4       fls <- dir(drtr,recursive=TRUE)
5       for (f in fls) {
6           # is f a directory?
7           f <- file.path(drtr,f)
8           if (!file.info(f)$isdir) {
9               tot <- tot + sum(scan(f,quiet=TRUE))
10          }
11      }
12      return(tot)
13  }
```

Note that this problem is a natural for recursion, which we discussed in Section 7.9. But here, R has done the recursion for us by allowing it as an option in dir(). Thus, in line 4, we set recursive=TRUE in order to find the files throughout the various levels of the directory tree.

To call file.info(), we need to account for the fact that the current filename *f* is relative to drtr, so our file *filea* would be referred to as *dir1/filea*. In order to form that pathname, we need to concatenate drtr, a slash, and filea. We could use the R string concatenation function paste() for this, but we would need a separate case for Windows, which uses a backslash instead of a slash. But file.path() does all that for us.

Some commentary pertaining to line 8 is in order. The function file.info() returns information about f as a data frame, one of whose columns is isdir, with one row for each file and with row names being the filenames. That column consists of Boolean values indicating whether each file is a directory. In line 8, then, we can detect whether the current file *f* is a directory. If *f* is an ordinary file, we go ahead and add its contents to our running total.

10.3   Accessing the Internet

R's socket facilities give the programmer access to the Internet's TCP/IP protocol. For readers who are not familiar with this protocol, we begin with an overview of TCP/IP.

10.3.1 Overview of TCP/IP

TCP/IP is quite complex, so the overview here will be something of an over-simplification, but we'll cover enough for you to understand what R's socket functions are doing.

For our purposes here, the term *network* refers to a set of computers connected together locally, without going through the Internet. This typically consists of all the computers in a home, all the computers in a smaller business, and so on. The physical medium between them is usually an Ethernet connection of some form.

The Internet, as its name implies, connects networks. A network in the Internet is connected to one or more other networks via *routers*, which are special-purpose computers that connect two or more networks together. Every computer on the Internet has an Internet Protocol (IP) address. This is numeric, but it can be stated in characters, as in *www.google.com*, which is then translated into the numeric address by the Domain Name Service.

However, the IP address is not enough. When A sends a message to B, there may be several applications at computer B that are receiving Internet messages, such as web browsing, email service, and so on. How does the operating system at B know to which of these to send the message from A? The answer is that A will specify a *port number* in addition to the IP address. The port number indicates which program running at B is intended as the recipient. And A will also have a port number so that the response from B reaches the correct application at A.

When A wishes to send something to B, it writes to a software entity called a *socket*, using a system call syntactically similar to the one for writing to a file. In the call, A specifies B's IP address and the port number to which A wishes to send a message. B has a socket, too, and it writes its responses to A in that socket. We say there is a *connection* between A and B via those sockets, but that doesn't mean anything physical—it's just an agreement between A and B to exchange data.

Applications follow a *client/server* model. Say a web server is running at B, at the standard port for the Web, port 80. The server at B is *listening* at port 80. Again, this term should not be taken literally; it just means that the server program has made a function call that notifies the operating system that the server program is willing to have connections at port 80. When network node A requests such a connection, the function call at the server returns, and the connection is set up.

If you are a nonprivileged user and write some kind of server program—say in R!—you must assign a port number above 1024.

NOTE   *If a server program is taken down or crashes, there may be a few seconds' delay before the same port is reusable again.*

10.3.2 Sockets in R

A very important point to keep in mind is that all the bytes sent by A to B during the time the connection between them exists are collectively considered *one big message*. Say A sends one line of text of 8 characters and then another of 20 characters. From A's point of view, that's two lines, but to TCP/IP, it's just 28 characters of a yet incomplete message. Splitting that long message back into lines can take a bit of doing. R provides various functions for this purpose, including the following:

- readLines() and writeLines(): These allow you to program as if TCP/IP were sending messages line by line, even though this is not actually the case. If your application is naturally viewed in terms of lines, these two functions can be quite handy.

- serialize() and unserialize(): You can use these to send R objects, such as a matrix or the complex output of a call to a statistical function. The object is converted to character string form by the sender and then converted back to the original object form at the receiver.

- readBin() and writeBin(): These are for sending data in binary form. (Recall the comment on terminology at the beginning of Section 10.2.2.)

Each of these functions operates on R connections, as you'll see in the next example.

It's important to choose the right function for each job. If you have a long vector, for example, using serialize() and unserialize() may be more convenient but far more time-consuming. This is not only because numbers must be converted to and from their character representations but also because the character representation is typically much longer, which means greater transmission time.

Here are two other R socket functions:

- socketConnection(): This establishes an R connection via sockets. You specify the port number in the argument port, and state whether a server or client is to be created, by setting the argument server to TRUE or FALSE, respectively. In the client case, you must also supply the server's IP address in the argument host.

- socketSelect(): This is useful when a server is connected to multiple clients. Its main argument, socklist, is a list of connections, and its return value is the sublist of connections that have data ready for the server to read.

10.3.3   Extended Example: Implementing Parallel R

Some statistical analyses have very long runtimes, so there naturally has been quite a bit of interest in "parallel R," in which several R processes cooperate on a given task. Another possible reason to "go parallel" is memory limitations. If one machine does not have enough memory for the task at hand, it may help to pool the memories of several machines in some way. Chapter 16 gives an introduction to this important topic.

Sockets play a key role in many parallel R packages. The cooperating R processes could be either on the same machine or on separate machines. In the latter case (and even the former), a natural approach to implementing parallelism is to use R sockets. This is one of the choices in the snow package and in my Rdsm package (both available on CRAN, R's code repository; see this book's appendix for details), as follows:

- In snow, the server sends out work tasks to the clients. The clients perform their tasks and send the results back to the server, which assembles them into the final result. Communication is done with serialize() and unserialize(), and the server uses socketSelect() to determine which client results are ready.

- Rdsm implements a virtual shared-memory paradigm, and the server is used to store the shared variables. The clients contact the server whenever they need to read or write a shared variable. To optimize speed, communication between server and clients is done with readBin() and writebin(), instead of serialize() and unserialize().

Let's look at some of the socket-related details of Rdsm. First, here is the server code in which connections with the clients are set up, storing them in a list cons (there are ncon clients):

```
1   # set up socket connections with clients
2   #
3   cons <<- vector(mode="list",length=ncon)  # list of connections
4   # prevent connection from dying during debug or long compute spell
5   options("timeout"=10000)
6   for (i in 1:ncon) {
7      cons[[i]] <<-
8         socketConnection(port=port,server=TRUE,blocking=TRUE,open="a+b")
9      # wait to hear from client i
10     checkin <- unserialize(cons[[i]])
11  }
12  # send ACKs
13  for (i in 1:ncon) {
14     # send the client its ID number, and the group size
15     serialize(c(i,ncon),cons[[i]])
16  }
```

Since the client messages and server acknowledgments are short messages, serialize() and unserialize() are good enough for the purpose here.

The first part of the main loop of the server finds a ready client and reads from it.

```
1   repeat {
2      # any clients still there?
3      if (remainingclients == 0) break
4      # wait for service request, then read it
5      # find all the pending client requests
6      rdy <- which(socketSelect(cons))
7      # choose one
8      j <- sample(1:length(rdy),1)
```

```
9    con <- cons[[rdy[j]]]
10   # read client request
11   req <- unserialize(con)
```

Again serialize() and unserialize() are good enough here to read the short message from the client indicating what kind of operation—typically reading a shared variable or writing one—it's requesting. But the reads and writes of the shared variables themselves use the faster readBin() and writeBin() functions. Here's the write part:

```
# write data dt, of mode md (integer of double), to connection cn
binwrite <- function(dt,md,cn) {
    writeBin(dt,con=cn)
```

And here's the read part:

```
# read sz elements of mode md (integer of double) from connection cn
binread <- function(cn,md,sz) {
    return(readBin(con=cn,what=md,n=sz))
```

On the client side, the connection setup code is as follows:

```
1   options("timeout"=10000)
2   # connect to server
3   con <- socketConnection(host=host,port=port,blocking=TRUE,open="a+b")
4   serialize(list(req="checking in"),con)
5   # receive this client's ID and total number of clients from server
6   myidandnclnt <- unserialize(con)
7   myinfo <<-
8       list(con=con,myid=myidandnclnt[1],nclnt=myidandnclnt[2])
```

The code for reading from and writing to the server is similar to the preceding server examples.

11

STRING MANIPULATION

Although R is a statistical language with numeric vectors and matrices playing a central role, character strings are surprisingly important as well. Ranging from birth dates stored in medical research data files to text-mining applications, character data arises quite frequently in R programs. Accordingly, R has a number of string-manipulation utilities, many of which will be introduced in this chapter.

11.1 An Overview of String-Manipulation Functions

Here, we'll briefly review just some of the many string-manipulation functions R has to offer. Note that the call forms shown in this introduction are very simple, usually omitting many optional arguments. We'll use some of those arguments in our extended examples later in the chapter, but do check R's online help for further details.

11.1.1 grep()

The call grep(pattern,x) searches for a specified substring pattern in a vector x of strings. If x has *n* elements—that is, it contains *n* strings—then grep(pattern,x) will return a vector of length up to *n*. Each element of this vector will be the index in x at which a match of pattern as a substring of x[i]) was found.

Here's an example of using grep:

```
> grep("Pole",c("Equator","North Pole","South Pole"))
[1] 2 3
> grep("pole",c("Equator","North Pole","South Pole"))
integer(0)
```

In the first case, the string "Pole" was found in elements 2 and 3 of the second argument, hence the output (2,3). In the second case, string "pole" was not found anywhere, so an empty vector was returned.

11.1.2 nchar()

The call nchar(x) finds the length of a string x. Here's an example:

```
> nchar("South Pole")
[1] 10
```

The string "South Pole" was found to have 10 characters. C programmers, take note: There is no NULL character terminating R strings.

Also note that the results of nchar() will be unpredictable if x is not in character mode. For instance, nchar(NA) turns out to be 2, and nchar(factor("abc")) is 1. For more consistent results on nonstring objects, use Hadley Wickham's stringr package on CRAN.

11.1.3 paste()

The call paste(...) concatenates several strings, returning the result in one long string. Here are some examples:

```
> paste("North","Pole")
[1] "North Pole"
> paste("North","Pole",sep="")
[1] "NorthPole"
> paste("North","Pole",sep=".")
[1] "North.Pole"
> paste("North","and","South","Poles")
[1] "North and South Poles"
```

As you can see, the optional argument sep can be used to put something other than a space between the pieces being spliced together. If you specify sep as an empty string, the pieces won't have any character between them.

11.1.4 sprintf()

The call sprintf(...) assembles a string from parts in a formatted manner. Here's a simple example:

```
> i <- 8
> s <- sprintf("the square of %d is %d",i,i^2)
> s
[1] "the square of 8 is 64"
```

The name of the function is intended to evoke *string print* for "printing" to a string rather than to the screen. Here, we are printing to the string s.

What are we printing? The function says to first print "the square of" and then print the decimal value of i. (The term *decimal* here means in the base-10 number system, not that there will be a decimal point in the result.) The result is the string "the square of 8 is 64."

11.1.5 substr()

The call substr(x,start,stop) returns the substring in the given character position range start:stop in the given string x. Here's an example:

```
> substring("Equator",3,5)
[1] "uat"
```

11.1.6 strsplit()

The call strsplit(x,split) splits a string x into an R list of substrings based on another string split in x. Here's an example:

```
> strsplit("6-16-2011",split="-")
[[1]]
[1] "6"     "16"     "2011"
```

11.1.7 regexpr()

The call regexpr(pattern,text) finds the character position of the first instance of pattern within text, as in this example:

```
> regexpr("uat","Equator")
[1] 3
```

This reports that "uat" did indeed appear in "Equator," starting at character position 3.

11.1.8 gregexpr()

The call gregexpr(pattern,text) is the same as regexpr(), but it finds all instances of pattern. Here's an example:

```
> gregexpr("iss","Mississippi")
[[1]]
[1] 2 5
```

This finds that "iss" appears twice in "Mississippi," starting at character positions 2 and 5.

11.2 Regular Expressions

When dealing with string-manipulation functions in programming languages, the notion of *regular expressions* sometimes arises. In R, you must pay attention to this point when using the string functions grep(), grepl(), regexpr(), gregexpr(), sub(), gsub(), and strsplit().

A regular expression is a kind of wild card. It's shorthand to specify broad classes of strings. For example, the expression "[au]" refers to any string that contains either of the letters *a* or *u*. You could use it like this:

```
> grep("[au]",c("Equator","North Pole","South Pole"))
[1] 1 3
```

This reports that elements 1 and 3 of ("Equator","North Pole","South Pole")—that is, "Equator" and "South Pole"—contain either an *a* or a *u*.

A period (.) represents any single character. Here's an example of using it:

```
> grep("o.e",c("Equator","North Pole","South Pole"))
[1] 2 3
```

This searches for three-character strings in which an *o* is followed by any single character, which is in turn followed by an *e*. Here is an example of the use of two periods to represent any pair of characters:

```
> grep("N..t",c("Equator","North Pole","South Pole"))
[1] 2
```

Here, we searched for four-letter strings consisting of an *N*, followed by any pair of characters, followed by a *t*.

A period is an example of a *metacharacter*, which is a character that is not to be taken literally. For example, if a period appears in the first argument of grep(), it doesn't actually mean a period; it means any character.

But what if you want to search for a period using grep()? Here's the naive approach:

```
> grep(".",c("abc","de","f.g"))
[1] 1 2 3
```

The result should have been 3, not (1,2,3). This call failed because periods are metacharacters. You need to *escape* the metacharacter nature of the period, which is done via a backslash:

```
> grep("\\.",c("abc","de","f.g"))
[1] 3
```

Now, didn't I say *a* backslash? Then why are there two? Well, the sad truth is that the backslash itself must be escaped, which is accomplished by its own backslash! This goes to show how arcanely complex regular expressions can become. Indeed, a number of books have been written on the subject of regular expressions (for various programming languages). As a start in learning about the topic, refer to R's online help (type ?regex).

11.2.1   Extended Example: Testing a Filename for a Given Suffix

Suppose we wish to test for a specified suffix in a filename. We might, for instance, want to find all HTML files (those with suffix *.html*, *.htm*, and so on). Here is code for that:

```
1  testsuffix <- function(fn,suff) {
2     parts <- strsplit(fn,".",fixed=TRUE)
3     nparts <- length(parts[[1]])
4     return(parts[[1]][nparts] == suff)
5  }
```

Let's test it.

```
> testsuffix("x.abc","abc")
[1] TRUE
> testsuffix("x.abc","ac")
[1] FALSE
> testsuffix("x.y.abc","ac")
[1] FALSE
> testsuffix("x.y.abc","abc")
[1] TRUE
```

How does the function work? First note that the call to strsplit() on line 2 returns a list consisting of one element (because fn is a one-element vector)—a vector of strings. For example, calling testsuffix("x.y.abc","abc") will result in parts being a list consisting of a three-element vector with elements x, y, and abc. We then pick up the last element and compare it to suff.

A key aspect is the argument fixed=TRUE. Without it, the splitting argument . (called split in the list of strsplit()'s formal arguments) would have been treated as a regular expression. Without setting fixed=TRUE, strsplit() would have just separated all the letters.

Of course, we could also escape the period, as follows:

```
testsuffix <- function(fn,suff) {
    parts <- strsplit(fn,"\\.")
    nparts <- length(parts[[1]])
    return(parts[[1]][nparts] == suff)
}
```

Let's check to see if it still works.

```
> testsuffix("x.y.abc","abc")
[1] TRUE
```

Here's another way to do the suffix-test code that's a bit more involved but a good illustration:

```
testsuffix <- function(fn,suff) {
    ncf <- nchar(fn)  # nchar() gives the string length
    # determine where the period would start if suff is the suffix in fn
    dotpos <- ncf - nchar(suff) + 1
    # now check that suff is there
    return(substr(fn,dotpos,ncf)==suff)
}
```

Let's look at the call to substr() here, again with fn = "x.ac" and suff = "abc". In this case, dotpos will be 1, which means there should be a period at the first character in fn if there is an abc suffix. The call to substr() then becomes substr("x.ac",1,4), which extracts the substring in character positions 1 through 4 of x.ac. That substring will be x.ac, which is not abc, so the filename's suffix is found not to be the latter.

11.2.2 *Extended Example: Forming Filenames*

Suppose we want to create five files, *q1.pdf* through *q5.pdf*, consisting of histograms of 100 random $N(0,i^2)$ variates. We could execute the following code:

```
for (i in 1:5)  {
    fname <- paste("q",i,".pdf")
    pdf(fname)
    hist(rnorm(100,sd=i))
    dev.off()
}
```

The main point in this example is the string manipulation we use to create the filename fname. For more details about the graphics operations used in this example, refer to Section 12.3.

The paste() function concatenates the string "q" with the string form of the number i. For example, when i = 2, the variable fname will be q 2 .pdf. However, that isn't quite what we want. On Linux systems, filenames with embedded spaces create headaches, so we want to remove the spaces. One solution is to use the sep argument, specifying an empty string for the separator, as follows:

```
for (i in 1:5)  {
    fname <- paste("q",i,".pdf",sep="")
    pdf(fname)
    hist(rnorm(100,sd=i))
    dev.off()
}
```

Another approach is to employ the sprintf() function, borrowed from C:

```
for (i in 1:5)  {
    fname <- sprintf("q%d.pdf",i)
    pdf(fname)
    hist(rnorm(100,sd=i))
    dev.off()
}
```

For floating-point quantities, note also the difference between %f and %g formats:

```
> sprintf("abc%fdef",1.5)
[1] "abc1.500000def"
> sprintf("abc%gdef",1.5)
[1] "abc1.5def"
```

The %g format eliminated the superfluous zeros.

11.3   Use of String Utilities in the edtdbg Debugging Tool

The internal code of the edtdbg debugging tool, which will be discussed in Section 13.4, makes heavy use of string utilities. A typical example of such usage is the dgbsendeditcmd() function:

```
# send command to editor
dbgsendeditcmd <- function(cmd) {
    syscmd <- paste("vim --remote-send ",cmd," --servername ",vimserver,sep="")
    system(syscmd)
}
```

What is going on here? The main point is that `edtdbg` sends remote commands to the Vim text editor. For instance, if you are running Vim with a server name of 168 and you want the cursor in Vim to move to line 12, you could type this into a terminal (shell) window:

```
vim --remote-send 12G --servername 168
```

The effect would be the same as if you had physically typed 12G at the Vim window. Since 12G is the Vim command to move the cursor to line 12, that's what would occur. Consider this call:

```
paste("vim --remote-send ",cmd," --servername ",vimserver,sep="")
```

Here, `cmd` is the string `"12G"`, `vimserver` is 168, and `paste()` concatenates all the indicated strings. The argument `sep=""` says to use the empty string as separator in this concatenation—that is, no separation. Thus, `paste()` returns the following:

```
vim --remote-send 12G --servername 168
```

Another core element in the operation of `edtdbg` is that the program has arranged, via a call to R's `sink()` function, to record to the file *dbgsink* most output from R's debugger in your R window. (The `edtdbg` utility works in concert with that debugger.) That information includes the line numbers of your positions in your source file as you step through it using R's debugger.

The line position information in the debugger output looks like this:

```
debug at cities.r#16: {
```

So, there is code in `edtdbg` to determine the latest line in *dbgsink* that begins with "debug at." That line is then placed, as a string, in a variable named `debugline`. The following code then extracts the line number (16 in the example) and the source filename/Vim buffer name (*cities.r* here):

```
linenumstart <- regexpr("#",debugline) + 1
buffname <- substr(debugline,10,linenumstart-2)
colon <- regexpr(":",debugline)
linenum <- substr(debugline,linenumstart,colon-1)
```

The call to `regexpr()` determines where in `debugline` the # character is located (character 18 in this example). Adding 1 to that gives the position of the line number within `debugline`.

To get the buffer name, using the preceding example as a guide, we see that the name comes after debug at and ends just before the #. Since "debug at" contains nine characters, the buffer name will start at position 10—hence the 10 in the call,

```
substr(debugline,10,linenumstart-2)
```

The end of the buffer name field is at linenumstart-2, as it is just before the #, which precedes the start of the line number. The line number computation is then similar.

Another illustrative example of edtdbg's internal code is its use of the strsplit() function. For example, at one point, it prints out a prompt to the user:

```
kbdin <- readline(prompt="enter number(s) of fns you wish to toggle dbg: ")
```

As you can see, the user's response is stored in kbdin. It will consist of a set of numbers separated by spaces, such as this:

```
1 4 5
```

We need to extract the numbers from the string 1 4 5 into an integer vector. This is done first via strsplit(), which produces three strings: "1", "4", and "5". Then we call as.integer() to convert from characters to numbers:

```
tognums <- as.integer(strsplit(kbdin,split=" ")[[1]])
```

Note that the output of strsplit() is an R list, in this case consisting of one element, which is in turn the vector ("1","4","5"). This leads to the expression [[1]] in the example.

12

GRAPHICS

R has a very rich set of graphics facilities. The R home page (*http://www.r-project.org/*) has a few colorful examples, but to really appreciate R's graphical power, browse through the R Graph Gallery at *http://addictedtor.free.fr/graphiques.*

In this chapter, we cover the basics of using R's base, or traditional, graphics package. This will give you enough foundation to start working with graphics in R. If you're interested in pursuing R graphics further, you may want to refer to the excellent books on the subject.[1]

12.1 Creating Graphs

To begin, we'll look at the foundational function for creating graphs: plot(). Then we'll explore how to build a graph, from adding lines and points to attaching a legend.

---

[1] These include Hadley Wickham, *ggplot2: Elegant Graphics for Data Analysis* (New York: Springer-Verlag, 2009); Dianne Cook and Deborah F. Swayne, *Interactive and Dynamic Graphics for Data Analysis: With R and GGobi* (New York: Springer-Verlag, 2007); Deepayan Sarkar, *Lattice: Multivariate Data Visualization with R* (New York: Springer-Verlag, 2008); and Paul Murrell, *R Graphics* (Boca Raton, FL: Chapman and Hall/CRC, 2011).

12.1.1   The Workhorse of R Base Graphics: The plot() Function

The plot() function forms the foundation for much of R's base graphing operations, serving as the vehicle for producing many different kinds of graphs. As mentioned in Section 9.1.1, plot() is a generic function, or a placeholder for a family of functions. The function that is actually called depends on the class of the object on which it is called.

Let's see what happens when we call plot() with an X vector and a Y vector, which are interpreted as a set of pairs in the (x,y) plane.

```
> plot(c(1,2,3), c(1,2,4))
```

This will cause a window to pop up, plotting the points (1,1), (2,2), and (3,4), as shown in Figure 12-1. As you can see, this is a very plain-Jane graph. We'll discuss adding some of the fancy bells and whistles later in the chapter.

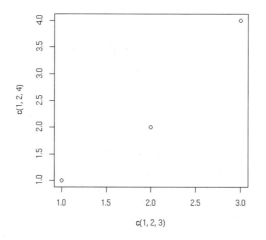

Figure 12-1: Simple point plot

NOTE   *The points in the graph in Figure 12-1 are denoted by empty circles. If you want to use a different character type, specify a value for the named argument pch (for point character).*

The plot() function works in stages, which means you can build up a graph in stages by issuing a series of commands. For example, as a base, we might first draw an empty graph, with only axes, like this:

```
> plot(c(-3,3), c(-1,5), type = "n", xlab="x", ylab="y")
```

This draws axes labeled *x* and *y*. The horizontal (*x*) axis ranges from −3 to 3. The vertical (*y*) axis ranges from −1 to 5. The argument type="n" means that there is nothing in the graph itself.

12.1.2 Adding Lines: The abline() Function

We now have an empty graph, ready for the next stage, which is adding
a line:

```
> x <- c(1,2,3)
> y <- c(1,3,8)
> plot(x,y)
> lmout <- lm(y ~ x)
> abline(lmout)
```

After the call to plot(), the graph will simply show the three points, along
with the *x*- and *y*- axes with hash marks. The call to abline() then adds a line
to the current graph. Now, which line is this?

As you learned in Section 1.5, the result of the call to the linear-regression
function lm() is a class instance containing the slope and intercept of the fitted line, as well as various other quantities that don't concern us here. We've
assigned that class instance to lmout. The slope and intercept will now be in
lmout$coefficients.

So, what happens when we call abline()? This function simply draws
a straight line, with the function's arguments treated as the intercept and
slope of the line. For instance, the call abline(c(2,1)) draws this line on whatever graph you've built up so far:

$$y = 2 + 1 \cdot x$$

But abline() is written to take special action if it is called on a regression
object (though, surprisingly, it is not a generic function). Thus, it will pick
up the slope and intercept it needs from lmout$coefficients and plot that
line. It superimposes this line onto the current graph, the one that graphs
the three points. In other words, the new graph will show both the points
and the line, as in Figure 12-2.

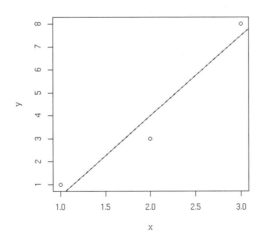

Figure 12-2: Using abline()

You can add more lines using the lines() function. Though there are many options, the two basic arguments to lines() are a vector of *x*-values and a vector of *y*-values. These are interpreted as (*x,y*) pairs representing points to be added to the current graph, with lines connecting the points. For instance, if X and Y are the vectors (1.5,2.5) and (3,3), you could use this call to add a line from (1.5,3) to (2.5,3) to the present graph:

```
> lines(c(1.5,2.5),c(3,3))
```

If you want the lines to "connect the dots," but don't want the dots themselves, include type="l" in your call to lines() or to plot(), as follows:

```
> plot(x,y,type="l")
```

You can use the lty parameter in plot() to specify the type of line, such as solid or dashed. To see the types available and their codes, enter this command:

```
> help(par)
```

12.1.3   Starting a New Graph While Keeping the Old Ones

Each time you call plot(), directly or indirectly, the current graph window will be replaced by the new one. If you don't want that to happen, use the command for your operating system:

- On Linux systems, call X11().
- On a Mac, call quartz().
- On Windows, call windows().

For instance, suppose you wish to plot two histograms of vectors X and Y and view them side by side. On a Linux system, you would type the following:

```
> hist(x)
> x11()
> hist(y)
```

12.1.4   Extended Example: Two Density Estimates on the Same Graph

Let's plot nonparametric density estimates (these are basically smoothed histograms) for two sets of examination scores in the same graph. We use the function density() to generate the estimates. Here are the commands we issue:

```
> d1 = density(testscores$Exam1,from=0,to=100)
> d2 = density(testscores$Exam2,from=0,to=100)
```

```
> plot(d1,main="",xlab="")
> lines(d2)
```

First, we compute nonparametric density estimates from the two variables, saving them in objects d1 and d2 for later use. We then call plot() to draw the curve for exam 1, at which point the plot looks like Figure 12-3. We then call lines() to add exam 2's curve to the graph, producing Figure 12-4.

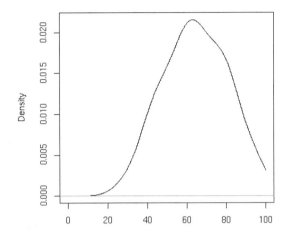

Figure 12-3: Plot of first density

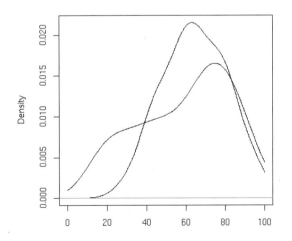

Figure 12-4: Addition of second density

Note that we asked R to use blank labels for the figure as a whole and for the *x*-axis. Otherwise, R would have gotten such labels from d1, which would have been specific to exam 1.

Also note that we needed to plot exam 1 first. The scores there were less diverse, so the density estimate was narrower and taller. Had we plotted exam 2, with its shorter curve, first, exam 1's curve would have been too tall for the plot window. Here, we first ran the two plots separately to see which was taller, but let's consider a more general situation.

Say we wish to write a broadly usable function that will plot several density estimates on the same graph. For this, we would need to automate the process of determining which density estimate is tallest. To do so, we would use the fact that the estimated density values are contained in the y component of the return value from the call to density(). We would then call max() on each density estimate and use which.max() to determine which density estimate is the tallest.

The call to plot() both initiates the plot and draws the first curve. (Without specifying type="l", only the points would have been plotted.) The call to lines() then adds the second curve.

12.1.5   Extended Example: More on the Polynomial Regression Example

In Section 9.1.7, we defined a class "polyreg" that facilitates fitting polynomial regression models. Our code there included an implementation of the generic print() function. Let's now add one for the generic plot() function:

```
1   # polyfit(x,maxdeg) fits all polynomials up to degree maxdeg; y is
2   # vector for response variable, x for predictor; creates an object of
3   # class "polyreg", consisting of outputs from the various regression
4   # models, plus the original data
5   polyfit <- function(y,x,maxdeg) {
6      pwrs <- powers(x,maxdeg)  # form powers of predictor variable
7      lmout <- list()  # start to build class
8      class(lmout) <- "polyreg"  # create a new class
9      for (i in 1:maxdeg) {
10        lmo <- lm(y ~ pwrs[,1:i])
11        # extend the lm class here, with the cross-validated predictions
12        lmo$fitted.xvvalues <- lvoneout(y,pwrs[,1:i,drop=F])
13        lmout[[i]] <- lmo
14     }
15     lmout$x <- x
16     lmout$y <- y
17     return(lmout)
18  }
19
20  # generic print() for an object fits of class "polyreg":  print
21  # cross-validated mean-squared prediction errors
22  print.polyreg <- function(fits) {
23     maxdeg <- length(fits) - 2  # count lm() outputs only, not $x and $y
```

```
24    n <- length(fits$y)
25    tbl <- matrix(nrow=maxdeg,ncol=1)
26    cat("mean squared prediction errors, by degree\n")
27    colnames(tbl) <- "MSPE"
28    for (i in 1:maxdeg) {
29       fi <- fits[[i]]
30       errs <- fits$y - fi$fitted.xvvalues
31       spe <- sum(errs^2)
32       tbl[i,1] <- spe/n
33    }
34    print(tbl)
35 }
36
37 # generic plot(); plots fits against raw data
38 plot.polyreg <- function(fits) {
39    plot(fits$x,fits$y,xlab="X",ylab="Y")  # plot data points as background
40    maxdg <- length(fits) - 2
41    cols <- c("red","green","blue")
42    dg <- curvecount <- 1
43    while (dg < maxdg) {
44       prompt <- paste("RETURN for XV fit for degree",dg,"or type degree",
45          "or q for quit ")
46       rl <- readline(prompt)
47       dg <- if (rl == "") dg else if (rl != "q") as.integer(rl) else break
48       lines(fits$x,fits[[dg]]$fitted.values,col=cols[curvecount%%3 + 1])
49       dg <- dg + 1
50       curvecount <- curvecount + 1
51    }
52 }
53
54 # forms matrix of powers of the vector x, through degree dg
55 powers <- function(x,dg) {
56    pw <- matrix(x,nrow=length(x))
57    prod <- x
58    for (i in 2:dg) {
59       prod <- prod * x
60       pw <- cbind(pw,prod)
61    }
62    return(pw)
63 }
64
65 # finds cross-validated predicted values; could be made much faster via
66 # matrix-update methods
67 lvoneout <- function(y,xmat) {
68    n <- length(y)
69    predy <- vector(length=n)
70    for (i in 1:n) {
```

```
71      # regress, leaving out ith observation
72      lmo <- lm(y[-i] ~ xmat[-i,])
73      betahat <- as.vector(lmo$coef)
74      # the 1 accommodates the constant term
75      predy[i] <- betahat %*% c(1,xmat[i,])
76    }
77    return(predy)
78 }
79
80 # polynomial function of x, coefficients cfs
81 poly <- function(x,cfs) {
82    val <- cfs[1]
83    prod <- 1
84    dg <- length(cfs) - 1
85    for (i in 1:dg) {
86       prod <- prod * x
87       val <- val + cfs[i+1] * prod
88    }
89 }
```

As noted, the only new code is plot.polyreg(). For convenience, the code is reproduced here:

```
# generic plot(); plots fits against raw data
plot.polyreg <- function(fits) {
   plot(fits$x,fits$y,xlab="X",ylab="Y")  # plot data points as background
   maxdg <- length(fits) - 2
   cols <- c("red","green","blue")
   dg <- curvecount <- 1
   while (dg < maxdg) {
      prompt <- paste("RETURN for XV fit for degree",dg,"or type degree",
         "or q for quit ")
      rl <- readline(prompt)
      dg <- if (rl == "") dg else if (rl != "q") as.integer(rl) else break
      lines(fits$x,fits[[dg]]$fitted.values,col=cols[curvecount%%3 + 1])
      dg <- dg + 1
      curvecount <- curvecount + 1
   }
}
```

As before, our implementation of the generic function takes the name of the class, which is plot.polyreg() here.

The while loop iterates through the various polynomial degrees. We cycle through three colors, by setting the vector cols; note the expression curvecount %%3 for this purpose.

The user can choose either to plot the next sequential degree or select a different one. The query, both user prompt and reading of the user's reply, is done in this line:

```
rl <- readline(prompt)
```

We use the R string function paste() to assemble a prompt, offering the user a choice of plotting the next fitted polynomial, plotting one of a different degree, or quitting. The prompt appears in the interactive R window in which we issued the plot() call. For instance, after taking the default choice twice, the command window looks like this:

```
> plot(lmo)
RETURN for XV fit for degree 1 or type degree or q for quit
RETURN for XV fit for degree 2 or type degree or q for quit
RETURN for XV fit for degree 3 or type degree or q for quit
```

The plot window looks like Figure 12-5.

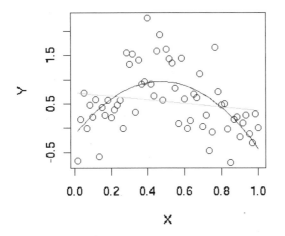

Figure 12-5: Plotting a polynomial fit

12.1.6 Adding Points: The points() Function

The points() function adds a set of (x,y) points, with labels for each, to the currently displayed graph. For instance, in our first example, suppose we entered this command:

```
points(testscores$Exam1,testscores$Exam3,pch="+")
```

The result would be to superimpose onto the current graph the points of the exam scores from that example, using plus signs (+) to mark them.

As with most of the other graphics functions, there are many options, such as point color and background color. For instance, if you want a yellow background, type this command:

```
> par(bg="yellow")
```

Now your graphs will have a yellow background, until you specify otherwise.

As with other functions, to explore the myriad of options, type this:

```
> help(par)
```

12.1.7   Adding a Legend: The legend() Function

The legend() function is used, not surprisingly, to add a legend to a multi-curve graph. This could tell the viewer something like, "The green curve is for the men, and the red curve displays the data for the women." Type the following to see some nice examples:

```
> example(legend)
```

12.1.8   Adding Text: The text() Function

Use the text() function to place some text anywhere in the current graph. Here's an example:

```
text(2.5,4,"abc")
```

This writes the text "abc" at the point (2.5,4) in the graph. The center of the string, in this case "b," would go at that point.

To see a more practical example, let's add some labels to the curves in our exam scores graph, as follows:

```
> text(46.7,0.02,"Exam 1")
> text(12.3,0.008,"Exam 2")
```

The result is shown in Figure 12-6.

In order to get a certain string placed exactly where you want it, you may need to engage in some trial and error. Or you may find the locator() function to be a much quicker way to go, as detailed in the next section.

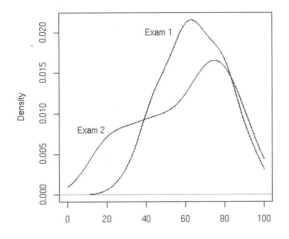

Figure 12-6: Placing text

12.1.9 Pinpointing Locations: The locator() Function

Placing text exactly where you wish can be tricky. You could repeatedly try different *x*- and *y*-coordinates until you find a good position, but the locator() function can save you a lot of trouble. You simply call the function and then click the mouse at the desired spot in the graph. The function returns the *x*- and *y*-coordinates of your click point. Specifically, typing the following will tell R that you will click in one place in the graph:

```
locator(1)
```

Once you click, R will tell you the exact coordinates of the point you clicked. Call locator(2) to get the locations of two places, and so on. (Warning: Make sure to include the argument.)

Here is a simple example:

```
> hist(c(12,5,13,25,16))
> locator(1)
$x
[1] 6.239237

$y
[1] 1.221038
```

This has R draw a histogram and then calls `locator()` with the argument 1, indicating we will click the mouse once. After the click, the function returns a list with components x and y, the *x*- and *y*-coordinates of the point where we clicked.

To use this information to place text, combine it with `text()`:

```
> text(locator(1),"nv=75")
```

Here, `text()` was expecting an *x*-coordinate and a *y*-coordinate, specifying the point at which to draw the text "nv=75." The return value of `locator()` supplied those coordinates.

12.1.10   Restoring a Plot

R has no "undo" command. However, if you suspect you may need to undo your next step when building a graph, you can save it using `recordPlot()` and then later restore it with `replayPlot()`.

Less formally but more conveniently, you can put all the commands you're using to build up a graph in a file and then use `source()`, or cut and paste with the mouse, to execute them. If you change one command, you can redo the whole graph by sourcing or copying and pasting your file.

For our current graph, for instance, we could create file named `examplot.R` with the following contents:

```
d1 = density(testscores$Exam1,from=0,to=100)
d2 = density(testscores$Exam2,from=0,to=100)
plot(d1,main="",xlab="")
lines(d2)
text(46.7,0.02,"Exam 1")
text(12.3,0.008,"Exam 2")
```

If we decide that the label for exam 1 was a bit too far to the right, we can edit the file and then either do the copy-and-paste or execute the following:

```
> source("examplot.R")
```

12.2   Customizing Graphs

You've seen how easy it is to build simple graphs in stages, starting with plot(). Now you can begin to enhance those graphs, using the many options R provides.

12.2.1   Changing Character Sizes: The cex Option

The cex (for *character expand*) function allows you to expand or shrink characters within a graph, which can be very useful. You can use it as a named parameter in various graphing functions. For instance, you may wish to draw the text "abc" at some point, say (2.5,4), in your graph but with a larger font, in order to call attention to this particular text. You could do this by typing the following:

```
text(2.5,4,"abc",cex = 1.5)
```

This prints the same text as in our earlier example but with characters 1.5 times the normal size.

12.2.2   Changing the Range of Axes: The xlim and ylim Options

You may wish to have the ranges on the *x*- and *y*-axes of your plot be broader or narrower than the default. This is especially useful if you will be displaying several curves in the same graph.

You can adjust the axes by specifying the xlim and/or ylim parameters in your call to plot() or points(). For example, ylim=c(0,90000) specifies a range on the *y*-axis of 0 to 90,000.

If you have several curves and do not specify xlim and/or ylim, you should draw the tallest curve first so there is room for all of them. Otherwise, R will fit the plot to the first one your draw and then cut off taller ones at the top! We took this approach earlier, when we plotted two density estimates on the same graph (Figures 12-3 and 12-4). Instead, we could have first found the highest values of the two density estimates. For d1, we find the following:

```
> d1

Call:
        density.default(x = testscores$Exam1, from = 0, to = 100)

Data: testscores$Exam1 (39 obs.);        Bandwidth 'bw' = 6.967

       x                 y
 Min.   :   0   Min.   :1.423e-07
 1st Qu.: 25   1st Qu.:1.629e-03
 Median : 50   Median :9.442e-03
 Mean   : 50   Mean   :9.844e-03
 3rd Qu.: 75   3rd Qu.:1.756e-02
 Max.   :100   Max.   :2.156e-02
```

So, the largest y-value is 0.022. For d2, it was only 0.017. That means we should have plenty of room if we set ylim at 0.03. Here is how we could draw the two plots on the same picture:

```
> plot(c(0, 100), c(0, 0.03), type = "n", xlab="score", ylab="density")
> lines(d2)
> lines(d1)
```

First we drew the bare-bones plot—just axes without innards, as shown in Figure 12-7. The first two arguments to plot() give xlim and ylim, so that the lower and upper limits on the Y axis will be 0 and 0.03. Calling lines() twice then fills in the graph, yielding Figures 12-8 and 12-9. (Either of the two lines() calls could come first, as we've left enough room.)

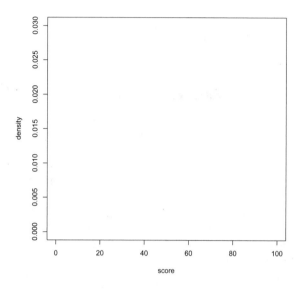

Figure 12-7: Axes only

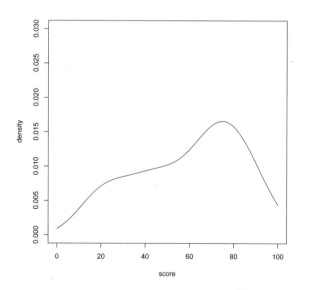

Figure 12-8: Addition of d2

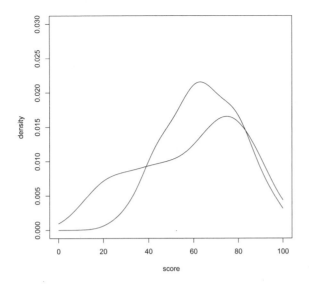

Figure 12-9: Addition of d1

12.2.3 Adding a Polygon: The polygon() Function

You can use polygon() to draw arbitrary polygonal objects. For example, the following code draws the graph of the function $f(x) = 1 - e^{-x}$ and then adds a rectangle that approximates the area under the curve from $x = 1.2$ to $x = 1.4$.

```
> f <- function(x) return(1-exp(-x))
> curve(f,0,2)
> polygon(c(1.2,1.4,1.4,1.2),c(0,0,f(1.3),f(1.3)),col="gray")
```

The result is shown in Figure 12-10.

In the call to polygon() here, the first argument is the set of *x*-coordinates for the rectangle, and the second argument specifies the *y*-coordinates. The third argument specifies that the rectangle in this case should be shaded in solid gray.

As another example, we could use the density argument to fill the rectangle with striping. This call specifies 10 lines per inch:

```
> polygon(c(1.2,1.4,1.4,1.2),c(0,0,f(1.3),f(1.3)),density=10)
```

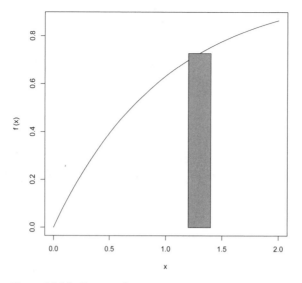

Figure 12-10: Rectangular area strip

12.2.4 Smoothing Points: The lowess() and loess() Functions

Just plotting a cloud of points, connected or not, may give you nothing but an uninformative mess. In many cases, it is better to smooth out the data by fitting a nonparametric regression estimator such as lowess().

Let's do that for our test score data. We'll plot the scores of exam 2 against those of exam 1:

```
> plot(testscores)
> lines(lowess(testscores))
```

The result is shown in Figure 12-11.

A newer alternative to lowess() is loess(). The two functions are similar but have different defaults and other options. You need some advanced knowledge of statistics to appreciate the differences. Use whichever you find gives better smoothing.

12.2.5 Graphing Explicit Functions

Say you want to plot the function $g(t) = (t^2 + 1)^{0.5}$ for t between 0 and 5. You could use the following R code:

```
g <- function(t) { return ((t^2+1)^0.5) }  # define g()
x <- seq(0,5,length=10000)  # x = [0.0004, 0.0008, 0.0012,..., 5]
y <- g(x)  # y = [g(0.0004), g(0.0008), g(0.0012), ..., g(5)]
plot(x,y,type="l")
```

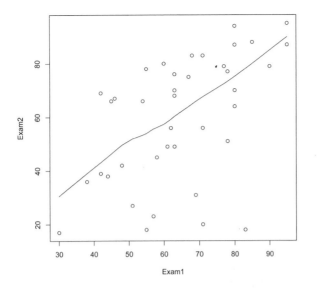

Figure 12-11: Smoothing the exam score relation

But you could avoid some work by using the curve() function, which basically uses the same method:

```
> curve((x^2+1)^0.5,0,5)
```

If you are adding this curve to an existing plot, use the add argument:

```
> curve((x^2+1)^0.5,0,5,add=T)
```

The optional argument n has the default value 101, meaning that the function will be evaluated at 101 equally spaced points in the specified range of x.

Use just enough points for visual smoothness. If you find 101 is not enough, experiment with higher values of n.

You can also use plot(), as follows:

```
> f <- function(x) return((x^2+1)^0.5)
> plot(f,0,5)  # the argument must be a function name
```

Here, the call plot() leads to calling plot.function(), the implementation of the generic plot() function for the function class.

Again, the approach is your choice; use whichever one you prefer.

12.2.6   Extended Example: Magnifying a Portion of a Curve

After you use curve() to graph a function, you may want to "zoom in" on one portion of the curve. You could do this by simply calling curve() again on the same function but with a restricted x range. But suppose you wish to display the original plot and the close-up one in the same picture. Here, we will develop a function, which we'll name inset(), to do this.

In order to avoid redoing the work that curve() did in plotting the original graph, we will modify its code slightly to save that work, via a return value. We can do this by taking advantage of the fact that you can easily inspect the code of R functions written in R (as opposed to the fundamental R functions written in C), as follows:

```
1  > curve
2  function (expr, from = NULL, to = NULL, n = 101, add = FALSE,
3      type = "l", ylab = NULL, log = NULL, xlim = NULL, ...)
4  {
5      sexpr <- substitute(expr)
6      if (is.name(sexpr)) {
7  # ...lots of lines omitted here...
8      x <- if (lg != "" && "x" %in% strsplit(lg, NULL)[[1]]) {
9          if (any(c(from, to) <= 0))
10             stop("'from' and 'to' must be > 0 with log=\"x\"")
11         exp(seq.int(log(from), log(to), length.out = n))
12     }
13     else seq.int(from, to, length.out = n)
14     y <- eval(expr, envir = list(x = x), enclos = parent.frame())
15     if (add)
16         lines(x, y, type = type, ...)
17     else plot(x, y, type = type, ylab = ylab, xlim = xlim, log = lg, ...)
18  }
```

The code forms vectors x and y, consisting of the x- and y-coordinates of the curve to be plotted, at n equally spaced points in the range of x. Since we'll make use of those in inset(), let's modify this code to return x and y. Here's the modified version, which we've named crv():

```
1  > crv
2  function (expr, from = NULL, to = NULL, n = 101, add = FALSE,
3      type = "l", ylab = NULL, log = NULL, xlim = NULL, ...)
4  {
5      sexpr <- substitute(expr)
6      if (is.name(sexpr)) {
7  # ...lots of lines omitted here...
8      x <- if (lg != "" && "x" %in% strsplit(lg, NULL)[[1]]) {
9          if (any(c(from, to) <= 0))
10             stop("'from' and 'to' must be > 0 with log=\"x\"")
11         exp(seq.int(log(from), log(to), length.out = n))
12     }
13     else seq.int(from, to, length.out = n)
14     y <- eval(expr, envir = list(x = x), enclos = parent.frame())
15     if (add)
```

```
16    lines(x, y, type = type, ...)
17    else plot(x, y, type = type, ylab = ylab, xlim = xlim, log = lg, ...)
18    return(list(x=x,y=y))  # this is the only modification
19  }
```

Now we can get to our inset() function.

```
1   # savexy:  list consisting of x and y vectors returned by crv()
2   # x1,y1,x2,y2:  coordinates of rectangular region to be magnified
3   # x3,y3,x4,y4:  coordinates of inset region
4   inset <- function(savexy,x1,y1,x2,y2,x3,y3,x4,y4) {
5      rect(x1,y1,x2,y2)  # draw rectangle around region to be magnified
6      rect(x3,y3,x4,y4)  # draw rectangle around the inset
7      # get vectors of coordinates of previously plotted points
8      savex <- savexy$x
9      savey <- savexy$y
10     # get subscripts of xi our range to be magnified
11     n <- length(savex)
12     xvalsinrange <- which(savex >= x1 & savex <= x2)
13     yvalsforthosex <- savey[xvalsinrange]
14     # check that our first box contains the entire curve for that X range
15     if (any(yvalsforthosex < y1 | yvalsforthosex > y2)) {
16        print("Y value outside first box")
17        return()
18     }
19     # record some differences
20     x2mnsx1 <- x2 - x1
21     x4mnsx3 <- x4 - x3
22     y2mnsy1 <- y2 - y1
23     y4mnsy3 <- y4 - y3
24     # for the ith point in the original curve, the function plotpt() will
25     # calculate the position of this point in the inset curve
26     plotpt <- function(i) {
27        newx <- x3 + ((savex[i] - x1)/x2mnsx1) * x4mnsx3
28        newy <- y3 + ((savey[i] - y1)/y2mnsy1) * y4mnsy3
29        return(c(newx,newy))
30     }
31     newxy <- sapply(xvalsinrange,plotpt)
32     lines(newxy[1,],newxy[2,])
33  }
```

Let's try it out.

```
xyout <- crv(exp(-x)*sin(1/(x-1.5)),0.1,4,n=5001)
inset(xyout,1.3,-0.3,1.47,0.3,  2.5,-0.3,4,-0.1)
```

The resulting plot looks like Figure 12-12.

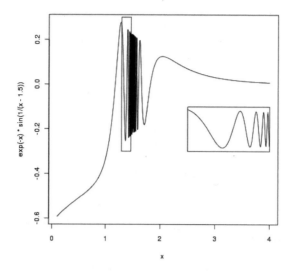

Figure 12-12: Adding an inset graph

12.3   Saving Graphs to Files

The R graphics display can consist of various graphics devices. The default device is the screen. If you want to save a graph to a file, you must set up another device.

Let's go through the basics of R graphics devices first to introduce R graphics device concepts, and then discuss a second approach that is much more direct and convenient.

12.3.1   R Graphics Devices

Let's open a file:

```
> pdf("d12.pdf")
```

This opens the file *d12.pdf.* We now have two devices open, as we can confirm:

```
> dev.list()
X11 pdf
  2   3
```

The screen is named X11 when R runs on Linux. (It's named windows on Windows systems.) It is device number 2 here. Our PDF file is device number 3. Our active device is the PDF file:

```
> dev.cur()
pdf
  3
```

All graphics output will now go to this file instead of to the screen. But what if we wish to save what's already on the screen?

12.3.2   Saving the Displayed Graph

One way to save the graph currently displayed on the screen is to reestablish the screen as the current device and then copy it to the PDF device, which is 3 in our example, as follows:

```
> dev.set(2)
X11
  2
> dev.copy(which=3)
pdf
  3
```

But actually, it is best to set up a PDF device as shown earlier and then rerun whatever analyses led to the current screen. This is because the copy operation can result in distortions due to mismatches between screen devices and file devices.

12.3.3   Closing an R Graphics Device

Note that the PDF file we create is not usable until we close it, which we do as follows:

```
> dev.set(3)
pdf
  3
> dev.off()
X11
  2
```

You can also close the device by exiting R, if you're finished working with it. But in future versions of R, this behavior may not exist, so it's probably better to proactively close.

12.4 Creating Three-Dimensional Plots

R offers a number of functions to plot data in three dimensions such as
persp() and wireframe(), which draw surfaces, and cloud(), which draws three-
dimensional scatter plots. Here, we'll look at a simple example that uses
wireframe().

```
> library(lattice)
> a <- 1:10
> b <- 1:15
> eg <- expand.grid(x=a,y=b)
> eg$z <- eg$x^2 + eg$x * eg$y
> wireframe(z ~ x+y, eg)
```

First, we load the lattice library. Then the call to expand.grid() creates
a data frame, consisting of two columns named x and y, in all possible combinations of the values of the two inputs. Here, a and b had 10 and 15 values, respectively, so the resulting data frame will have 150 rows. (Note that
the data frame that is input to wireframe() does not need to be created by
expand.grid().)

We then added a third column, named z, as a function of the first two
columns. Our call to wireframe() creates the graph. The arguments, given
in regression model form, specify that z is to be graphed against x and y. Of
course, z, x, and y refer to names of columns in eg. The result is shown in
Figure 12-13.

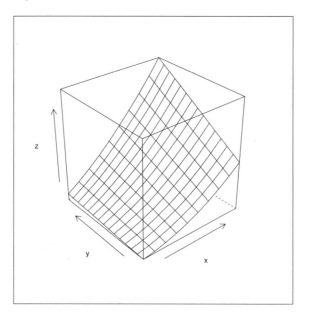

Figure 12-13: Example of using wireframe()

All the points are connected as a surface (like connecting points by lines in two dimensions). In contrast, with cloud(), the points are isolated.

For wireframe(), the (x,y) pairs must form a rectangular grid, though not necessarily be evenly spaced.

The three-dimensional plotting functions have many different options. For instance, a nice one for wireframe() is shade=T, which makes the data easier to see. Many functions, some with elaborate options, and whole new graphics packages work at a higher (read "more convenient and powerful") level of abstraction than R's base graphics package. For more information, refer to the books cited in footnote 1 at the beginning of this chapter.

13

DEBUGGING

 Programmers often find that they spend more time debugging a program than actually writing it. Good debugging skills are invaluable. In this chapter, we'll discuss debugging in R.

13.1 Fundamental Principles of Debugging

> Beware of bugs in the above code; I have only proved it correct, not tried it.
>
> —Donald Knuth, pioneer of computer science

Though debugging is an art rather than a science, it involves some fundamental principles. Here, we'll look at some debugging best practices.

13.1.1 The Essence of Debugging: The Principle of Confirmation

As Pete Salzman and I said in our book on debugging, *The Art of Debugging, with GDB, DDD, and Eclipse* (No Starch Press, 2008), the principle of confirmation is the essence of debugging.

Fixing a buggy program is a process of confirming, one by one, that the many things you *believe* to be true about the code actually *are* true. When you find that one of your assumptions is *not* true, you have found a clue to the location (if not the exact nature) of a bug.

Another way of saying this is, "Surprises are good!" For example, say you have the following code:

```
x <- y^2 + 3*g(z,2)
w <- 28
if (w+q > 0) u <- 1 else v <- 10
```

Do you think the value of your variable x should be 3 after x is assigned? Confirm it! Do you think the else will be executed, not the if on that third line? Confirm it!

Eventually, one of these assertions that you are so sure of will turn out to not confirm. Then you will have pinpointed the likely location of the error, thus enabling you to focus on the nature of the error.

13.1.2   Start Small

At least at the beginning of the debugging process, stick to small, simple test cases. Working with large data objects may make it harder to think about the problem.

Of course, you should eventually test your code on large, complicated cases, but start small.

13.1.3   Debug in a Modular, Top-Down Manner

Most good software developers agree that code should be written in a modular manner. Your first-level code should not be longer than, say, a dozen lines, with much of it consisting of function calls. And those functions should not be too lengthy and should call other functions if necessary. This makes the code easier to organize during the writing stage and easier for others to understand when it comes time for the code to be extended.

You should debug in a top-down manner, too. Suppose that you have set the debug status of your function f() (that is, you have called debug(f), to be explained shortly) and f() contains this line:

```
y <- g(x,8)
```

You should take an "innocent until proven guilty" approach to g(). Do *not* call debug(g) yet. Execute that line and see if g() returns the value you expect. If it does, then you've just avoided the time-consuming process of single-stepping through g(). If g() returns the wrong value, then now is the time to call debug(g).

13.1.4 Antibugging

You may adopt some "antibugging" strategies as well. Suppose you have a section of code in which a variable x should be positive. You could insert this line:

```
stopifnot(x > 0)
```

If there is a bug earlier in the code that renders x equal to, say, −12, the call to `stopifnot()` will bring things to a halt right there, with an error message like this:

```
Error: x > 0 is not TRUE
```

(C programmers may notice the similarity to C's assert statement.)

After fixing a bug and testing the new code, you might want to keep that code handy so you can check later that the bug did not somehow reappear.

13.2   Why Use a Debugging Tool?

In the old days, programmers would perform the debugging confirmation process by temporarily inserting print statements into their code and rerunning the program to see what printed out. For example, to confirm that x = 3 in our previous code, we would insert into our code a statement that printed the value of x and do something similar for the if-else, like this:

```
x <- y^2 + 3*g(z,2)
cat("x =",x,"\n")
w <- 28
if (w+q > 0) {
    u <- 1
    print("the 'if' was done")
} else {
    v <- 10
    print("the 'else' was done")
}
```

We would rerun the program and inspect the feedback printed out. We would then remove the print statements and put in new ones to track down the next bug.

This manual process is fine for one or two cycles, but it gets really tedious during a long debugging session. And worse, all that editing work distracts your attention, making it harder to concentrate on finding the bug.

So, debugging by inserting print statements into your code is slow, cumbersome, and distracting. If you are serious about programming in any particular language, you should seek a good debugging tool for that language. Using a debugging tool will make it much easier to query the values of variables, check whether the if or the else gets executed, and so on. Moreover, if your bug causes an execution error, debugging tools can analyze it for you, possibly providing major clues as to the source of the error. All of this will increase your productivity substantially.

13.3   Using R Debugging Facilities

The R base package includes a number of debugging facilities, and more functional debugging packages are also available. We'll discuss both the base facilities and other packages, and our extended example will present a fully detailed debugging session.

13.3.1   Single-Stepping with the debug() and browser() Functions

The core of R's debugging facility consists of the *browser*. It allows you to single-step through your code, line by line, taking a look around as you go. You can invoke the browser through a call to either the debug() or browser() function.

R's debugging facility is specific to individual functions. If you believe there is a bug in your function f(), you can make the call debug(f) to set the debug status for the function f(). This means that from that point onward, each time you call the function, you will automatically enter the browser at the beginning of the function. Calling undebug(f) will unset the debug status of the function so that entry to the function will no longer invoke the browser.

On the other hand, if you place a call to browser() at some line within f(), the browser will be invoked only when execution reaches that line. You then can single-step through your code until you exit the function. If you believe the bug's location is not near the beginning of the function, you probably don't want to be single-stepping from the beginning, so this approach is more direct.

Readers who have used C debuggers such as GDB (the GNU debugger) will find similarity here, but some aspects will come as a surprise. As noted, for instance, debug() is called on the function level, not on the overall program level. If you believe you have bugs in several of your functions, you'll need to call debug() on each one.

It can become tedious to call debug(f) and then undebug(f) when you just want to go through one debugging session for f(). Starting with R 2.10, one can now call debugonce() instead; calling debugonce(f) puts f() into debugging status the first time you execute it, but that status is reversed immediately upon exit from the function.

13.3.2   Using Browser Commands

While you are in the browser, the prompt changes from > to Browse[d]>. (Here, d is the depth of the call chain.) You may submit any of the following commands at that prompt:

- n (for *next*): Tells R to execute the next line and then pause again. Hitting ENTER causes this action, too.

- c (for *continue*): This is like n, except that several lines of code may be executed before the next pause. If you are currently in a loop, this command will result in the remainder of the loop being executed and then pausing upon exit from the loop. If you are in a function but not in a loop, the remainder of the function will be executed before the next pause.

- Any R command: While in the browser, you are still in R's interactive mode and thus can query the value of, say, x by simply typing x. Of course, if you have a variable with the same name as a browser command, you must explicitly call something like print(), as in print(n).

- where: This prints a *stack trace*. It displays what sequence of function calls led execution to the current location.

- Q: This quits the browser, bringing you back to R's main interactive mode.

13.3.3   Setting Breakpoints

Calling debug(f) places a call to browser() at the beginning of f(). However, this may be too coarse a tool in some cases. If you suspect that the bug is in the middle of the function, it's wasteful to trudge through all the intervening code.

The solution is to set *breakpoints* at certain key locations of your code—places where you want execution to be paused. How can this be done in R? You can call browser directly or use the setBreakpoint() function (with R version 2.10 and later).

13.3.3.1   Calling browser() Directly

You can set a breakpoint by simply inserting calls to browser() at the places of interest in your code. This has the effect, essentially, of setting breakpoints there.

You can make invoking the browser conditional so that it is entered only in specified situations. Use the expr argument to define those situations. For instance, suppose you suspect that your bug arises only when a certain variable s is larger than 1. You could use this code:

```
browser(s > 1)
```

The browser will be invoked only if s is larger than 1. The following would have the same effect:

```
if (s > 1) browser()
```

Calling the browser directly, rather than entering the debugger via debug() is very useful in situations in which you have a loop with many iterations and the bug surfaces only after, say, the 50th iteration. If the loop index is i, then you could write this:

```
if (i > 49) browser()
```

That way, you would avoid the tedium of stepping through the first 49 iterations!

13.3.3.2 Using the setBreakpoint() Function

Starting with R 2.10, you can use setBreakpoint() in the format

```
setBreakpoint(filename,linenumber)
```

This will result in browser() being called at line *linenumber* of our source file *filename*.

This is especially useful when you are in the midst of using the debugger, single-stepping through code. Say you are currently at line 12 of your source file *x.R* and want to have a breakpoint at line 28. Instead of exiting the debugger, adding a call to browser() at line 28, and then re-entering the function, you could simply type this:

```
> setBreakpoint("x.R",28)
```

You could then resume execution within the debugger, say by issuing the c command.

The setBreakpoint() function works by calling the trace() function, discussed in the next section. Thus, to cancel the breakpoint, you cancel the trace. For instance, if we had called setBreakpoint() at a line in the function g(), we would cancel the breakpoint by typing the following:

```
> untrace(g)
```

You can call setBreakpoint() whether or not you are currently in the debugger. If you are not currently running the debugger and you execute the affected function and hit the breakpoint during that execution, you will be put into the browser automatically. This is similar to the case of browser(), but using this approach, you save yourself the trouble of changing your code via your text editor.

13.3.4 Tracking with the trace() Function

The trace() function is flexible and powerful, though it takes some initial effort to learn. We will discuss some of the simpler usage forms here, beginning with the following:

```
> trace(f,t)
```

This call instructs R to call the function t() every time we enter the function f(). For instance, say we wish to set a breakpoint at the beginning of the function gy(). We could use this command:

```
> trace(gy,browser)
```

This has the same effect as placing the command browser() in our source code for gy(), but it's quicker and more convenient than inserting such a line, saving the file, and rerunning source() to load in the new version of the file. Calling trace() does *not* change your source file, though it does change a temporary version of your file maintained by R. It would also be quicker and more convenient to undo, by simply running untrace:

```
> untrace(gy)
```

You can turn tracing on or off globally by calling tracingState(), using the argument TRUE to turn it on or FALSE to turn it off.

13.3.5 Performing Checks After a Crash with the traceback() and debugger() Functions

Say your R code crashes when you are not running the debugger. There is still a debugging tool available to you after the fact. You can do a "post-mortem" by simply calling traceback(). It will tell you in which function the problem occurred and the call chain that led to that function.

You can get a lot more information if you set up R to dump frames in the event of a crash:

```
> options(error=dump.frames)
```

If you've done this, then after a crash, run this command:

```
> debugger()
```

You will then be presented with a choice of levels of function calls to view. For each one that you choose, you can take a look at the values of the variables there. After browsing through one level, you can return to the debugger() main menu by hitting N.

You can arrange to automatically enter the debugger by writing this code:

```
> options(error=recover)
```

Note, though, that if you do choose this automatic route, it will whisk you into the debugger, even if you simply have a syntax error (not a useful time to enter the debugger).

To turn off any of this behavior, type the following:

```
> options(error=NULL)
```

You'll see a demonstration of this approach in the next section.

13.3.6   Extended Example: Two Full Debugging Sessions

Now that we've looked at R's debugging tools, let's try using them to find and fix code problems. We'll begin with a simple example and then move on to a more complicated one.

13.3.6.1   Debugging Finding Runs of Ones

First recall our extended example of finding runs of 1s in Chapter 2. Here is a buggy version of the code:

```
1  findruns <- function(x,k) {
2     n <- length(x)
3     runs <- NULL
4     for (i in 1:(n-k)) {
5        if (all(x[i:i+k-1]==1)) runs <- c(runs,i)
6     }
7     return(runs)
8  }
```

Let's try it on a small test case:

```
> source("findruns.R")
> findruns(c(1,0,0,1,1,0,1,1,1),2)
[1] 3 4 6 7
```

The function was supposed to report runs at indices 4, 7, and 8, but it found some indices that it shouldn't have and missed some as well. Something is wrong. Let's enter the debugger and take a look around.

```
> debug(findruns)
> findruns(c(1,0,0,1,1,0,1,1,1),2)
debugging in: findruns(c(1, 0, 0, 1, 1, 0, 1, 1, 1), 2)
debug at findruns.R#1: {
```

```
    n <- length(x)
    runs <- NULL
    for (i in 1:(n - k)) {
        if (all(x[i:i + k - 1] == 1))
            runs <- c(runs, i)
    }
    return(runs)
}
attr(,"srcfile")
findruns.R
```

So, according to the principle of confirmation, let's first make sure our test vector was received correctly:

```
Browse[2]> x
[1] 1 0 0 1 1 0 1 1 1
```

So far, so good. Let's step through the code a bit. We hit n a couple of times to single-step through the code.

```
Browse[2]> n
debug at findruns.R#2: n <- length(x)
Browse[2]> n
debug at findruns.R#3: runs <- NULL
Browse[2]> print(n)
[1] 9
```

Note that after each single step, R tells us which statement would be the *next* one to execute. In other words, at the time we executed print(n), we had *not* yet executed the assignment of NULL to runs.

Note, too, that although normally you can print out the value of a variable by simply typing its name, we could not do so here for our variable n, because n is also the abbreviation for the debugger's next command. Thus, we needed print().

At any rate, we found that the length of our test vector was 9, confirming what we knew. Now, let's single-step some more, getting into the loop.

```
Browse[2]> n
debug at findruns.R#4: for (i in 1:(n - k + 1)) {
    if (all(x[i:i + k - 1] == 1))
        runs <- c(runs, i)
}
Browse[2]> n
debug at findruns.R#4: i
Browse[2]> n
debug at findruns.R#5: if (all(x[i:i + k - 1] == 1)) runs <- c(runs, i)
```

Since k is 2—that is, we are checking for runs of length 2— the if() statement should be checking the first two elements of x, which are (1,0). Let's confirm:

```
Browse[2]> x[i:i + k - 1]
[1] 0
```

So, it did *not* confirm. Let's check that we have the correct subscript range, which should be 1:2. Is it?

```
Browse[2]> i:i + k - 1
[1] 2
```

Also wrong. Well, how about i and k? They should be 1 and 2, respectively. Are they?

```
Browse[2]> i
[1] 1
Browse[2]> k
[1] 2
```

Well, those do confirm. Thus, our problem must be with the expression i:i + k - 1. After some thought, we realize there is an operator precedence problem there, and we correct it to i:(i + k - 1).

Is it okay now?

```
> source("findruns.R")
> findruns(c(1,0,0,1,1,0,1,1,1),2)
[1] 4 7
```

No, as mentioned, it should be (4,7,8).

Let's set a breakpoint inside the loop and take a closer look.

```
> setBreakpoint("findruns.R",5)
/home/nm/findruns.R#5:
 findruns step 4,4,2 in <environment: R_GlobalEnv>
> findruns(c(1,0,0,1,1,0,1,1,1),2)
findruns.R#5
Called from: eval(expr, envir, enclos)
Browse[1]> x[i:(i+k-1)]
[1] 1 0
```

Good, we're dealing with the first two elements of the vector, so our bug fix is working so far. Let's look at the second iteration of the loop.

```
Browse[1]> c
findruns.R#5
Called from: eval(expr, envir, enclos)
```

```
Browse[1]> i
[1] 2
Browse[1]> x[i:(i+k-1)]
[1] 0 0
```

That's right, too. We could go another iteration, but instead, let's look at the last iteration, a place where bugs frequently arise in loops. So, let's add a conditional breakpoint, as follows:

```
findruns <- function(x,k) {
    n <- length(x)
    runs <- NULL
    for (i in 1:(n-k)) {
        if (all(x[i:(i+k-1)]==1)) runs <- c(runs,i)
        if (i == n-k) browser()  # break in last iteration of loop
    }
    return(runs)
}
```

And now run it again.

```
> source("findruns.R")
> findruns(c(1,0,0,1,1,0,1,1,1),2)
Called from: findruns(c(1, 0, 0, 1, 1, 0, 1, 1, 1), 2)
Browse[1]> i
[1] 7
```

This shows the last iteration was for i = 7. But the vector is nine elements long, and k = 2, so our last iteration should be i = 8. Some thought then reveals that the range in the loop should have been written as follows:

```
for (i in 1:(n-k+1)) {
```

By the way, note that the breakpoint that we set using setBreakpoint() is no longer valid, now that we've replaced the old version of the object findruns.

Subsequent testing (not shown here) indicates the code now works. Let's move on to a more complex example.

13.3.6.2   Debugging Finding City Pairs

Recall our code in Section 3.4.2, which found the pair of cities with the closest distance between them. Here is a buggy version of that code:

```
1    # returns the minimum value of d[i,j], i != j, and the row/col attaining
2    # that minimum, for square symmetric matrix d; no special policy on
3    # ties;
4    # motivated by distance matrices
```

```
 5   mind <- function(d) {
 6       n <- nrow(d)
 7       add a column to identify row number for apply()
 8       dd <- cbind(d,1:n)
 9       wmins <- apply(dd[-n,],1,imin)
10       wmins will be 2xn, 1st row being indices and 2nd being values
11       i <- which.min(wmins[1,])
12       j <- wmins[2,i]
13       return(c(d[i,j],i,j))
14   }
15
16    finds the location, value of the minimum in a row x
17   imin <- function(x) {
18       n <- length(x)
19       i <- x[n]
20       j <- which.min(x[(i+1):(n-1)])
21       return(c(j,x[j]))
22   }
```

Let's use R's debugging tools to find and fix the problems.
We'll run it first on a small test case:

```
> source("cities.R")
> m <- rbind(c(0,12,5),c(12,0,8),c(5,8,0))
> m
     [,1] [,2] [,3]
[1,]    0   12    5
[2,]   12    0    8
[3,]    5    8    0
> mind(m)
Error in mind(m) : subscript out of bounds
```

Not an auspicious start! Unfortunately, the error message doesn't tell us where the code blew up. But the debugger will give us that information:

```
> options(error=recover)
> mind(m)
Error in mind(m) : subscript out of bounds

Enter a frame number, or 0 to exit

1: mind(m)

Selection: 1
Called from: eval(expr, envir, enclos)


Browse[1]> where
```

```
where 1: eval(expr, envir, enclos)
where 2: eval(quote(browser()), envir = sys.frame(which))
where 3 at cities.R#13: function ()
{
    if (.isMethodsDispatchOn()) {
        tState <- tracingState(FALSE)
...
```

Okay, so the problem occurred in mind() rather than imin() and in particular at line 13. It still could be the fault of imin(), but for now, let's deal with the former.

NOTE   *There is another way we could have determined that the blowup occurred on line 13. We would enter the debugger as before but probe the local variables. We could reason that if the subscript bounds error had occurred at line 9, then the variable* wmins *would not have been set, so querying it would give us an error message like* Error: object 'wmins' not found. *On the other hand, if the blowup occurred on line 13, even j would have been set.*

Since the error occurred with d[i,j], let's look at those variables:

```
Browse[1]> d
     [,1] [,2] [,3]
[1,]    0   12    5
[2,]   12    0    8
[3,]    5    8    0
Browse[1]> i
[1] 2
Browse[1]> j
[1] 12
```

This is indeed a problem—d only has three columns, yet j, a column subscript, is 12.

Let's look at the variable from which we gleaned j, wmins:

```
Browse[1]> wmins
     [,1] [,2]
[1,]    2    1
[2,]   12   12
```

If you recall how the code was designed, column k of wmins is supposed to contain information about the minimum value in row k of d. So here wmins is saying that in the first row (k = 1) of d,(0,12,5), the minimum value is 12, occurring at index 2. But it should be 5 at index 3. So, something went wrong with this line:

```
wmins <- apply(dd[-n, ], 1, imin)
```

There are several possibilities here. But since ultimately imin() is called, we can check them all from within that function. So, let's set the debug status of imin(), quit the debugger, and rerun the code.

```
Browse[1]> Q
> debug(imin)
> mind(m)
debugging in: FUN(newX[, i], ...)
debug at cities.R#17: {
    n <- length(x)
    i <- x[n]
    j <- which.min(x[(i + 1):(n - 1)])
    return(c(j, x[j]))
}
...
```

So, we're in imin(). Let's see if it properly received the first row of dd, which should be (0,12,5,1).

```
Browse[4]> x
[1]  0 12  5  1
```

It's confirmed. This seems to indicate that the first two arguments to apply() were correct and that the problem is instead within imin(), though that remains to be seen.

Let's single-step through, occasionally typing confirmational queries:

```
Browse[2]> n
debug at cities.r#17: n <- length(x)
Browse[2]> n
debug at cities.r#18: i <- x[n]
Browse[2]> n
debug at cities.r#19: j <- which.min(x[(i + 1):(n - 1)])
Browse[2]> n
debug at cities.r#20: return(c(j, x[j]))
Browse[2]> print(n)
[1] 4
Browse[2]> i
[1] 1
Browse[2]> j
[1] 2
```

Recall that we designed our call which.min(x[(i + 1):(n - 1)] to look only at the above-diagonal portion of this row. This is because the matrix is symmetric and because we don't want to consider the distance between a city and itself.

But the value j = 2 does not confirm. The minimum value in (0,12,5) is 5, which occurs at index 3 of that vector, not index 2. Thus, the problem is in this line:

```
j <- which.min(x[(i + 1):(n - 1)])
```

What could be wrong?

After taking a break, we realize that although the minimum value of (0,12,5) occurs at index 3 of that vector, that is *not* what we asked which.min() to find for us. Instead, that i + 1 term means we asked for the index of the minimum in (12,5), which is 2.

We did ask which.min() for the correct information, but we failed to use it correctly, because we do want the index of the minimum in (0,12,5). We need to adjust the output of which.min() accordingly, as follows:

```
j <- which.min(x[(i+1):(n-1)])
k <- i + j
return(c(k,x[k]))
```

We make the fix and try again.

```
> mind(m)
Error in mind(m) : subscript out of bounds

Enter a frame number, or 0 to exit

1: mind(m)

Selection:
```

Oh no, *another* bounds error! To see where the blowup occurred this time, we issue the where command as before, and we find it was at line 13 again. What about i and j now?

```
Browse[1]> i
[1] 1
Browse[1]> j
[1] 5
```

The value of j is still wrong; it cannot be larger than 3, as we have only three columns in this matrix. On the other hand, i is correct. The overall minimum value in dd is 5, occurring in row 1, column 3.

So, let's check the source of j again, the matrix wmins:

```
Browse[1]> wmins
     [,1] [,2]
[1,]   3    3
[2,]   5    8
```

Well, there are the 3 and 5 in column 1, just as should be the case. Remember, column 1 here contains the information for row 1 in d, so wmins is saying that the minimum value in row 1 is 5, occurring at index 3 of that row, which is correct.

After taking another break, though, we realize that while wmins is correct, our *use* of it isn't. We have the rows and columns of that matrix mixed up. This code:

```
i <- which.min(wmins[1,])
j <- wmins[2,i]
```

should be like this:

```
i <- which.min(wmins[2,])
j <- wmins[1,i]
```

After making that change and resourcing our file, we try it out.

```
> mind(m)
[1] 5 1 3
```

This is correct, and subsequent tests with larger matrices worked, too.

13.4 Moving Up in the World: More Convenient Debugging Tools

As just seen, R's debugging tools are effective. However, they're not very convenient. Fortunately, there are various tools that make the process easier. In approximate chronological order of development, they are as follows:

- The debug package by Mark Bravington

- My edtdbg package, which works with the Vim and Emacs text editors

- Vitalie Spinu's ess-tracebug, which runs under Emacs (with the same goals as edtdbg but with more Emacs-specific features)

- REvolution Analytics' Integrated Development Environment (IDE)

NOTE   *As of this writing (July 2011), work is in progress by the teams that develop the StatET and RStudio IDEs to add debugging tools.*

All of these tools are cross-platform, working on Linux, Windows, and Mac systems, with the exception of the REvolution Analytics product. That IDE is available only on Windows systems with Microsoft Visual Studio. All of the tools are open source or free, again with the exception of the REvolution Analytics product.

So, what do these packages have to offer? To me, one of the biggest problems with R's built-in debugging tools is the lack of a window that shows the big picture—a window displaying your R code with a cursor that moves through the code as you single-step through it. For example, consider this excerpt from our previous browser output:

```
Browse[2]> n
debug at cities.r#17: n <- length(x)
Browse[2]> n
debug at cities.r#18: i <- x[n]
```

This is nice, but where are these lines in our code? Most GUI debuggers for other languages feature a window showing the user's source code, with a symbol indicating the next line to be executed. All of the R tools listed at the start of this section remedy this lack in core R. The Bravington `debug` package creates a separate window for exactly this purpose. The other tools have your text editor double as that window, thus saving space on your screen compared to using `debug`.

In addition, these tools allow you to set breakpoints and handle other debugging operations without moving your screen's cursor from the editor window to your R execution window. This is convenient and saves typing as well, greatly enhancing your ability to concentrate on the real task at hand: finding your bugs.

Let's consider the cities example again. I opened the GVim text editor on my source file in conjunction with `edtdbg`, did some startup for `edtdbg`, and then hit the [(left bracket) key twice to single-step twice through the code. The resulting GVim window is shown in Figure 13-1.

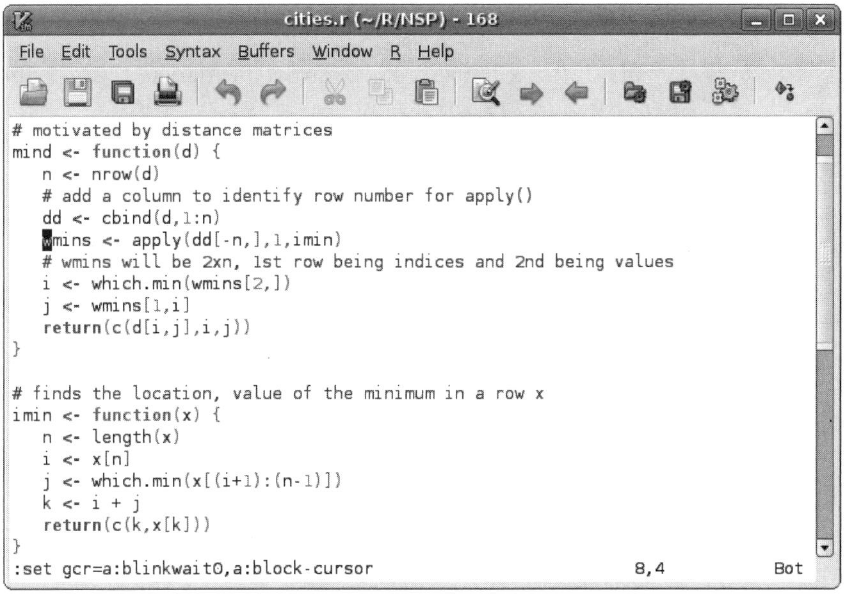
cities.r (~/R/NSP) - 168
File Edit Tools Syntax Buffers Window R Help
# motivated by distance matrices
mind <- function(d) {
n <- nrow(d)
# add a column to identify row number for apply()
dd <- cbind(d,1:n)
wmins <- apply(dd[-n,],1,imin)
# wmins will be 2xn, 1st row being indices and 2nd being values
i <- which.min(wmins[2,])
j <- wmins[1,i]
return(c(d[i,j],i,j))
}
# finds the location, value of the minimum in a row x
imin <- function(x) {
n <- length(x)
i <- x[n]
j <- which.min(x[(i+1):(n-1)])
k <- i + j
return(c(k,x[k]))
}
:set gcr=a:blinkwait0,a:block-cursor
8,4
Bot

Figure 13-1: Source window in edtdbg

Operation of edtdbg for Emacs is the same as shown here, just with different keystrokes used for the commands. For instance, F8 is used for single-stepping instead of [.

First, note that the editor's cursor is now on this line:

```
wmins <- apply(dd[-n, ], 1, imin)
```

This shows the line to be executed next.

Whenever I want to single-step a line, I simply hit the [key while I'm in the editor window. The editor then tells the browser to execute its n command, without my needing to move the mouse to the R execution window, and then the editor moves its cursor to the next line. I can also hit] for the browser's c command. Each time I execute a line or lines in this manner, the editor's cursor moves right along.

Whenever I make a change to my source code, typing ,src (the comma is part of the command) into my GVim window will tell R to call source() on it. Each time I want to rerun my code, I hit ,dt. I rarely, if ever, need to move my mouse away from the editor window to the R window and back. In essence, the editor has become my debugger in addition to providing its editing operations.

13.5   Ensuring Consistency in Debugging Simulation Code

If you're doing anything with random numbers, you'll need to be able to reproduce the same stream of numbers each time you run your program during the debugging session. Without this, your bugs may not be reproducible, making them even harder to fix.

The set.seed() function controls this by reinitializing the random number sequence to a given value.

Consider this example:

```
[1] 0.8811480 0.2853269 0.5864738
> runif(3)
[1] 0.5775979 0.4588383 0.8354707
> runif(3)
[1] 0.4155105 0.4852900 0.6591892
> runif(3)
> set.seed(8888)
> runif(3)
[1] 0.5775979 0.4588383 0.8354707
> set.seed(8888)
> runif(3)
[1] 0.5775979 0.4588383 0.8354707
```

The call runif(3) generates three random numbers from the uniform distribution on the interval (0,1). Each time we make that call, we will get a different set of three numbers. But with set.seed(), we can start over and get the same sequence of numbers.

13.6 Syntax and Runtime Errors

The most common syntax errors will be lack of matching parentheses, brackets, braces, or quotation marks. When you encounter a syntax error, this is the first thing you should check and double-check. I highly recommend that you use a text editor that does parentheses matching and syntax coloring for R, such as Vim or Emacs.

Be aware that often when you get a message saying there is a syntax error on a certain line, the error may actually be in a much earlier line. This can occur with any language, but R seems especially prone to it.

If it just isn't obvious to you where your syntax error is, I recommend selectively commenting out some of your code, better enabling you to pinpoint the location of the syntax problem. Generally, it helps to follow a binary search approach: Comment out half of your code (being careful to maintain syntax integrity) and see if the same error arises. If it does, it's in the remaining half; otherwise, it's in the half you deleted. Then cut that half in half, and so on.

You may sometimes get messages like the following:

```
There were 50 or more warnings (use warnings() to see the first 50)
```

These should be heeded—run `warnings()` as suggested. The problem could range from nonconvergence of an algorithm to misspecification of a matrix argument to a function. In many cases, the program output may be invalid, though it may well be fine, too, say with this message:

```
Fitted probabilities numerically 0 or 1 occurred in: glm...
```

In some cases, you may find it useful to issue this command:

```
> options(warn=2)
```

This instructs R to turn warnings into actual errors and makes the locations of the warnings easier to find.

13.7 Running GDB on R Itself

This section may be of interest to you even if you are not trying to fix a bug in R. For example, you may have written some C code to interface to R (covered in Chapter 15) and found it to be buggy. In order to run GDB on that C function, you must first run R itself through GDB.

Or, you may be interested in the internals of R, say to determine how you can write efficient R code, and wish to explore the internals by stepping through the R source code with a debugging tool such as GDB.

Although you can invoke R through GDB from a shell command line (see Section 15.1.4), for our purposes here, I suggest using separate windows for R and GDB. Here's the procedure:

1. Start R in one window, as usual.

2. In another window, determine the ID number of your R process. In UNIX family systems, for instance, this is obtained by something like `ps -a`.

3. In that second window, submit GDB's `attach` command with the R process number.

4. Submit the `continue` command to GDB.

You can set breakpoints in the R source code either before continuing or by interrupting GDB later with CTRL-C. See Section 15.1.4 for details for debugging C code called from R. If, on the other hand, you wish to use GDB to explore the R source code, note the following.

The R source code is dominated by S expression pointers (SEXPs), which are pointers to C structs that contain an R variable's value, type, and so on. You can use the R internal function `Rf_PrintValue(s)` to inspect SEXP values. For example, if the SEXP is named s, then in GDB, type this:

```
call Rf_PrintValue(s)
```

This prints the value.

14

PERFORMANCE ENHANCEMENT: SPEED AND MEMORY

In computer science curricula, a common theme is the trade-off between time and space. In order to have a fast-running program, you may need to use more memory space. On the other hand, in order to conserve memory space, you might need to settle for slower code. In the R language, this trade-off is of particular interest for the following reasons:

- R is an interpreted language. Many of the commands are written in C and thus do run in fast machine code. But other commands, and your own R code, are pure R and thus interpreted. So, there is a risk that your R application may run more slowly than you would like.

- All objects in an R session are stored in memory. More precisely, all objects are stored in R's memory address space. R places a limit of $2^{31} - 1$ bytes on the size of any object, even on 64-bit machines and even if you have a lot of RAM. Yet some applications do encounter larger objects.

This chapter will suggest ways that you can enhance the performance of your R code, taking into account the time/space trade-off.

14.1 Writing Fast R Code

What can be done to make R code faster? Here are the main tools available to you:

- Optimize your R code through vectorization, use of byte-code compilation, and other approaches.

- Write the key, CPU-intensive parts of your code in a compiled language such as C/C++.

- Write your code in some form of parallel R.

The first approach will be covered in this chapter, and the other approaches are covered in Chapters 15 and 16.

To optimize your R code, you need to understand R's functional programming nature and the way R uses memory.

14.2 The Dreaded for Loop

The r-help discussion listserv for R often has questions about how to accomplish various tasks without for loops. There seems to be a feeling that programmers should avoid these loops at all costs.[1] Those who pose the queries usually have the goal of speeding up their code.

It's important to understand that simply rewriting code to avoid loops will not necessarily make the code faster. However, in some cases, dramatic speedup may be attained, usually through vectorization.

14.2.1 Vectorization for Speedup

Sometimes, you can use vectorization instead of looping. For example, if x and y are vectors of equal lengths, you can write this:

```
z <- x + y
```

This is not only more compact, but even more important, it is faster than using this loop:

```
for (i in 1:length(x)) z[i] <- x[i] + y[i]
```

Let's do a quick timing comparison:

```
> x <- runif(1000000)
> y <- runif(1000000)
```

---

[1] By contrast, while loops pose much more of a challenge, because they are difficult to vectorize effectively.

```
> z <- vector(length=1000000)
> system.time(z <- x + y)
   user  system elapsed
  0.052   0.016   0.068
> system.time(for (i in 1:length(x)) z[i] <- x[i] + y[i])
   user  system elapsed
  8.088   0.044   8.175
```

What a difference! The version without a loop was more than 120 times faster in elapsed time. While timings may vary from one run to another (a second run of the loop version had elapsed time of 22.958), in some cases, "delooping" R code can really pay off.

It's worth discussing some of the sources of slowdown in the loop version. What may not be obvious to programmers coming to R from other languages is that numerous function calls are involved in the loop version of the previous code:

- Though syntactically the loop looks innocuous, for() is, in fact, a function.

- The colon : looks even more innocuous, but it's a function too. For instance, 1:10 is actually the : function called on the arguments 1 and 10:

```
> ":"(1,10)
 [1]  1  2  3  4  5  6  7  8  9 10
```

- Each vector subscript operation represents a function call, with calls to [for the two reads and to [<- in the case of the write.

Function calls can be time-consuming, as they involve setting up stack frames and the like. Suffering that time penalty at every iteration of the loop adds up to a big slowdown.

By contrast, if we were to write this in C, there would be no function calls. Indeed, that is essentially what happens in our first code snippet. There are function calls there as well, namely a call to + and one to ->, but each is called only once, not 1,000,000 times, as in the loop version. Thus, the first version of the code is much faster.

One type of vectorization is *vector filtering* For instance, let's rewrite our function oddcount() from Section 1.3:

```
oddcount <- function(x) return(sum(x%%2==1))
```

There is no explicit loop here, and even though R will internally loop through the array, this will be done in native machine code. Again, the anticipated speedup does occur.

```
> x <- sample(1:1000000,100000,replace=T)
> system.time(oddcount(x))
   user  system elapsed
```

```
  0.012   0.000   0.015
> system.time(
+   {
+   c <- 0
+   for (i in 1:length(x))
+       if (x[i] %% 2 == 1) c <- c+1
+   return(c)
+   }
+ )
   user   system elapsed
  0.308   0.000   0.310
```

You might wonder whether it matters in this case, since even the loop version of the code took less than a second to run. But if this code had been part of an enclosing loop, with many iterations, the difference could be important indeed.

Examples of other vectorized functions that may speed up your code are ifelse(), which(), where(), any(), all(), cumsum(), and cumprod(). In the matrix case, you can use rowSums(), colSums(), and so on. In "all possible combinations" types of settings, combin(), outer(), lower.tri(), upper.tri(), or expand.grid() may be just what you need.

Though apply() eliminates an explicit loop, it is actually implemented in R rather than C and thus will usually not speed up your code. However, the other apply functions, such as lapply(), can be very helpful in speeding up your code.

14.2.2   Extended Example: Achieving Better Speed in a Monte Carlo Simulation

In some applications, simulation code can run for hours, days, or even months, so speedup methods are of high interest. Here, we'll look at two simulation examples.

To begin, let's consider the following code from Section 8.6:

```
sum <- 0
nreps <- 100000
for (i in 1:nreps) {
   xy <- rnorm(2)  # generate 2 N(0,1)s
   sum <- sum + max(xy)
}
print(sum/nreps)
```

Here's a revision (hopefully faster):

```
nreps <- 100000
xymat <- matrix(rnorm(2*nreps),ncol=2)
```

```
maxs <- pmax(xymat[,1],xymat[,2])
print(mean(maxs))
```

In this code, we generate all the random variates at once, storing them in a matrix xymat, with one (X,Y) pair per row:

```
xymat <- matrix(rnorm(2*nreps),ncol=2)
```

Next, we find all the max(X,Y) values, storing those values in maxs, and then simply call mean().

It's easier to program, and we believe it will be faster. Let's check that. I had the original code in the file *MaxNorm.R* and the improved version in *MaxNorm2.R*.

```
> system.time(source("MaxNorm.R"))
[1] 0.5667599
   user  system elapsed
  1.700   0.004   1.722
> system.time(source("MaxNorm2.R"))
[1] 0.5649281
   user  system elapsed
  0.132   0.008   0.143
```

The speedup is dramatic, once again.

NOTE   *We achieved an increase in speed, at the expense of using more memory, by keeping our random numbers in an array instead of generating and discarding them one pair at a time. As mentioned earlier, the time/space trade-off is a common one in the computing world and in the R world in particular.*

We attained an excellent speedup in this example, but it was misleadingly easy. Let's look at a slightly more complicated example.

Our next example is a classic exercise from elementary probability courses. Urn 1 contains ten blue marbles and eight yellow ones. In urn 2, the mixture is six blue and six yellow. We draw a marble at random from urn 1, transfer it to urn 2, and then draw a marble at random from urn 2. What is the probability that that second marble is blue? This is easy to find analytically, but we'll use simulation. Here is the straightforward way:

```
1  # perform nreps repetitions of the marble experiment, to estimate
2  # P(pick blue from Urn 2)
3  sim1 <- function(nreps)  {
4     nb1 <- 10  # 10 blue marbles in Urn 1
5     n1 <- 18 # number of marbles in Urn 1 at 1st pick
6     n2 <- 13 # number of marbles in Urn 2 at 2nd pick
7     count <- 0  # number of repetitions in which get blue from Urn 2
8     for (i in 1:nreps)  {
9        nb2 <- 6  # 6 blue marbles orig. in Urn 2
```

```
10    # pick from Urn 1 and put in Urn 2; is it blue?
11    if (runif(1) < nb1/n1) nb2 <- nb2 + 1
12    # pick from Urn 2; is it blue?
13    if (runif(1) < nb2/n2) count <- count + 1
14    }
15    return(count/nreps)  # est. P(pick blue from Urn 2)
16  }
```

Here is how we can do it without loops, using apply():

```
1   sim2 <- function(nreps)  {
2     nb1 <- 10
3     nb2 <- 6
4     n1 <- 18
5     n2 <- 13
6     # pre-generate all our random numbers, one row per repetition
7     u <- matrix(c(runif(2*nreps)),nrow=nreps,ncol=2)
8     # define simfun for use in apply(); simulates one repetition
9     simfun <- function(rw) {
10       # rw ("row") is a pair of random numbers
11       # choose from Urn 1
12       if (rw[1] < nb1/n1) nb2 <- nb2 + 1
13       # choose from Urn 2, and return boolean on choosing blue
14       return (rw[2] < nb2/n2)
15    }
16    z <- apply(u,1,simfun)
17    # z is a vector of booleans but they can be treated as 1s, 0s
18    return(mean(z))
19  }
```

Here, we set up a matrix u with two columns of $U(0,1)$ random variates. The first column is used for our simulation of drawing from urn 1, and the second for drawing from urn 2. This way, we generate all our random numbers at once, which might save a bit of time, but the main point is to set up for using apply(). Toward that goal, our function simfun() works on one repetition of the experiment—that is, one row of u. We set up the call to apply() to go through all of the nreps repetitions.

Note that since the function simfun() is declared within sim2(), the locals of sim2()—n1, n2, nb1, and nb2—are available as globals of simfun(). Also, since a Boolean vector will automatically be changed by R to 1s and 0s, we can find the fraction of TRUE values in the vector by simply calling mean().

Now, let's compare performance.

```
> system.time(print(sim1(100000)))
[1] 0.5086
   user  system elapsed
  2.465   0.028   2.586
> system.time(print(sim2(10000)))
```

```
[1] 0.5031
   user  system elapsed
  2.936   0.004   3.027
```

In spite of the many benefits of functional programming, this approach using apply() didn't help. Instead, things got worse. Since this could be simply due to random sampling variation, I ran the code several times again, with similar results.

So, let's look at vectorizing this simulation.

```
1  sim3 <- function(nreps)  {
2     nb1 <- 10
3     nb2 <- 6
4     n1 <- 18
5     n2 <- 13
6     u <- matrix(c(runif(2*nreps)),nrow=nreps,ncol=2)
7     # set up the condition vector
8     cndtn <- u[,1] <= nb1/n1 & u[,2] <= (nb2+1)/n2 |
9             u[,1] > nb1/n1 & u[,2] <= nb2/n2
10    return(mean(cndtn))
11 }
```

The main work is done in this statement:

```
cndtn <- u[,1] <= nb1/n1 & u[,2] <= (nb2+1)/n2 |
        u[,1] > nb1/n1 & u[,2] <= nb2/n2
```

To get that, we reasoned out which conditions would lead to choosing a blue marble on the second pick, coded them, and then assigned them to cndtn.

Remember that <= and & are functions; in fact, they are vector functions, so they should be fast. Sure enough, this brings quite an improvement:

```
> system.time(print(sim3(10000)))
[1] 0.4987
   user  system elapsed
  0.060   0.016   0.076
```

In principle, the approach we took to speed up the code here could be applied to many other Monte Carlo simulations. However, it's clear that the analog of the statement that computes cndtn would quickly become quite complex, even for seemingly simple applications.

Moreover, the approach would not work in "infinite-stage" situations, meaning an unlimited number of time steps. Here, we are considering the marble example as being two-stage, with two columns to the matrix u.

14.2.3 Extended Example: Generating a Powers Matrix

Recall in Section 9.1.7, we needed to generate a matrix of powers of our predictor variable. We used the following code:

```
# forms matrix of powers of the vector x, through degree dg
powers1 <- function(x,dg) {
   pw <- matrix(x,nrow=length(x))
   prod <- x  # current product
   for (i in 2:dg) {
      prod <- prod * x
      pw <- cbind(pw,prod)
   }
   return(pw)
}
```

One glaring problem is that cbind() is used to build up the output matrix, column by column. This is very costly in terms of memory-allocation time. It's much better to allocate the full matrix at the beginning, even though it will be empty, as this will mean incurring the cost of only one memory-allocation operation.

```
# forms matrix of powers of the vector x, through degree dg
powers2 <- function(x,dg) {
   pw <- matrix(nrow=length(x),ncol=dg)
   prod <- x  # current product
   pw[,1] <- prod
   for (i in 2:dg) {
      prod <- prod * x
      pw[,i] <- prod
   }
   return(pw)
}
```

And indeed, powers2() is a lot faster.

```
> x <- runif(1000000)
> system.time(powers1(x,8))
   user   system elapsed
  0.776    0.356   1.334
> system.time(powers2(x,8))
   user   system elapsed
  0.388    0.204   0.593
```

And yet, `powers2()` still contains a loop. Can we do better? It would seem that this setting is perfect for `outer()`, whose call form is

```
outer(X,Y,FUN)
```

This call applies the function `FUN()` to all possible pairs of elements of `X` and elements of `Y`. The default value of `FUN` is multiplication.

Here, we can write the following:

```
powers3 <- function(x,dg) return(outer(x,1:dg,"^"))
```

For each combination of element of x and element of 1:dg (resulting in length(x) × dg combinations in all), `outer()` calls the exponentiation function ^ on that combination, placing the results in a length(x) × dg matrix. This is exactly what we need, and as a bonus, the code is quite compact. But is the code faster?

```
> system.time(powers3(x,8))
   user  system elapsed
  1.336   0.204   1.747
```

What a disappointment! Here, we're using a fancy R function, with very compact code, but getting the worst performance of the three functions.

And it gets even worse. Here's what happens if we try to make use of `cumprod()`:

```
> powers4
function(x,dg) {
   repx <- matrix(rep(x,dg),nrow=length(x))
   return(t(apply(repx,1,cumprod)))
}
> system.time(powers4(x,8))
   user  system elapsed
 28.106   1.120  83.255
```

In this example, we made multiple copies of x, since the powers of a number n are simply `cumprod(c(1,n,n,n...))`. But in spite of dutifully using two C-level R functions, the performance was disastrous.

The moral of the story is that performance issues can be unpredictable. All you can do is be armed with an understanding of the basic issues, vectorization, and the memory aspects explained next and then try various approaches.

14.3 Functional Programming and Memory Issues

Most R objects are *immutable*, or unchangeable. Thus, R operations are implemented as functions that reassign to the given object, a trait that can have performance implications.

14.3.1 Vector Assignment Issues

As an example of some of the issues that can arise, consider this simple-looking statement:

```
z[3] <- 8
```

As noted in Chapter 7, this assignment is more complex than it seems. It is actually implemented via the replacement function "[<-" through this call and assignment:

```
z <- "[<-"(z,3,value=8)
```

An internal copy of z is made, element 3 of the copy is changed to 8, and then the resulting vector is reassigned to z. And recall that the latter simply means that z is pointed to the copy.

In other words, even though we are ostensibly changing just one element of the vector, the semantics say that *the entire vector is recomputed*. For a long vector, this would slow down the program considerably. The same would be true for a shorter vector if it were assigned from within a loop of our code.

In some situations, R does take some measures to mitigate this impact, but it is a key point to consider when aiming for fast code. You should be mindful of this when working with vectors (including arrays). If your code seems to be running unexpectedly slowly, assignment of vectors should be a prime area of suspicion.

14.3.2 Copy-on-Change Issues

A related issue is that R (usually) follows a *copy-on-change* policy. For instance, if we execute the following in the previous setting:

```
> y <- z
```

then initially y shares the same memory area with z. But if either of them changes, then a copy is made in a different area of memory, and the changed variable will occupy the new area of memory. However, only the *first* change is affected, as the relocating of the moved variable means there are no longer any sharing issues. The function tracemem() will report such memory relocations.

Though R usually adheres to copy-on-change semantics, there are exceptions. For example, R doesn't exhibit the location-change behavior in the following setting:

```
> z <- runif(10)
> tracemem(z)
[1] "<0x88c3258>"
> z[3] <- 8
> tracemem(z)
[1] "<0x88c3258>"
```

The location of z didn't change; it was at memory address 0x88c3258 both before and after the assignment to z[3] was executed. Thus, although you should be vigilant about location change, you also can't assume it.

Let's look at the times involved.

```
> z <- 1:10000000
> system.time(z[3] <- 8)
   user  system elapsed
  0.180   0.084   0.265
> system.time(z[33] <- 88)
   user  system elapsed
      0       0       0
```

In any event, if copying is done, the vehicle is R's internal function duplicate(). (The function is called duplicate1() in recent versions of R.) If you're familiar with the GDB debugging tool and your R build includes debugging information, you can explore the circumstances under which a copy is performed.

Following the guide in Section 15.1.4, start up R with GDB, step through R through GDB, and place a breakpoint at duplicate1(). Each time you break at that function, submit this GDB command:

```
call Rf_PrintValue(s)
```

This will print the value of s (or whatever variable is of interest).

14.3.3   Extended Example: Avoiding Memory Copy

This example, though artificial, will demonstrate the memory-copy issues discussed in the previous section.

Suppose we have a large number of unrelated vectors and, among other things, we wish to set the third element of each to 8. We could store the vectors in a matrix, one vector per row. But since they are unrelated, maybe even of different lengths, we may consider storing them in a list.

But things can get very subtle when it comes to R performance issues, so let's try it out.

```
> m  <- 5000
> n <- 1000
> z <- list()
> for (i in 1:m) z[[i]] <- sample(1:10,n,replace=T)
> system.time(for (i in 1:m) z[[i]][3] <- 8)
   user  system elapsed
  0.288   0.024   0.321
> z <- matrix(sample(1:10,m*n,replace=T),nrow=m)
> system.time(z[,3] <- 8)
   user  system elapsed
  0.008   0.044   0.052
```

Except for system time (again), the matrix formulation did better. One of the reasons is that in the list version, we encounter the memory-copy problem in each iteration of the loop. But in the matrix version, we encounter it only once. And, of course, the matrix version is vectorized.

But what about using lapply() on the list version?

```
>
> set3 <- function(lv) {
+     lv[3] <- 8
+     return(lv)
+ }
> z <- list()
> for (i in 1:m) z[[i]] <- sample(1:10,n,replace=T)
> system.time(lapply(z,set3))
   user  system elapsed
  0.100   0.012   0.112
```

It's hard to beat vectorized code.

14.4   Using Rprof() to Find Slow Spots in Your Code

If you think your R code is running unnecessarily slowly, a handy tool for finding the culprit is Rprof(), which gives you a report of (approximately) how much time your code is spending in each of the functions it calls. This is important, as it may not be wise to optimize *every* section of your program. Optimization may come at the expense of coding time and code clarity, so it's of value to know where optimization would really help.

14.4.1   Monitoring with Rprof()

Let's demonstrate using Rprof() with our three versions of code to find a powers matrix from the previous extended example. We'll call Rprof() to get the monitor started, run our code, and then call Rprof() with a NULL argument to stop the monitoring. Finally, we'll call `summaryRprof()` to see the results.

```
> x <- runif(1000000)
> Rprof()
> invisible(powers1(x,8))
> Rprof(NULL)
> summaryRprof()
$by.self
          self.time self.pct total.time total.pct
"cbind"        0.74     86.0       0.74      86.0
"*"            0.10     11.6       0.10      11.6
"matrix"       0.02      2.3       0.02       2.3
"powers1"      0.00      0.0       0.86     100.0


$by.total
          total.time total.pct self.time self.pct
"powers1"       0.86     100.0      0.00      0.0
"cbind"         0.74      86.0      0.74     86.0
"*"             0.10      11.6      0.10     11.6
"matrix"        0.02       2.3      0.02      2.3


$sampling.time
[1] 0.86
```

We see immediately that the runtime of our code is dominated by calls to `cbind()`, which as we noted in the extended example is indeed slowing things down.

By the way, the call to `invisible()` in this example is used to suppress output. We certainly don't want to see the 1,000,000-row matrix returned by `powers1()` here!

Profiling `powers2()` does not show any obvious bottlenecks.

```
> Rprof()
> invisible(powers2(x,8))
> Rprof(NULL)
> summaryRprof()
$by.self
          self.time self.pct total.time total.pct
"powers2"      0.38     67.9       0.56     100.0
"matrix"       0.14     25.0       0.14      25.0
"*"            0.04      7.1       0.04       7.1


$by.total
          total.time total.pct self.time self.pct
"powers2"       0.56     100.0      0.38     67.9
"matrix"        0.14      25.0      0.14     25.0
"*"             0.04       7.1      0.04      7.1
```

```
$sampling.time
[1] 0.56
```

What about powers3(), the promising approach that didn't pan out?

```
> Rprof()
> invisible(powers3(x,8))
> Rprof(NULL)
> summaryRprof()
$by.self
          self.time self.pct total.time total.pct
"FUN"          0.94     56.6       0.94      56.6
"outer"        0.72     43.4       1.66     100.0
"powers3"      0.00      0.0       1.66     100.0

$by.total
          total.time total.pct self.time self.pct
"outer"         1.66     100.0      0.72     43.4
"powers3"       1.66     100.0      0.00      0.0
"FUN"           0.94      56.6      0.94     56.6

$sampling.time
[1] 1.66
```

The function logging the largest amount of time was FUN(), which as noted in our extended example is simply multiplication. For each pair of elements of x here, one of the elements is multiplied by the other; that is, a product of two scalars is found. In other words, no vectorization! No wonder it was slow.

14.4.2   How Rprof() Works

Let's explore in a bit more detail what Rprof() does. Every 0.02 seconds (the default value), R inspects the call stack to determine which function calls are in effect at that time. It writes the result of each inspection to a file, by default *Rprof.out*. Here is an excerpt of that file from our run of powers3():

```
...
"outer" "powers3"
"outer" "powers3"
"outer" "powers3"
"FUN" "outer" "powers3"
"FUN" "outer" "powers3"
"FUN" "outer" "powers3"
"FUN" "outer" "powers3"
...
```

So, Rprof() often found that at inspection time, powers3() had called outer(), which in turn had called FUN(), the latter being the currently executing function. The function summaryRprof() conveniently summarizes all those lines in the file, but you may find that looking at the file itself reveals more insights in some cases.

Note, too, that Rprof() is no panacea. If the code you're profiling produces many function calls (including indirect calls, triggered when your code calls some function that then calls another within R), the profiling output may be hard to decipher. This is arguably the case for the output from powers4():

```
$by.self
             self.time self.pct total.time total.pct
"apply"          19.46     67.5      27.56      95.6
"lapply"          4.02     13.9       5.68      19.7
"FUN"             2.56      8.9       2.56       8.9
"as.vector"       0.82      2.8       0.82       2.8
"t.default"       0.54      1.9       0.54       1.9
"unlist"          0.40      1.4       6.08      21.1
"!"               0.34      1.2       0.34       1.2
"is.null"         0.32      1.1       0.32       1.1
"aperm"           0.22      0.8       0.22       0.8
"matrix"          0.14      0.5       0.74       2.6
"!="              0.02      0.1       0.02       0.1
"powers4"         0.00      0.0      28.84     100.0
"t"               0.00      0.0      28.10      97.4
"array"           0.00      0.0       0.22       0.8

$by.total
             total.time total.pct self.time self.pct
"powers4"         28.84     100.0      0.00      0.0
"t"               28.10      97.4      0.00      0.0
"apply"           27.56      95.6     19.46     67.5
"unlist"           6.08      21.1      0.40      1.4
"lapply"           5.68      19.7      4.02     13.9
"FUN"              2.56       8.9      2.56      8.9
"as.vector"        0.82       2.8      0.82      2.8
"matrix"           0.74       2.6      0.14      0.5
"t.default"        0.54       1.9      0.54      1.9
"!"                0.34       1.2      0.34      1.2
"is.null"          0.32       1.1      0.32      1.1
"aperm"            0.22       0.8      0.22      0.8
"array"            0.22       0.8      0.00      0.0
"!="               0.02       0.1      0.02      0.1

$sampling.time
[1] 28.84
```

14.5 Byte Code Compilation

Starting with version 2.13, R has included a *byte code compiler*, which you can use to try to speed up your code. Consider our example from Section 14.2.1. As a trivial example, we showed that

```
z <- x + y
```

was much faster than

```
for (i in 1:length(x)) z[i] <- x[i] + y[i]
```

Again, that was obvious, but just to get an idea of how byte code compilation works, let's give it a try:

```
> library(compiler)
> f <- function() for (i in 1:length(x)) z[i] <<- x[i] + y[i]
> cf <- cmpfun(f)
> system.time(cf())
   user  system elapsed
  0.845   0.003   0.848
```

We created a new function, cf(), from the original f(). The new code's run time was 0.848 seconds, much faster than the 8.175 seconds the non-compiled version took. Granted, it still wasn't as fast as the straightforward vectorized code, but it is clear that byte code compilation has potential. You should try it whenever you need faster code.

14.6 Oh No, the Data Doesn't Fit into Memory!

As mentioned earlier, all objects in an R session are stored in memory. R places a limit of $2^{31} - 1$ bytes on the size of any object, regardless of word size (32-bit versus 64-bit) and the amount of RAM in your machine. However, you really should not consider this an obstacle. With a little extra care, applications that have large memory requirements can indeed be handled well in R. Some common approaches are chunking and using R packages for memory management.

14.6.1 Chunking

One option involving no extra R packages at all is to read in your data from a disk file one chunk at a time. For example, suppose that our goal is to find means or proportions of some variables. We can use the skip argument in read.table().

Say our data set has 1,000,000 records and we divide them into 10 chunks (or more—whatever is needed to cut the data down to a size so it fits in memory). Then we set skip = 0 on our first read, set skip = 100000 the second time, and so on. Each time we read in a chunk, we calculate the counts or totals for that chunk and record them. After reading all the chunks, we add up all the counts or totals in order to calculate our grand means or proportions.

As another example, suppose we are performing a statistical operation, say calculating principle components, in which we have a huge number of rows—that is, a huge number of observations—but the number of variables is manageable. Again, chunking could be the solution. We apply the statistical operation to each chunk and then average the results over all the chunks. My mathematical research shows that the resulting estimators are statistically efficient in a wide class of statistical methods.

14.6.2   Using R Packages for Memory Management

Again looking at a bit more sophistication, there are alternatives for accommodating large memory requirements in the form of some specialized R packages.

One such package is RMySQL, an R interface to SQL databases. Using it requires some database expertise, but this package provides a much more efficient and convenient way to handle large data sets. The idea is to have SQL do its variable/case selection operations for you back at the database end and then read the resulting selected data as it is produced by SQL. Since the latter will typically be much smaller than the overall data set, you will likely be able to circumvent R's memory restriction.

Another useful package is biglm, which does regression and generalized linear-model analysis on very large data sets. It also uses chunking but in a different manner: Each chunk is used to update the running totals of sums needed for the regression analysis and then discarded.

Finally, some packages do their own storage management independently of R and thus can deal with very large data sets. The two most commonly used today are ff and bigmemory. The former sidesteps memory constraints by storing data on disk instead of memory, essentially transparently to the programmer. The highly versatile bigmemory package does the same, but it can store data not only on disk but also in the machine's main memory, which is ideal for multicore machines.

15

INTERFACING R TO OTHER LANGUAGES

 R is a great language, but it can't do everything well. Thus, it is sometimes desirable to call code written in other languages from R. Conversely, when working in other great languages, you may encounter tasks that could be better done in R.

R interfaces have been developed for a number of other languages, from ubiquitous languages like C to esoteric ones like the Yacas computer algebra system. This chapter will cover two interfaces: one for calling C/C++ from R and the other for calling R from Python.

15.1 Writing C/C++ Functions to Be Called from R

You may wish to write your own C/C++ functions to be called from R. Typically, the goal is performance enhancement, since C/C++ code may run much faster than R, even if you use vectorization and other R optimization techniques to speed things up.

Another possible goal in dropping down to the C/C++ level is specialized I/O. For example, R uses the TCP protocol in layer 3 of the standard Internet communication system, but UDP can be faster in some settings.

To work in UDP, you need C/C++, which requires an interface to R for those languages.

R actually offers two C/C++ interfaces via the functions .C() and .Call(). The latter is more versatile but requires some knowledge of R's internal structures, so we'll stick with .C() here.

15.1.1 Some R-to-C/C++ Preliminaries

In C, two-dimensional arrays are stored in row-major order, in contrast to R's column-major order. For instance, if you have a 3-by-4 array, the element in the second row and second column is element number 5 of the array when viewed linearly, since there are three elements in the first column and this is the second element in the second column. Also keep in mind that C subscripts begin at 0, rather than at 1, as with R.

All the arguments passed from R to C are received by C as pointers. Note that the C function itself must return void. Values that you would ordinarily return must be communicated through the function's arguments, such as result in the following example.

15.1.2 Example: Extracting Subdiagonals from a Square Matrix

Here, we will write C code to extract subdiagonals from a square matrix. (Thanks to my former graduate assistant, Min-Yu Huang, who wrote an earlier version of this function.) Here's the code for the file *sd.c*:

```
#include <R.h>  // required

// arguments:
//    m:  a square matrix
//    n:  number of rows/columns of m
//    k:  the subdiagonal index--0 for main diagonal, 1 for first
//        subdiagonal, 2 for the second, etc.
//    result:  space for the requested subdiagonal, returned here

void subdiag(double *m, int *n, int *k, double *result)
{
  int nval = *n, kval = *k;
  int stride = nval + 1;
  for (int i = 0, j = kval; i < nval-kval; ++i, j+= stride)
    result[i] = m[j];
}
```

The variable stride alludes to a concept from the parallel-processing community. Say we have a matrix in 1,000 columns and our C code is looping through all the elements in a given column, from top to bottom. Again, since C uses row-major order, consecutive elements in the column are 1,000 elements apart from each other if the matrix is viewed as one long vector.

Here, we would say that we are traversing that long vector with a stride of 1,000—that is, accessing every thousandth element.

15.1.3 Compiling and Running Code

You compile your code using R. For example, in a Linux terminal window, we could compile our file like this:

```
% R CMD SHLIB sd.c
gcc -std=gnu99 -I/usr/share/R/include        -fpic  -g -02 -c sd.c -o sd.o
gcc -std=gnu99 -shared  -o sd.so sd.o   -L/usr/lib/R/lib -lR
```

This would produce the dynamic shared library file *sd.so*.

Note that R has reported how it invoked GCC in the output of the example. You can also run these commands by hand if you have special requirements, such as special libraries to be linked in. Also note that the locations of the *include* and *lib* directories may be system-dependent.

NOTE   *GCC is easily downloadable for Linux systems. For Windows, it is included in Cygwin, an open source package available from* http://www.cygwin.com/.

We can then load our library into R and call our C function like this:

```
> dyn.load("sd.so")
> m <- rbind(1:5, 6:10, 11:15, 16:20, 21:25)
> k <- 2
> .C("subdiag", as.double(m), as.integer(dim(m)[1]), as.integer(k),
result=double(dim(m)[1]-k))
[[1]]
 [1]  1  6 11 16 21  2  7 12 17 22  3  8 13 18 23  4  9 14 19 24  5 10 15 20 25

[[2]]
[1] 5

[[3]]
[1] 2

$result
[1] 11 17 23
```

For convenience here, we've given the name result to both the formal argument (in the C code) and the actual argument (in the R code). Note that we needed to allocate space for result in our R code.

As you can see from the example, the return value takes on the form of a list consisting of the arguments in the R call. In this case, the call had four arguments (in addition to the function name), so the returned list has four components. Typically, some of the arguments will be changed during execution of the C code, as was the case here with result.

15.1.4   Debugging R/C Code

Chapter 13 discussed a number of tools and methods for debugging R code. However, the R/C interface presents an extra challenge. The problem in using a debugging tool such as GDB here is that you must first apply it to R itself.

The following is a walk-through of the R/C debugging steps using GDB on our previous *sd.c* code as the example.

```
$ R -d gdb
GNU gdb 6.8-debian
...
(gdb) run
Starting program: /usr/lib/R/bin/exec/R
...
> dyn.load("sd.so")
>    # hit ctrl-c here
Program received signal SIGINT, Interrupt.
0xb7ffa430 in __kernel_vsyscall ()
(gdb) b subdiag
Breakpoint 1 at 0xb77683f3: file sd.c, line 3.
(gdb) continue
Continuing.

Breakpoint 1, subdiag (m=0x92b9480, n=0x9482328, k=0x9482348, result=0x9817148)
    at sd.c:3
3          int nval = *n, kval = *k;
(gdb)
```

So, what happened in this debugging session?

1. We launched the debugger, GDB, with R loaded into it, from a command line in a terminal window:

   ```
   R -d gdb
   ```

2. We told GDB to run R:

   ```
   (gdb) run
   ```

3. We loaded our compiled C code into R as usual:

   ```
   > dyn.load("sd.so")
   ```

4. We hit the CTRL-C interrupt key pair to pause R and put us back at the GDB prompt.

5. We set a breakpoint at the entry to subdiag():

   ```
   (gdb) b subdiag
   ```

6. We told GDB to resume executing R (we needed to hit the ENTER key a second time in order to get the R prompt):

```
(gdb) continue
```

We then executed our C code:

```
> m <- rbind(1:5, 6:10, 11:15, 16:20, 21:25)
> k <- 2
> .C("subdiag", as.double(m), as.integer(dim(m)[1]), as.integer(k),
+ result=double(dim(m)[1]-k))

Breakpoint 1, subdiag (m=0x942f270, n=0x96c3328, k=0x96c3348, result=0x9a58148)
    at subdiag.c:46
46 if (*n < 1) error("n < 1\n");
```

At this point, we can use GDB to debug as usual. If you're not familiar with GDB, you may want to try one of the many quick tutorials on the Web. Table 15-1 lists some of the most useful commands.

Table 15-1: Common GDB Commands

Command	Description
l	List code lines
b	Set breakpoint
r	Run/rerun
n	Step to next statement
s	Step into function call
p	Print variable or expression
c	Continue
h	Help
q	Quit

15.1.5   Extended Example: Prediction of Discrete-Valued Time Series

Recall our example in Section 2.5.2 where we observed 0- and 1-valued data, one per time period, and attempted to predict the value in any period from the previous k values, using majority rule. We developed two competing functions for the job, preda() and predb(), as follows:

```
# prediction in discrete time series; 0s and 1s; use k consecutive
# observations to predict the next, using majority rule; calculate the
# error rate
preda <- function(x,k) {
    n <- length(x)
    k2 <- k/2
    # the vector pred will contain our predicted values
    pred <- vector(length=n-k)
```

```
    for (i in 1:(n-k)) {
        if (sum(x[i:(i+(k-1))]) >= k2) pred[i] <- 1 else pred[i] <- 0
    }
    return(mean(abs(pred-x[(k+1):n])))
}

predb <- function(x,k) {
    n <- length(x)
    k2 <- k/2
    pred <- vector(length=n-k)
    sm <- sum(x[1:k])
    if (sm >= k2) pred[1] <- 1 else pred[1] <- 0
    if (n-k >= 2) {
        for (i in 2:(n-k)) {
            sm <- sm + x[i+k-1] - x[i-1]
            if (sm >= k2) pred[i] <- 1 else pred[i] <- 0
        }
    }
    return(mean(abs(pred-x[(k+1):n])))
}
```

Since the latter avoids duplicate computation, we speculated it would be faster. Now is the time to check that.

```
> y <- sample(0:1,100000,replace=T)
> system.time(preda(y,1000))
   user  system elapsed
  3.816   0.016   3.873
> system.time(predb(y,1000))
   user  system elapsed
  1.392   0.008   1.427
```

Hey, not bad! That's quite an improvement.

However, you should always ask whether R already has a fine-tuned function that will suit your needs. Since we're basically computing a moving average, we might try the filter() function, with a constant coefficient vector, as follows:

```
predc <- function(x,k) {
    n <- length(x)
    f <- filter(x,rep(1,k),sides=1)[k:(n-1)]
    k2 <- k/2
    pred <- as.integer(f >= k2)
    return(mean(abs(pred-x[(k+1):n])))
}
```

That's even more compact than our first version. But it's a lot harder to read, and for reasons we will explore soon, it may not be so fast. Let's check.

```
> system.time(predc(y,1000))
   user  system elapsed
  3.872   0.016   3.945
```

Well, our second version remains the champion so far. This actually should be expected, as a look at the source code shows. Typing the following shows the source for that function:

```
> filter
```

This reveals (not shown here) that filter1() is called. The latter is written in C, which should give us some speedup, but it still suffers from the duplicate computation problem—hence the slowness.

So, let's write our own C code.

```c
#include <R.h>

void predd(int *x, int *n, int *k, double *errrate)
{
    int nval = *n, kval = *k, nk = nval - kval, i;
    int sm = 0;  // moving sum
    int errs = 0;  // error count
    int pred;  // predicted value
    double k2 = kval/2.0;
    // initialize by computing the initial window
    for (i = 0; i < kval; i++) sm += x[i];
    if (sm >= k2) pred = 1; else pred = 0;
    errs = abs(pred-x[kval]);
    for (i = 1; i < nk; i++) {
        sm = sm + x[i+kval-1] - x[i-1];
        if (sm >= k2) pred = 1; else pred = 0;
        errs += abs(pred-x[i+kval]);
    }
    *errrate = (double) errs / nk;
}
```

This is basically predb() from before, "hand translated" into C. Let's see if it will outdo predb().

```
> system.time(.C("predd",as.integer(y),as.integer(length(y)),as.integer(1000),
+   errrate=double(1)))
   user  system elapsed
  0.004   0.000   0.003
```

The speedup is breathtaking.

You can see that writing certain functions in C can be worth the effort. This is especially true for functions that involve iteration, as R's own iteration constructs, such as for(), are slow.

15.2   Using R from Python

Python is an elegant and powerful language, but it lacks built-in facilities for statistical and data manipulation, two areas in which R excels. This section demonstrates how to call R from Python, using RPy, one of the most popular interfaces between the two languages.

15.2.1   Installing RPy

RPy is a Python module that allows access to R from Python. For extra efficiency, it can be used in conjunction with NumPy.

You can build the module from the source, available from *http://rpy .sourceforge.net*, or download a prebuilt version. If you are running Ubuntu, simply type this:

```
sudo apt-get install python-rpy
```

To load RPy from Python (whether in Python interactive mode or from code), execute the following:

```
from rpy import *
```

This will load a variable r, which is a Python class instance.

15.2.2   RPy Syntax

Running R from Python is in principle quite simple. Here is an example of a command you might run from the >>> Python prompt:

```
>>> r.hist(r.rnorm(100))
```

This will call the R function rnorm() to produce 100 standard normal variates and then input those values into R's histogram function, hist().

As you can see, R names are prefixed by r., reflecting the fact that Python wrappers for R functions are members of the class instance r.

The preceding code will, if not refined, produce ugly output, with your (possibly voluminous!) data appearing as the graph title and the *x*-axis label. You can avoid this by supplying a title and label, as in this example:

```
>>> r.hist(r.rnorm(100),main='',xlab='')
```

RPy syntax is sometimes less simple than these examples would lead you to believe. The problem is that R and Python syntax may clash. For instance, consider a call to the R linear model function lm(). In our example, we will predict b from a.

```
>>> a = [5,12,13]
>>> b = [10,28,30]
>>> lmout = r.lm('v2 ~ v1',data=r.data_frame(v1=a,v2=b))
```

This is somewhat more complex than it would have been if done directly in R. What are the issues here?

First, since Python syntax does not include the tilde character, we needed to specify the model formula via a string. Since this is done in R anyway, this is not a major departure.

Second, we needed a data frame to contain our data. We created one using R's data.frame() function. In order to form a period in an R function name, we need to use an underscore on the Python end. Thus we called r.data_frame(). Note that in this call, we named the columns of our data frame v1 and v2 and then used these in our model formula.

The output object is a Python dictionary (analog of R's list type), as you can see here (in part):

```
>>> lmout
{'qr': {'pivot': [1, 2], 'qr': array([[ -1.73205081, -17.32050808],
       [  0.57735027,  -6.164414   ],
       [  0.57735027,   0.78355007]]), 'qraux':
```

You should recognize the various attributes of lm() objects here. For example, the coefficients of the fitted regression line, which would be contained in lmout$coefficients if this were done in R, are here in Python as lmout['coefficients']. So, you can access those coefficients accordingly, for example like this:

```
>>> lmout['coefficients']
{'v1': 2.5263157894736841, '(Intercept)': -2.5964912280701729}
>>> lmout['coefficients']['v1']
2.5263157894736841
```

You can also submit R commands to work on variables in R's namespace, using the function r(). This is convenient if there are many syntax clashes. Here is how we could run the wireframe() example in Section 12.4 in RPy:

```
>>> r.library('lattice')
>>> r.assign('a',a)
>>> r.assign('b',b)
>>> r('g <- expand.grid(a,b)')
>>> r('g$Var3 <- g$Var1^2 + g$Var1 * g$Var2')
>>> r('wireframe(Var3 ~ Var1+Var2,g)')
>>> r('plot(wireframe(Var3 ~ Var1+Var2,g))')
```

First, we used `r.assign()` to copy a variable from Python's namespace to R's. We then ran `expand.grid()` (with a period in the name instead of an underscore, since we are running in R's namespace), assigning the result to g. Again, the latter is in R's namespace. Note that the call to `wireframe()` did not automatically display the plot, so we needed to call `plot()`.

The official documentation for RPy is at *http://rpy.sourceforge.net/rpy/doc/rpy.pdf*. Also, you can find a useful presentation, "RPy—R from Python," at *http://www.daimi.au.dk/~besen/TBiB2007/lecture-notes/rpy.html*.

16

PARALLEL R

 Since many R users have very large computational needs, various tools for some kind of parallel operation of R have been devised. This chapter is devoted to parallel R.

Many a novice in parallel processing has, with great anticipation, written parallel code for some application only to find that the parallel version actually ran more slowly than the serial one. For reasons to be discussed in this chapter, this problem is especially acute with R.

Accordingly, understanding the nature of parallel-processing hardware and software is crucial to success in the parallel world. These issues will be discussed here in the context of common platforms for parallel R.

We'll start with a few code examples and then move to general performance issues.

16.1   The Mutual Outlinks Problem

Consider a network graph of some kind, such as web links or links in a social network. Let A be the *adjacency matrix* of the graph, meaning that, say, A[3,8] is 1 or 0, depending on whether there is a link from node 3 to node 8.

For any two vertices, say any two websites, we might be interested in mutual outlinks—that is, outbound links that are common to two sites. Suppose that we want to find the mean number of mutual outlinks, averaged over all pairs of websites in our data set. This mean can be found using the following outline, for an n-by-n matrix:

```
1  sum = 0
2  for i = 0...n-1
3     for j = i+1...n-1
4        for k = 0...n-1 sum = sum + a[i][k]*a[j][k]
5  mean = sum / (n*(n-1)/2)
```

Given that our graph could contain thousands—even millions—of websites, our task could entail quite large amounts of computation. A common approach to dealing with this problem is to divide the computation into smaller chunks and then process each of the chunks simultaneously, say on separate computers.

Let's say that we have two computers at our disposal. We might have one computer handle all the odd values of i in the for i loop in line 2 and have the second computer handle the even values. Or, since dual-core computers are fairly standard these days, we could take this same approach on a single computer. This may sound simple, but a number of major issues can arise, as you'll learn in this chapter.

16.2   Introducing the snow Package

Luke Tierney's snow (Simple Network of Workstations) package, available from the CRAN R code repository, is arguably the simplest, easiest-to-use form of parallel R and one of the most popular.

NOTE   *The CRAN Task View page on parallel R,* http://cran.r-project.org/web/views/HighPerformanceComputing.html, *has a fairly up-to-date list of available parallel R packages.*

To see how snow works, here's code for the mutual outlinks problem described in the previous section:

```
1  # snow version of mutual links problem
2
3  mtl <- function(ichunk,m) {
4     n <- ncol(m)
5     matches <- 0
6     for (i in ichunk) {
7        if (i < n) {
8           rowi <- m[i,]
9           matches <- matches +
10             sum(m[(i+1):n,] %*% rowi)
11        }
12     }
13     matches
14  }
```

```
15
16   mutlinks <- function(cls,m) {
17      n <- nrow(m)
18      nc <- length(cls)
19      # determine which worker gets which chunk of i
20      options(warn=-1)
21      ichunks <- split(1:n,1:nc)
22      options(warn=0)
23      counts <- clusterApply(cls,ichunks,mtl,m)
24      do.call(sum,counts) / (n*(n-1)/2)
25   }
```

Suppose we have this code in the file *SnowMutLinks.R*. Let's first discuss how to run it.

16.2.1   *Running snow Code*

Running the above snow code involves the following steps:

1. Load the code.

2. Load the snow library.

3. Form a snow cluster.

4. Set up the adjacency matrix of interest.

5. Run your code on that matrix on the cluster you formed.

Assuming we are running on a dual-core machine, we issue the following commands to R:

```
> source("SnowMutLinks.R")
> library(snow)
> cl <- makeCluster(type="SOCK",c("localhost","localhost"))
> testm <- matrix(sample(0:1,16,replace=T),nrow=4)
> mutlinks(cl,testm)
[1] 0.6666667
```

Here, we are instructing snow to start two new R processes on our machine (localhost is a standard network name for the local machine), which I will refer to here as *workers*. I'll refer to the original R process—the one in which we type the preceding commands—as the *manager*. So, at this point, three instances of R will be running on the machine (visible by running the ps command if you are in a Linux environment, for example).

The workers form a *cluster* in snow parlance, which we have named cl. The snow package uses what is known in the parallel-processing world as a *scatter/gather* paradigm, which works as follows:

1. The manager partitions the data into chunks and parcels them out to the workers (scatter phase).

2. The workers process their chunks.

3. The manager collects the results from the workers (gather phase) and combines them as appropriate to the application.

We have specified that communication between the manager and workers will be via network sockets (covered in Chapter 10).

Here's a test matrix to check the code:

```
> testm
  [,1] [,2] [,3] [,4]
[1,]   1    0    0    1
[2,]   0    0    0    0
[3,]   1    0    1    1
[4,]   0    1    0    1
```

Row 1 has zero outlinks in common with row 2, two in common with row 3, and one in common with row 4. Row 2 has zero outlinks in common with the rest, but row 3 has one in common with row 4. That is a total of four mutual outlinks out of $4 \times 3/2 = 6$ pairs—hence, the mean value of $4/6 = 0.6666667$, as you saw earlier.

You can make clusters of any size, as long as you have the machines. In my department, for instance, I have machines whose network names are pc28, pc29, and pc30. Each machine is dual core, so I could create a six-worker cluster as follows:

```
> cl6 <- makeCluster(type="SOCK",c("pc28","pc28","pc29","pc29","pc30","pc30"))
```

16.2.2 Analyzing the snow Code

Now let's see how the mutlinks() function works. First, we sense how many rows the matrix m has, in line 17, and the number of workers in our cluster, in line 18.

Next, we need to determine which worker will handle which values of i in the for i loop in our outline code shown earlier in Section 16.1. R's split() function is well suited for this. For instance, in the case of a 4-row matrix and a 2-worker cluster, that call produces the following:

```
> split(1:4,1:2)
$`1`
[1] 1 3

$`2`
[1] 2 4
```

An R list is returned whose first element is the vector (1,3) and the second is (2,4). This will set up having one R process work on the odd values of i and the other work on the even values, as we discussed earlier. We ward off the warnings that split() would give us ("data length is not a multiple of split variable") by calling options().

The real work is done in line 23, where we call the snow function clusterApply(). This function initiates a call to the same specified function (mtl() here), with some arguments specific to each worker and some optional arguments common to all. So, here's what the call in line 23 does:

1. Worker 1 will be directed to call the function mtl() with the arguments ichunks[[1]] and m.

2. Worker 2 will call mtl() with the arguments ichunks[[2]] and m, and so on for all workers.

3. Each worker will perform its assigned task and then return the result to the manager.

4. The manager will collect all such results into an R list, which we have assigned here to counts.

At this point, we merely need to sum all the elements of counts. Well, I shouldn't say "merely," because there is a little wrinkle to iron out in line 24.

R's sum() function is capable of acting on several vector arguments, like this:

```
> sum(1:2,c(4,10))
[1] 17
```

But here, counts is an R list, not a (numeric) vector. So we rely on do.call() to extract the vectors from counts, and then we call sum() on them.

Note lines 9 and 10. As you know, in R, we try to vectorize our computation wherever possible for better performance. By casting things in matrix-times-vector terms, we replace the for j and for k loops in the outline in Section 16.1 by a single vector-based expression.

16.2.3   How Much Speedup Can Be Attained?

I tried this code on a 1000-by-1000 matrix m1000. I first ran it on a 4-worker cluster and then on a 12-worker cluster. In principle, I should have had speedups of 4 and 12, respectively. But the actual elapsed times were 6.2 seconds and 5.0 seconds. Compare these figures to the 16.9 seconds runtime in nonparallel form. (The latter consisted of the call mtl(1:1000,m1000).) So, I attained a speedup of about 2.7 instead of a theoretical 4.0 for a 4-worker cluster and 3.4 rather than 12.0 on the 12-node system. (Note that some timing variation occurs from run to run.) What went wrong?

In almost any parallel-processing application, you encounter *overhead*, or "wasted" time spent on noncomputational activity. In our example, there is overhead in the form of the time needed to send our matrix from the manager to the workers. We also encountered a bit of overhead in sending the function mtl() itself to the workers. And when the workers finish their tasks, returning their results to the manager causes some overhead, too. We'll discuss this in detail when we talk about general performance considerations in in Section 16.4.1.

16.2.4 Extended Example: K-Means Clustering

To learn more about the capabilities of snow, we'll look at another example, this one involving k-means clustering (KMC).

KMC is a technique for exporatory data analysis. In looking at scatter plots of your data, you may have the perception that the observations tend to cluster into groups, and KMC is a method for finding such groups. The output consists of the centroids of the groups.

The following is an outline of the algorithm:

```
1  for iter = 1,2,...,niters
2    set vector and count totals to 0
3    for i = 1,...,nrow(m)
4      set j = index of the closest group center to m[i,]
5      add m[i,] to the vector total for group j, v[j]
6      add 1 to the count total for group j, c[j]
7    for j = 1,...,ngrps
8      set new center of group j = v[j] / c[j]
```

Here, we specify niters iterations, with initcenters as our initial guesses for the centers of the groups. Our data is in the matrix m, and there are ngrps groups.

The following is the snow code to compute KMC in parallel:

```
1  # snow version of k-means clustering problem
2
3  library(snow)
4
5  # returns distances from x to each vector in y;
6  # here x is a single vector and y is a bunch of them;
7  # define distance between 2 points to be the sum of the absolute values
8  # of their componentwise differences; e.g., distance between (5,4.2) and
9  # (3,5.6) is 2 + 1.4 = 3.4
10 dst <- function(x,y) {
11   tmpmat <- matrix(abs(x-y),byrow=T,ncol=length(x)) # note recycling
12   rowSums(tmpmat)
13 }
14
15 # will check this worker's mchunk matrix against currctrs, the current
16 # centers of the groups, returning a matrix; row j of the matrix will
17 # consist of the vector sum of the points in mchunk closest to jth
18 # current center, and the count of such points
19 findnewgrps <- function(currctrs) {
20   ngrps <- nrow(currctrs)
21   spacedim <- ncol(currctrs) # what dimension space are we in?
```

```
22    # set up the return matrix
23    sumcounts <- matrix(rep(0,ngrps*(spacedim+1)),nrow=ngrps)
24    for (i in 1:nrow(mchunk)) {
25       dsts <- dst(mchunk[i,],t(currctrs))
26       j <- which.min(dsts)
27       sumcounts[j,] <- sumcounts[j,] + c(mchunk[i,],1)
28    }
29    sumcounts
30 }
31
32 parkm <- function(cls,m,niters,initcenters) {
33    n <- nrow(m)
34    spacedim <- ncol(m) # what dimension space are we in?
35    # determine which worker gets which chunk of rows of m
36    options(warn=-1)
37    ichunks <- split(1:n,1:length(cls))
38    options(warn=0)
39    # form row chunks
40    mchunks <- lapply(ichunks,function(ichunk) m[ichunk,])
41    mcf <- function(mchunk) mchunk <<- mchunk
42    # send row chunks to workers; each chunk will be a global variable at
43    # the worker, named mchunk
44    invisible(clusterApply(cls,mchunks,mcf))
45    # send dst() to workers
46    clusterExport(cls,"dst")
47    # start iterations
48    centers <- initcenters
49    for (i in 1:niters) {
50       sumcounts <- clusterCall(cls,findnewgrps,centers)
51       tmp <- Reduce("+",sumcounts)
52       centers <- tmp[,1:spacedim] / tmp[,spacedim+1]
53       # if a group is empty, let's set its center to 0s
54       centers[is.nan(centers)] <- 0
55    }
56    centers
57 }
```

The code here is largely similar to our earlier mutual outlinks example. However, there are a couple of new snow calls and a different kind of usage of an old call.

Let's start with lines 39 through 44. Since our matrix m does not change from one iteration to the next, we definitely do not want to resend it to the workers repeatedly, exacerbating the overhead problem. Thus, first we need to send each worker its assigned chunk of m, just once. This is done in line 44 via snow's clusterApply() function, which we used earlier but need to get creative with here. In line 41, we define the function mcf(), which will, running on a worker, accept the worker's chunk from the manager and then keep it as a global variable mchunk on the worker.

Line 46 makes use of a new snow function, clusterExport(), whose job it is to make copies of the manager's global variables at the workers. The variable in question here is actually a function, dst(). Here is why we need to send it separately: The call in line 50 will send the function findnewgrps() to the workers, but although that function calls dst(), snow will not know to send the latter as well. Therefore we send it ourselves.

Line 50 itself uses another new snow call, clusterCall(). This instructs each worker to call findnewgrps(), with centers as argument.

Recall that each worker has a different matrix chunk, so this call will work on different data for each worker. This once again brings up the controversy regarding the use of global variables, discussed in Section 7.8.4. Some software developers may be troubled by the use of a hidden argument in findnewgrps(). On the other hand, as mentioned earlier, using mchunk as an argument would mean sending it to the workers repeatedly, compromising performance.

Finally, take a look at line 51. The snow function clusterApply() always returns an R list. In this case, the return value is in sumcounts, each element of which is a matrix. We need to sum the matrices, producing a totals matrix. Using R's sum() function wouldn't work, as it would total all the elements of the matrices into a single number. Matrix addition is what we need.

Calling R's Reduce() function will do the matrix addition. Recall that any arithmetic operation in R is implemented as a function; in this case, it is implemented as the function "+". The recall to Reduce() then successively applies "+" to the elements of the list sumcounts. Of course, we could just write a loop to do this, but using Reduce() may give us a small performance boost.

16.3   Resorting to C

As you've seen, using parallel R may greatly speed up your R code. This allows you to retain the convenience and expressive power of R, while still ameliorating large runtimes in big applications. If the parallelized R gives you sufficiently good performance, then all is well.

Nevertheless, parallel R is still R and thus still subject to the performance issues covered in Chapter 14. Recall that one solution offered in that chapter was to write a performance-critical portion of your code in C and then call that code from your main R program. (The references to C here mean C or C++.) We will explore this from a parallel-processing viewpoint. Here, instead of writing parallel R, we write ordinary R code that calls parallel C. (I assume a knowledge of C.)

16.3.1   Using Multicore Machines

The C code covered here runs only on multicore systems, so we must discuss the nature of such systems.

You are probably familiar with dual-core machines. Any computer includes a CPU, which is the part that actually runs your program. In essence, a dual-core machine has two CPUs, a quad-core system has four, and so on. With multiple cores, you can do parallel computation!

This parallel computation is done with *threads*, which are analogous to snow's workers. In computationally intensive applications, you generally set up as many threads as there are cores, for example two threads in a dual-core machine. Ideally, these threads run simultaneously, though overhead issues do arise, as will be explained when we look at general performance issues in Section 16.4.1.

If your machine has multiple cores, it is structured as a *shared-memory* system. All cores access the same RAM. The shared nature of the memory makes communication between the cores easy to program. If a thread writes to a memory location, the change is visible to the other threads, without the programmer needing to insert code to make that happen.

16.3.2   Extended Example: Mutual Outlinks Problem in OpenMP

OpenMP is a very popular package for programming on multicore machines. To see how it works, here is the mutual outlinks example again, this time in R-callable OpenMP code:

```
1   #include <omp.h>
2   #include <R.h>
3
4   int tot;  // grand total of matches, over all threads
5
6   // processes row pairs (i,i+1), (i,i+2), ...
7   int procpairs(int i, int *m, int n)
8   {  int j,k,sum=0;
9      for (j = i+1; j < n; j++) {
10        for (k = 0; k < n; k++)
11           // find m[i][k]*m[j][k] but remember R uses col-major order
12           sum += m[n*k+i] * m[n*k+j];
13     }
14     return sum;
15  }
16
17  void mutlinks(int *m, int *n, double *mlmean)
18  {  int nval = *n;
19     tot = 0;
20     #pragma omp parallel
21     {  int i,mysum=0,
22           me = omp_get_thread_num(),
23           nth = omp_get_num_threads();
24        // in checking all (i,j) pairs, partition the work according to i;
25        // this thread me will handle all i that equal me mod nth
26        for (i = me; i < nval; i += nth) {
```

```
27        mysum += procpairs(i,m,nval);
28      }
29      #pragma omp atomic
30      tot += mysum;
31    }
32    int divisor = nval * (nval-1) / 2;
33    *mlmean = ((float) tot)/divisor;
34  }
```

16.3.3   Running the OpenMP Code

Again, compilation follows the recipe in Chapter 15. We do need to link in
the OpenMP library, though, by using the -fopenmp and -lgomp options. Suppose our source file is *romp.c.* Then we use the following commands to run
the code:

```
gcc -std=gnu99 -fopenmp -I/usr/share/R/include -fpic -g -O2 -c romp.c -o romp.o
gcc -std=gnu99 -shared -o romp.so romp.o -L/usr/lib/R/lib -lR -lgomp
```

Here's an R test:

```
> dyn.load("romp.so")
> Sys.setenv(OMP_NUM_THREADS=4)
> n <- 1000
> m <- matrix(sample(0:1,n^2,replace=T),nrow=n)
> system.time(z <- .C("mutlinks",as.integer(m),as.integer(n),result=double(1)))
   user   system  elapsed
  0.830   0.000   0.218
> z$result
[1] 249.9471
```

The typical way to specify the number of threads in OpenMP is through
an operating system environment variable, OMP_NUM_THREADS. R is capable of
setting operating system environment variables with the Sys.setenv() function. Here, I set the number of threads to 4, because I was running on a
quad-core machine.

Note the runtime—only 0.2 seconds! This compares to the 5.0-second
time we saw earlier for a 12-node snow system. This might be surprising to
some readers, as our code in the snow version was vectorized to a fair degree,
as mentioned earlier. Vectorizing is good, but again, R has many hidden
sources of overhead, so C might do even better.

NOTE   *I tried R's new byte-compilation function cmpfun(), but mtl() actually became slower.*

Thus, if you are willing to write part of your code in parallel C, dramatic
speedups may be possible.

16.3.4 OpenMP Code Analysis

OpenMP code is C, with the addition of *pragmas* that instruct the compiler to insert some library code to perform OpenMP operations. Look at line 20, for instance. When execution reaches this point, the threads will be activated. Each thread then executes the block that follows—lines 21 through 31—in parallel.

A key point is variable scope. All the variables within the block starting on line 21 are local to their specific threads. For example, we've named the total variable in line 21 mysum because each thread will maintain its own sum. By contrast, the global variable tot on line 4 is held in common by all the threads. Each thread makes its contribution to that grand total on line 30.

But even the variable nval on line 18 is held in common with all the threads (during the execution of mutlinks()), as it is declared outside the block beginning on line 21. So, even though it is a local variable in terms of C scope, it is global to all the threads. Indeed, we could have declared tot on that line, too. It needs to be shared by all the threads, but since it's not used outside mutlinks(), it could have been declared on line 18.

Line 29 contains another pragma, atomic. This one applies only to the single line following it—line 30, in this case—rather than to a whole block. The purpose of the atomic pragma is to avoid what is called a *race condition* in parallel-processing circles. This term describes a situation in which two threads are updating a variable at the same time, which may produce incorrect results. The atomic pragma ensures that line 30 will be executed by only one thread at a time. Note that this implies that in this section of the code, our parallel program becomes temporarily serial, which is a potential source of slowdown.

Where is the manager's role in all of this? Actually, the manager is the original thread, and it executes lines 18 and 19, as well as .C(), the R function that makes the call to mutlinks(). When the worker threads are activated in line 21, the manager goes dormant. The worker threads become dormant once they finish line 31. At that point, the manager resumes execution. Due to the dormancy of the manager while the workers are executing, we do want to have as many workers as our machine has cores.

The function procpairs() is straightforward, but note the manner in which the matrix m is being accessed. Recall from the discussion in Chapter 15 on interfacing R to C that the two languages store matrices differently: column by column in R and row-wise in C. We need to be aware of that difference here. In addition, we have treated the matrix m as a one-dimensional array, as is common in parallel C code. In other words, if n is, say, 4, then we treat m as a vector of 16 elements. Due to the column-major nature of R matrix storage, the vector will consist first of the four elements of column 1, then the four of column 2, and so on. To further complicate matters, we must keep in mind that array indices in C start at 0, instead of starting at 1 as in R.

Putting all of this together yields the multiplication in line 12. The factors here are the (k,i) and (k,j) elements of the version of m in the C code, which are the (i+1,k+1) and (j+1,k+1) elements back in the R code.

16.3.5 Other OpenMP Pragmas

OpenMP includes a wide variety of possible operations—far too many to list here. This section provides an overview of some OpenMP pragmas that I consider especially useful.

16.3.5.1 The omp barrier Pragma

The parallel-processing term *barrier* refers to a line of code at which the threads rendezvous. The syntax for the omp barrier pragma is simple:

```
#pragma omp barrier
```

When a thread reaches a barrier, its execution is suspended until all other threads have reached that line. This is very useful for iterative algorithms; threads wait at a barrier at the end of every iteration.

Note that in addition to this explicit barrier invocation, some other pragmas place an implicit barrier following their blocks. These include single and parallel. There is an implied barrier immediately following line 31 in the previous listing, for example, which is why the manager stays dormant until all worker threads finish.

16.3.5.2 The omp critical Pragma

The block that follows this pragma is a *critical section*, meaning one in which only one thread is allowed to execute at a time. The omp critical pragma essentially serves the same purpose as the atomic pragma discussed earlier, except that the latter is limited to a single statement.

NOTE   *The OpenMP designers defined a special pragma for this single-statement situation in the hope that the compiler can translate this to an especially fast machine instruction.*

Here is the omp critical syntax:

```
1  #pragma omp critical
2  {
3      // place one or more statements here
4  }
```

16.3.5.3 The omp single Pragma

The block that follows this pragma is to be executed by only one of the threads. Here is the syntax for the omp single pragma:

```
1  #pragma omp single
2  {
3      // place one or more statements here
4  }
```

This is useful for initializing sum variables that are shared by the threads, for instance. As noted earlier, an automatic barrier is placed after the block. This should make sense to you. If one thread is initializing a sum, you wouldn't want other threads that make use of this variable to continue execution until the sum has been properly set.

You can learn more about OpenMP in my open source textbook on parallel processing at *http://heather.cs.ucdavis.edu/parprocbook*.

16.3.6 GPU Programming

Another type of shared-memory parallel hardware consists of graphics processing units (GPUs). If you have a sophisticated graphics card in your machine, say for playing games, you may not realize that it is also a very powerful computational device—so powerful that the slogan "A supercomputer on your desk!" is often used to refer to PCs equipped with high-end GPUs.

As with OpenMP, the idea here is that instead of writing parallel R, you write R code interfaced to parallel C. (Similar to the OpenMP case, *C* here means a slightly augmented version of the C language.) The technical details become rather complex, so I won't show any code examples, but an overview of the platform is worthwhile.

As mentioned, GPUs do follow the shared-memory/threads model, but on a much larger scale. They have dozens, or even hundreds, of cores (depending on how you define *core*). One major difference is that several threads can be run together in a block, which can produce certain efficiencies.

Programs that access GPUs begin their run on your machine's CPU, referred to as the *host*. They then start code running on the GPU, or *device*. This means that your data must be transferred from the host to the device, and after the device finishes its computation, the results must be transferred back to the host.

As of this writing, GPU programming has not yet become common among R users. The most common usage is probably through the CRAN package gputools, which consists of some matrix algebra and statistical routines callable from R. For instance, consider matrix inversion. R provides the function solve() for this, but a parallel alternative is available in gputools with the name gpuSolve().

For more about GPU programming, again see my book on parallel processing at *http://heather.cs.ucdavis.edu/parprocbook*.

16.4 General Performance Considerations

This section discusses some issues that you may find generally useful in parallelizing R applications. I'll present some material on the main sources of overhead and then discuss a couple of algorithmic issues.

16.4.1 Sources of Overhead

Having at least a rough idea of the physical causes of overhead is essential to successful parallel programming. Let's take a look at these in the contexts of the two main platforms, shared-memory and networked computers.

16.4.1.1 Shared-Memory Machines

As noted earlier, the memory sharing in multicore machines makes for easier programming. However, the sharing also produces overhead, since the two cores will bump into each other if they both try to access memory at the same time. This means that one of them will need to wait, causing overhead. That overhead is typically in the range of hundreds of nanoseconds (billionths of seconds). This sounds really small, but keep in mind that the CPU is working at a subnanosecond speed, so memory access often becomes a bottleneck.

Each core may also have a *cache*, in which it keeps a local copy of some of the shared memory. It's intended to reduce contention for memory among the cores, but it produces its own overhead, involving time spent in keeping the caches consistent with each other.

Recall that GPUs are special types of multicore machines. As such, they suffer from the problems I've described, and more. First, the *latency*, which is the time delay before the first bit arrives at the GPU from its memory after a memory read request, is quite long in GPUs.

There is also the overhead incurred in transferring data between the host and the device. The latency here is on the order of microseconds (millionths of seconds), an eternity compared to the nanosecond scale of the CPU and GPU.

GPUs have great performance potential for certain classes of applications, but overhead can be a major issue. The authors of gputools note that their matrix operations start achieving a speedup only at matrix sizes of 1000 by 1000. I wrote a GPU version of our mutual outlinks application, which turned out to have a runtime of 3.0 seconds—about half of the snow version but still far slower than the OpenMP implementation.

Again, there are ways of ameliorating these problems, but they require very careful, creative programming and a sophisticated knowledge of the physical GPU structure.

16.4.1.2 Networked Systems of Computers

As you saw earlier, another way to achieve parallel computation is through networked systems of computers. You still have multiple CPUs, but in this case, they are in entirely separate computers, each with its own memory.

As pointed out earlier, network data transfer causes overhead. Its latency is again on the order of microseconds. Thus, even accessing a small amount of data across the network incurs a major delay.

Also note that snow has additional overhead, as it changes numeric objects such as vectors and matrices to character form before sending them, say from the manager to the workers. Not only does this entail time for the conversion (both in changing from numeric to character form and in charging back to numeric at the receiver), but the character form tends to make for much longer messages, thus longer network transfer time.

Shared-memory systems can be networked together, which, in fact, we did in the previous example. We had a hybrid situation in which we formed snow clusters from several networked dual-core computers.

16.4.2   Embarrassingly Parallel Applications and Those That Aren't

It's no shame to be poor, but it's no great honor either.
—Tevye, *Fiddler on the Roof*

Man is the only animal that blushes, or needs to.
—Mark Twain

The term *embarrassingly parallel* is heard often in talk about parallel R (and in the parallel processing field in general). The word *embarrassing* alludes to the fact that the problems are so easy to parallelize that there is no intellectual challenge involved; they are embarrassingly easy.

Both of the example applications we've looked at here would be considered embarrassingly parallel. Parallelizing the for i loop for the mutual outlinks problem in Section 16.1 was pretty obvious. Partitioning the work in the KMC example in Section 16.2.4 was also natural and easy.

By contrast, most parallel sorting algorithms require a great deal of interaction. For instance, consider merge sort, a common method of sorting numbers. It breaks the vector to be sorted into two (or more) independent parts, say the left half and right half, which are then sorted in parallel by two processes. So far, this is embarrassingly parallel, at least after the vector is divided in half. But then the two sorted halves must be merged to produce the sorted version of the original vector, and that process is *not* embarrassingly parallel. It can be parallelized but in a more complex manner.

Of course, to paraphrase Tevye, it's no shame to have an embarrassingly parallel problem! It may not exactly be an honor, but it is a cause for celebration, as it is easy to program. More important, embarrassingly parallel problems tend to have low communication overhead, which is crucial to performance, as discussed earlier. In fact, when most people refer to embarrassingly parallel applications, they have this low overhead in mind.

But what about nonembarrassingly parallel applications? Unfortunately, parallel R code is simply not suitable for many of them for a very basic reason: the functional programming nature of R. As discussed in Section 14.3, a statement like this:

```
x[3] <- 8
```

is deceptively simple, because it can cause the entire vector x to be rewritten. This really compounds communication traffic problems. Accordingly, if your application is not embarrassingly parallel, your best strategy is probably to write the computationally intensive parts of the code in C, say using OpenMP or GPU programming.

Also, note carefully that even being embarrassingly parallel does not make an algorithm efficient. Some such algorithms can still have significant communication traffic, thus compromising performance.

Consider the KMC problem, run under snow. Suppose we were to set up a large enough number of workers so that each worker had relatively little work to do. In that case, the communication with the manager after each iteration would become a signficant portion of run time. In this situation, we would say that the *granularity* is too fine, and then probably switch to using fewer workers. We would then have larger tasks for each worker, thus a *coarser* granularity.

16.4.3   Static Versus Dynamic Task Assignment

Look again at the loop beginning on line 26 of our OpenMP example, reproduced here for convenience:

```
for (i = me; i < nval; i += nth) {
    mysum += procpairs(i,m,nval);
}
```

The variable me here was the thread number, so the effect of this code was that the various threads would work on nonoverlapping sets of values of i. We do want the values to be nonoverlapping, to avoid duplicate work and an incorrect count of total number of links, so the code was fine. But the point now is that we were, in effect, preassigning the tasks that each thread would handle. This is called *static* assignment.

An alternative approach is to revise the for loop to look something like this:

```
int nexti = 0;   // global variable
...
for ( ; myi < n; ) {   // revised "for" loop
    #pragma omp critical
    {
        nexti += 1;
        myi = nexti;
    }
    if (myi < n)  {
        mysum += procpairs(myi,m,nval);
        ...
    }
}
...
```

This is *dynamic* task assignment, in which it is not determined ahead of time which threads handle which values of i. Task assignment is done during execution. At first glance, dynamic assignment seems to have the potential for better performance. Suppose, for instance, that in a static assignment setting, one thread finishes its last value of i early, while another thread still has two values of i left to do. This would mean our program would finish somewhat later than it could. In parallel-processing parlance, we would have a *load balance* problem. With dynamic assignment, the thread that finished when there were two values of i left to handle could have taken up one of those values itself. We would have better balance and theoretically less overall runtime.

But don't jump to conclusions. As always, we have the overhead issue to reckon with. Recall that a critical pragma, used in the dynamic version of the code above, has the effect of temporarily rendering the program serial rather than parallel, thus causing a slowdown. In addition, for reasons too technical to discuss here, these pragmas may cause considerable cache activity overhead. So in the end, the dynamic code could actually be substantially slower than the static version.

Various solutions to this problem have been developed, such as an OpenMP construct named guided. But rather than present these, the point I wish to make is that they are unnecessary. In most situations, static assignment is just fine. Why is this the case?

You may recall that the standard deviation of the sum of independent, identically distributed random variables, divided by the mean of that sum, goes to zero as the number of terms goes to infinity. In other words, sums are approximately constant. This has a direct implication for our load-balancing concerns: Since the total work time for a thread in static assignment is the sum of its individual task times, that total work time will be approximately constant; there will be very little variation from thread to thread. Thus, they will all finish at pretty close to the same time, and we do not need to worry about load imbalance. Dynamic scheduling will not be necessary.

This reasoning does depend on a statistical assumption, but in practice, the assumption will typically be met sufficiently well for the outcome: Static scheduling does as well as dynamic in terms of uniformity of total work times across threads. And since static scheduling doesn't have the overhead problems of the dynamic kind, in most cases the static approach will give better performance.

There is one more aspect of this to discuss. To illustrate the issue, consider again the mutual outlinks example. Let's review the outline of the algorithm:

```
1   sum = 0
2   for i = 0...n-1
3       for j = i+1...n-1
4           for k = 0...n-1 sum = sum + a[i][k]*a[j][k]
5   mean = sum / (n*(n-1)/2)
```

Say n is 10000 and we have four threads, and consider ways to partition the for i loop. Naively, we might at first decide to have thread 0 handle the i values 0 through 2499, thread 1 handle 2500 through 4999, and so on. However, this would produce a severe load imbalance, since the thread that handles a given value of i does an amount of work proportional to n-i. That, in fact, is why we staggered the values of i in our actual code: Thread 0 handled the i values 0, 4, 8 ..., thread 1 worked on 1, 5, 9, ..., and so on, yielding good load balance.

The point then is that static assignment might require a bit more planning. One general approach to this is to randomly assign tasks (i values, in our case here) to threads (still doing so at the outset, before work begins). With a bit of forethought such as this, static assignment should work well in most applications.

16.4.4 Software Alchemy: Turning General Problems into Embarrassingly Parallel Ones

As discussed earlier, it's difficult to attain good performance from nonembarrassingly parallel algorithms. Fortunately, for statistical applications, there is a way to turn nonembarrassingly parallel problems into embarrassingly parallel ones. The key is to exploit some statistical properties.

To demonstrate the method, let's once again turn to our mutual outlinks problem. The method, applied with w workers on a links matrix m, consists of the following:

1. Break the rows of m into w chunks.

2. Have each worker find the mean number of mutual outlinks for pairs of vertices in its chunk.

3. Average the results returned by the workers.

It can be shown mathematically that for large problems (the only ones you would need parallel computing for anyway), this chunked approach gives the estimators of the same statistical accuracy as in the nonchunked method. But meanwhile, we've turned a nonparallel problem into not just a parallel one but an embarrassingly parallel one! The workers in the preceding outline compute entirely independently of each other.

This method should not be confused with the usual chunk-based approaches in parallel processing. In those, such as the merge-sort example discussed on page 347, the chunking is embarrassingly parallel, but the combining of results is not. By contrast, here the combining of results consists of simple averaging, thanks to the mathematical theory.

I tried this approach on the mutual outlinks problem in a 4-worker snow cluster. This reduced the runtime to 1.5 seconds. This is far better than the serial time of about 16 seconds, double the speedup obtained by the GPU and approaching comparability to the OpenMP time. And the theory showing that the two methods give the same statistical accuracy was confirmed as well. The chunked method found the mean number of mutual outlinks to be 249.2881, compared to 249.2993 for the original estimator.

16.5 Debugging Parallel R Code

Parallel R packages such as Rmpi, snow, foreach, and so on do not set up a terminal window for each process, thus making it impossible to use R's debugger on the workers. (My Rdsm package, which adds a threads capability to R, is an exception to this.)

What then can you do to debug apps for those packages? Let's consider snow for a concrete example.

First, you should debug the underlying single-worker function, such as mtl() in Section 16.2. Here, we would set up some artificial values of the arguments and then use R's ordinary debugging facilities.

Debugging the underlying function may be sufficient. However, the bug may be in the arguments themselves or in the way we set them up. Then things get more difficult.

It's even hard to print out trace information, such as values of variables, since print() won't work in the worker processes. The message() function may work for some of these packages; if not, you may need to resort to using cat() to write to a file.

A

INSTALLING R

This appendix covers the methods for installing R on your system. You can easily download and install the precompiled binaries, use your package manager on a UNIX-based system, or even install from source if you prefer.

A.1 Downloading R from CRAN

R, in both its base form and user-written packages, is available on the Comprehensive R Archive Network (CRAN) at the R home page, *http://www .r-project.org/.* Click CRAN and choose a site near you to download the appropriate base package for your operating system (OS).

For most users, installing R is quite simple, regardless of the platform. You can find precompiled binaries for Windows, Linux, and Mac OS X on CRAN. You should be able to simply download the appropriate file and install R.

A.2 Installing from a Linux Package Manager

Rather than using the precompiled binaries, if you're running a Linux distribution with a centralized package repository, such as Fedora or Ubuntu, you can install R using your OS's package manager. For example, if you're running Fedora, you can install R by typing the following at the command line:

```
$ yum install R
```

For a Debian-based system, such as Ubuntu, the command looks like this:

```
$ sudo apt-get install r-base
```

Check your distribution's documentation for more details on installing and removing packages.

A.3   Installing from Source

On Linux or other UNIX-based machines (probably including Mac OS X), you can also compile R's source code yourself. Simply unpack the source archive and follow the classic three-command installation procedure:

```
$ configure
$ make
$ make install
```

Note that you may need to run make install as root, depending on your write permissions and the location to which you're installing R. If you want to install to a nonstandard directory, say */a/b/c*, you can run configure with the --prefix parameter, like this:

```
$ configure --prefix=/a/b/c
```

This might be helpful if you're working on a shared machine and don't have write permissions to the standard installation directories like */usr*.

B

INSTALLING AND USING PACKAGES

One of the major strengths of R is that thousands of user-written packages are available on the Comprehensive R Archive Network (CRAN) at the R home page, *http://www.r-project.org/*. Package installation is easy in most cases, but there are nuances to be aware of for some of the specialty packages.

This appendix starts with some package basics and then explains how to load R packages from your hard drive and from the Web.

B.1 Package Basics

R uses packages to store groups of related pieces of software. The packages that are included with the R distribution are visible as subdirectories of your *library* directory in your R installation tree, as in */usr/lib/R/library*.

NOTE   *In the R community, the term* library *is often used in place of* package.

Some packages are loaded automatically when you start R, such as the *base* subdirectory. However, in order to save memory and time, R does not load all available packages automatically.

You can check which packages are currently loaded by typing this:

```
> .path.package()
```

B.2 Loading a Package from Your Hard Drive

If you need a package that is in your R installation but not loaded into memory yet, you can load it using the library() function. For instance, suppose you wish to generate multivariate normal random vectors. The function mvrnorm() in the package MASS does this. So, load the package as follows:

```
> library(MASS)
```

The mvrnorm() function will now be ready to use. And so will its documentation (before you loaded MASS, entering help(mvrnorm) would have generated an error message).

B.3 Downloading a Package from the Web

The package you want may not be in your R installation. One of the big advantages of open source software is that people love to share. People all over the world have written their own special-purpose R packages, placing them in the CRAN repository and elsewhere.

NOTE *User contributions to CRAN go through a vetting process and are generally of high quality. They are, however, not tested as thoroughly as R itself.*

B.3.1 Installing Packages Automatically

One way to install a package is to use the install_packages() function. For example, suppose you wish to use the mvtnorm package, which computes multivariate normal cumulative distribution functions and other quantities. First, choose a directory in which you wish to install the package (and maybe others in the future), say */a/b/c*. Then at the R prompt, type this:

```
> install.packages("mvtnorm","/a/b/c/")
```

This will cause R to automatically go to CRAN, download the package, compile it, and load it into a new directory: */a/b/c/mvtnorm*.

You do need to tell R where to find that package once it's installed, which you can do via the .libPaths() function:

```
> .libPaths("/a/b/c/")
```

This will add that new directory to the ones R was already using. If you use that directory often enough, you may wish to add that call to .libPaths() in your *.Rprofile* startup file in your home directory.

A call to `.libPaths()` without an argument will show you a list of all the places R will currently look for loading a package when requested.

B.3.2 Installing Packages Manually

Sometimes you need to install "by hand" to make modifications required to make a particular R package work on your system. The following example demonstrates how I did so in one particular instance, and it will serve as a case study on handling situations in which ordinary methods don't work.

NOTE   *Situations in which you need to install packages by hand typically are operating system dependent and require more computer expertise than is generally assumed in this book. For help in very specific cases, the* r-help *mailing list is invaluable. To access it, go to the R home page (*http://www.r-project.org/ *), click the FAQs link and then the R FAQ link, and scroll down to Section 2.9, "What mailing lists exist for R?"*

I wanted to install the `Rmpi` package on our department's instructional machines in the directory */home/matloff/R.* I tried using `install.packages()` first but found that the automated process could not find the MPI library on our machines. The problem was that R was looking for those files in */usr/local/lam,* whereas I knew they were in */usr/local/LAM.* Since these were public machines, not my own, I did not have the authority to change the name. So, I downloaded the `Rmpi` files in the packed form *Rmpi_0.5-3 .tar.gz.* I unpacked that file in my directory *~/tmp,* producing a directory named *~/tmp/Rmpi.*

If I had not experienced this problem, at this point, I could have just typed the following in a terminal window from within the *~/tmp* directory:

```
R CMD INSTALL -l /home/matloff/R  Rmpi
```

That command would install the package contained in *~/tmp/Rmpi,* placing it in */home/matloff/R.* This would have been an alternative to calling `install.packages()`.

But as noted, I had to deal with a problem. Within the *~/tmp/Rmpi* directory, there was a *configure* file, so I ran this command on my Linux command line:

```
configure --help
```

It told me that I could specify the location of my MPI files to `configure`, as follows:

```
configure --with-mpi=/usr/local/LAM
```

This applies if you run `configure` directly, but I ran it via R:

```
R CMD INSTALL -l /home/matloff/R Rmpi --configure-args=--with-mpi=/usr/local/LAM
```

Well, that seemed to work, in the sense that R did install the package, but R also noted that it had a problem with the threads library on our machines. Sure enough, when I tried to load Rmpi, I got a runtime error, saying that a certain threads function wasn't there.

I knew that our threads library was fine, so I went into the configure file and commented out two lines:

```
# if test $ac_cv_lib_pthread_main = yes; then
    MPI_LIBS="$MPI_LIBS -lpthread"
# fi
```

In other words, I forced it to use what I knew (or was fairly sure) would work. I then reran R CMD INSTALL, and the package loaded without any problems.

B.4   Listing the Functions in a Package

You can get a list of functions in a package by calling library() with the help argument. For instance, for help on the mvtnorm package, type one of the following:

*
  ```
  > library(help=mvtnorm)
  ```

*
  ```
  > help(package=mvtnorm)
  ```

INDEX

atomic pragma, 343
atomic vectors, 85–86
attr() function, 212

B

batch mode, 1
  help feature, 24
  running R in, 3
Bernoulli sequence, 204
biglm package, 321
bigmemory package, 321
binary files, 237
binary search tree, 177–182
body() function, 149, 151
Boolean operators, 145–146
braces, 144
brackets, 87–88
Bravington, Mark, 300
breakpoints, setting, 289–290
  calling browser() function directly,
    289–290
  using setbreakpoint() function, 290
breaks component, hist() function, 14
break statement, 141
browser commands, 289
browser() function
  setting breakpoints, 289–290
  single-stepping through code, 288
by() function, 126–127
byrow argument, matrix() function,
  61, 236
byte code compilation, 320

C

c %in% y set operation, 202
cache, 346
calculus, 192–193
categorical variables, 121
cbind() function, 12, 74–75, 106–107
c browser command, 289
cdf (cumulative distribution
  function), 193
ceiling() math function, 190
cell counts, changing to
  proportions, 130
cex option, changing graph character
  sizes with, 272–273
c() function, 56–57
Chambers, John, 226

character strings, 251–259
  defined, 11
  regular expressions, 254–257
    forming filenames example,
      256–257
    testing filename for given suffix
      example, 255–256
  string-manipulation functions,
    251–254
    gregexpr(), 254
    grep(), 252
    nchar(), 252
    paste(), 252–253
    regexpr(), 253–254
    sprintf(), 253
    strsplit(), 253
    substr(), 253
  use of string utilities in edtdbg debug-
    ging tool, 257–259
child nodes, binary search tree, 177
Chinese dialects, aids for learning,
  115–120
chi-square distribution, 193–194
chol() linear algebra function, 197
choose() set operation, 202
chunking memory, 320–321
class() function, 212
cleaner code, 172
client/server model, 247
closures, 151, 174–175
cloud() function, 282–283
cluster, snow package, 335
clusterApply() function, snow package,
  72, 337, 339–340
code files, 3
code safety, 41
col() function, 69–70
colon operator (:), 32–33
color images, 63
column-major order, matrix storage,
  59, 61
combinatorial simulation, 205–206
combn() function, 203
comdat$countabsamecomm component, 206
comdat$numabchosen component, 206
comdat$whosleft component, 206
comma-separated value (CSV) files, 103
comments, 3
complete.cases() function, 105–106
Comprehensive R Archive Network
  (CRAN), 24, 193, 353

mapsound() function, 115–116
marginal values, variable, 131
m argument, apply() function, 70
Markov chains, 199–201
MASS package, 23, 356
math functions, 189–193
   calculating probability example,
      190–191
   calculus, 192–193
   cumulative sums and products, 191
   minima and maxima, 191–192
matrices, 11–12, 59–83
   adding and deleting rows and col-
      umns, 73–78
      finding closest pair of vertices in
         graph example, 75–78
      resizing matrix, 73–75
   applying functions to rows and col-
      umns, 70–73
      apply() function, 70–72
      finding outliers example, 72–73
   avoiding unintended dimension
      reduction, 80–81
   linear algebra operations on, 196–201
   naming rows and columns, 81–82
   operations, 61–70
      filtering, 66–69
      generating covariance matrix
         example, 69–70
      image manipulation example,
         63–66
      linear algebra operations, 61
      matrix indexing, 62–63
   reading from files, 236
   vector/matrix distinction, 78–79
   as vectors, 28
matrix/array-like operations, 130–131
matrix class, 79
matrix() function, 60
matrix-inverse update method, 222
matrix-like operations, 104–109
   apply() function, 107
   extracting subdata frames, 104–105
   NA values, 105–106
   rbind() and cbind() functions,
      106–107
   salary study example, 108–109
matrix-multiplication operator, 12
maxima function, 191–192
max() math function, 190, 192
mean() function, 38

memory
   chunking, 320–321
   functional programming, 314–316
      avoiding memory copy example,
         315–316
      copy-on-change issues, 314–315
      vector assignment issues, 314
   using R packages for memory
      management, 321
merge() function, 109–110
merge sort method, numerical
   sorting, 347
merging data frames, 109–112
   employee database example,
      111–112
metacharacters, 254
methods() function, 210
microdata, 239
minima function, 191–192
min() math function, 190, 191
M/M/1 queue, 165, 168
modes
   batch, 1, 3, 24
   defined, 26
   interactive, 2–3
modulo operator, 44
monitor, accessing, 232–235
   using print() function, 234–235
   using readline() function, 234
   using scan() function, 232–234
Monte Carlo simulation, achieving better speed in, 308–311
multicore machines, 340–341
mutlinks() function, 336
mutual outlinks, 333–334, 341–342
mvrnorm() function, MASS package, 23, 356

N

named arguments, 146–147
names() function, 56
naming
   matrix rows and columns, 81–82
   vector elements, 56
NA values
   matrix-like operations, 105–106
   vectors, 43
n browser command, 289
nchar() function, 252
ncol() function, 79

negative subscripts, 32, 63
network, defined, 247
Newton-Raphson method, 192
next statement, 141
Nile data set, 5
noise, adding to image, 65–66
nominal variables, 121
nonlocals
    writing to with superassignment
        operator, 161–162
    writing with assign() function, 163
nonvector sets, looping control state-
        ments over, 143
nonvisible functions, 211
nreps values, 205
nrow() function, 79
NULL values, 44

O

object-oriented programming. *See* OOP
objects. *See also* managing objects
    first-class, 149
    immutable, 314
oddcount() function, 7, 140
omp barrier pragma, OpenMP, 344
omp critical pragma, OpenMP, 344
omp single pragma, OpenMP, 344–345
OOP (object-oriented programming),
        xxi, 207–230
    managing objects. *See* managing
        objects
    S3 classes. *See* S3 classes
    S4 classes, 222–226
        implementing generic function
            on, 225–226
        vs. S3 classes, 226
        writing, 223–225
OpenMP, 344–345
    code analysis, 343
    omp barrier pragma, 344
    omp critical pragma, 344
    omp single pragma, 344–345
operations
    list, 87–93
        adding and deleting list elements,
            88–90
        getting size of list, 90
        list indexing, 87–88
        text concordance example, 90–93

matrix, 61–70
    filtering, 66–69
    generating covariance matrix
        example, 69–70
    image manipulation example,
        63–66
    indexing, 62–63
    linear algebra operations, 61
matrix/array-like, 130–131
vector, 30–34
    arithmetic and logical operations,
        30–31
    colon operator (:), 32–33
    generating vector sequences with
        seq() function, 33–34
    repeating vector constants with
        rep() function, 34
    vector in, matrix out, 42–43
    vector in, vector out, 40–42
    vector indexing, 31–32
operator precedence, 33
order() function, 97, 194–195
outliers, 49

P

packages, 355–358
    installing
        automatically, 356–357
        manually, 357–358
    listing functions in, 358
    loading from hard drive, 356
parallel R, 333–351
    debugging, 351
        embarrassingly parallel applica-
            tions, 347–348
        turning general problems into, 350
    implementing, 248–250
    mutual outlinks, 333–334
    resorting to C, 340–345
        GPU programming, 345
        multicore machines, 340–341
        mutual outlinks, 341–342
        OpenMP code analysis, 343
        OpenMP pragmas, 344–345
        running OpenMP code, 342
    snow package, 334–340
        analyzing snow code, 336–337
        k-means clustering (KMC), 338–340
        running snow code, 335–336
        speedup, 337–338

running (*continued*)
   R, 1–2
      batch mode, 3
      first session, 4–7
      interactive mode, 2–3
   snow code, 335–336
runs of consecutive ones, finding, 35–37
runtime errors, 303

S

S (programming language), xix
S3 classes, 208–222
   class for storing upper-triangular
      matrices example, 214–219
   finding implementations of generic
      methods, 210–212
   generic functions, 208
   OOP in lm() function example,
      208–210
   procedure for polynomial regression
      example, 219–222
   vs. S4 classes, 226
   using inheritance, 214
   writing, 212–213
S4 classes, 222–226
   implementing generic function on,
      225–226
   vs. S3 classes, 226
   writing, 223–225
salary study, 108–109
Salzman, Pete, 285
sapply() function, 42
   applying functions to lists, 95
   using on data frames, 112–113
save() function, saving collection of
      objects with, 228
saving graphs to files, 280–281
scalars, 10
   Boolean operators, 145
   vectors, 26
scan() function, 142, 232–234
scatter/gather paradigm, 335–336
schedevnt() function, 165, 171
scope hierarchy, 152–155. *See also* envi-
      ronment and scope
sepsoundtone() function, 119
seq() function, 21, 33–34
serialize() function, 248
setbreakpoint() function, 290
setClass() function, 223

setdiff() set operation, 202
setequal() set operation, 202
setMethod() function, 225
set operations, 202–203
set.seed() function, 302
setting breakpoints, 289–290
   calling browser() function directly,
      289–290
   using setbreakpoint() function, 290
setwd() function, 245
S expression pointers (SEXPs), 304
shared-memory systems, 341, 346–347
shared-memory/threads model,
      GPUs, 345
Sherman-Morrison-Woodbury
      formula, 222
shortcuts
   help() function, 20
   help.search() function, 23
showframe() function, 158
sim global variable, 172–173
simplifying code, 172
simulation programming in R, 204–206
   built-in random variate generators,
      204–205
   combinatorial simulation, 205–206
   obtaining same random stream in
      repeated runs, 205
single brackets, 87–88
single-server queuing system, 168
sink() function, 258
sin() math function, 190
slots, S4 class, 224
snow package, 334–335
   implementing parallel R, 248–249
   k-means clustering (KMC), 338–340
   snow code
      analyzing, 336–337
      running, 335–336
   speedup, 337–338
socketConnection() function, 248
sockets, 247–248
socketSelect() function, 248
solve() function, 197
sorting, numerical, 194–196
sos package, 24
source, installing R from, 354
sourceval parameter, mapsound()
      function, 116
Spearman rank correlation, 49

top-level environment, 152
traceback() function, 291–292
trace() function, 291
tracemem() function, 314–315
training set, 37
transcendental functions, 40
transition probability, 200
treelike data structures, 177

U

Ubuntu, installing R on, 353–354
unclass() function, 229
union() set operation, 202
unlist() function, 93
unname() function, 94
unserialize() function, 248
upn argument, showframe() function, 158
upper-triangular matrices, class for storing, 214–219
URLs, accessing files on remote machines via, 243
u variable, 162

V

values
    assigning to submatrices, 62–63
    Boolean, 145–146
    list, accessing, 93–95
    NA, 43, 105–106
    NULL, 44
    return, 147–149
vanilla option, startup/shutdown, 20
variables
    assessing statistical relation of two, 49–51
    categorical, 121
    global, 9, 171–174
    nominal, 121
variable scope, 9
vector assignment issues, 314
vector cross product, 198–199
vector filtering, 307
vector-filtering capability, 176
vector functions, 311
vectorization
    defined, 25
    for speedup, 306–308
vectorized operations, 40
vector/matrix distinction, 78–79

vectors, 10, 25–57
    all() and any() functions, 35–39
        finding runs of consecutive ones example, 35–37
        predicting discrete-valued time series example, 37–39
    c() function, 56–57
    common operations, 30–34
        arithmetic and logical operations, 30–31
        colon operator (:), 32–33
        generating vector sequences with seq() function, 33–34
        repeating vector constants with rep() function, 34
        vector indexing, 31–32
    computing inner product of two, 196
    declarations, 28–29
    defined, 4
    elements
        adding and deleting, 26
        naming, 56
    filtering, 45–48
        generating indices for, 45–47
        with subset() function, 47
        with which() function, 47–48
    ifelse() function, 48–54
        assessing statistical relation of two variables example, 49–51
        recoding abalone data set example, 51–54
    linear algebra operations on, 196–201
    matrices and arrays as, 28
    NA value, 43
    NULL value, 44
    obtaining length of, 27
    recycling, 29–30
    scalars, 26
    testing vector equality, 54–55
    vectorized operations, 39–43
        vector in, matrix out, 42–43
        vector in, vector out, 40–42
vertices, graph, finding, 75–78

W

Web, downloading packages from, 356–358
    installing automatically, 356–357
    installing manually, 357–358

The Electronic Frontier Foundation (EFF) is the leading organization defending civil liberties in the digital world. We defend free speech on the Internet, fight illegal surveillance, promote the rights of innovators to develop new digital technologies, and work to ensure that the rights and freedoms we enjoy are enhanced — rather than eroded — as our use of technology grows.

PRIVACY
EFF has sued telecom giant AT&T for giving the NSA unfettered access to the private communications of millions of their customers. eff.org/nsa

FREE SPEECH
EFF's Coders' Rights Project is defending the rights of programmers and security researchers to publish their findings without fear of legal challenges. eff.org/freespeech

INNOVATION
EFF's Patent Busting Project challenges overbroad patents that threaten technological innovation. eff.org/patent

FAIR USE
EFF is fighting prohibitive standards that would take away your right to receive and use over-the-air television broadcasts any way you choose. eff.org/IP/fairuse

TRANSPARENCY
EFF has developed the Switzerland Network Testing Tool to give individuals the tools to test for covert traffic filtering. eff.org/transparency

INTERNATIONAL
EFF is working to ensure that international treaties do not restrict our free speech, privacy or digital consumer rights. eff.org/global

EFF.ORG

ELECTRONIC FRONTIER FOUNDATION

Protecting Rights and Promoting Freedom on the Electronic Frontier

EFF is a member-supported organization. Join Now! www.eff.org/support

UPDATES

Visit *http://www.nostarch.com/artofr.htm* for updates, errata, and more.

More no-nonsense books from **NO STARCH PRESS**

THE LINUX COMMAND LINE
A Complete Introduction
by WILLIAM E. SHOTTS, JR.
JANUARY 2012, 480 PP., $39.95
ISBN 978-1-59327-389-7

LEARN YOU SOME ERLANG FOR GREAT GOOD!
A Beginner's Guide
by FRED HÉBERT
JANUARY 2013, 624 PP., $49.95
ISBN 978-1-59327-435-1

PYTHON FOR KIDS
A Playful Introduction to Programming
by JASON R. BRIGGS
DECEMBER 2012, 344 PP., $34.95
ISBN 978-1-59327-407-8
full color

LEARN YOU A HASKELL FOR GREAT GOOD!
A Beginner's Guide
by MIRAN LIPOVAČA
APRIL 2011, 400 PP., $44.95
ISBN 978-1-59327-283-8

THE MANGA GUIDE™ TO STATISTICS
by SHIN TAKAHASHI *and* TREND-PRO CO., LTD
NOVEMBER 2008, 232 PP., $19.95
ISBN 978-1-59327-189-3

THINK LIKE A PROGRAMMER
An Introduction to Creative Problem Solving
by V. ANTON SPRAUL
AUGUST 2012, 256 PP., $34.95
ISBN 978-1-59327-424-5

PHONE:
800.420.7240 OR
415.863.9900

EMAIL:
SALES@NOSTARCH.COM

WEB:
WWW.NOSTARCH.COM

The Art of R Programming is set in New Baskerville, TheSansMono Condensed, Futura, and Dogma.

This book was printed and bound at Edwards Brothers Malloy in Ann Arbor, Michigan. The paper is 60# Husky Opaque, which is certified by the Sustainable Forestry Initiative (SFI).

The book uses a RepKover binding, in which the pages are bound together with a cold-set, flexible glue and the first and last pages of the resulting book block are attached to the cover with tape. The cover is not actually glued to the book's spine, and when open, the book lies flat and the spine doesn't crack.